MANIFEST DESTINY DENIED

America's First Intervention in Nicaragua

James T. Wall

Library of
Davidson College

UNIVERSITY
PRESS OF
AMERICA

327.73
W187m

Copyright © 1981 by
University Press of America, Inc.™
P.O. Box 19101, Washington, D.C. 20036

All rights reserved

Printed in the United States of America

ISBN: 0-8191-1973-3 (Perfect)
0-8191-1972-5 (Case)

Library of Congress Number: 81-40586

83-4017

TO PROFESSOR ROLAND E. DUNCAN

Mentor and Friend

restore order, but Trinidad Munoz, the Commander of Arms, intrigued to increase his own power and influence, and finally betrayed the party, reestablishing the capital at Leon. A new Conservative uprising, championed by Honduras and Costa Rica, overthrew Munoz in 1851 and again moved the government to Managua. The Conservatives made an effort to conciliate their opponents, this time by giving them minor posts in the cabinet. Liberal rejection of this olive branch spelled failure for the plan, and a period of attempted forceful suppression of the Liberals ensued.

Continual strife between Liberals and Conservatives in Nicaragua, during the period of the Federation and subsequent to the establishment of the Republic in 1838, had resulted in unprecedented ruin and destruction. Although the country was capable of producing indigo, sugar, rice, coffee, tobacco, and virtually every product known to a tropical region, agriculture and commerce had so stagnated that only plantains and Indian corn were cultivated for bare subsistence. Exploitable deposits of gold and silver in the district of Matagalpa in the Cordillera were ignored. Great tracts of commercial timber stood unharvested.

President Fruto Chamorro, a member of one of the leading Granadan families, resolved to halt Nicaragua's plunge into political anarchy and commercial impotence. His opportunity came in the election of 1853 when he secured a second term by defeating Francisco Castellon from Leon, a well-educated Liberal and former minister to England. William V. Wells, an American observer, later contended that neither candidate could muster the necessary two-thirds vote as required in the 1838 constitution, and that Chamorro claimed the election by default.[3]

In order to organize a strong government and ensure order, Chamorro decided to rescind and replace the Liberal Party-dictated constitution of 1838 which he regarded as anarchical. Anticipating the convening of a constituent assembly for the purpose of drafting a new charter, Chamorro deemed it expedient to eliminate, insofar as possible, the major Liberal opposition. In November, 1853, he charged Castellon, Maximo Jerez, Colonel Jose Maria Valle, Francisco Diaz, Manuel Cisneros, and Mateo Pineda, all leading citizens of the Occidental Department (in which Leon was located), with conspiracy against the government. Some Liberal agitation probably had resulted from dissatisfaction with Chamorro's unprecedented bid for a second term, and from the questionable circumstances surrounding his re-election.

---

[3] William V. Wells, Walker's Expedition to Nicaragua (New York: Stringer and Townsend, 1856), 46.

Yet, the tangible evidence, which Chamorro purported to have, remained in his "secret files" and was never subject to public disclosure.[4]

All but Castellon and Jerez escaped and went into exile in Honduras. After a short imprisonment, these two were also exiled on November 28, 1853, and forced to join their colleagues. Early in 1854, Chamorro proceeded to call a constituent assembly. A Conservative constitution was drafted and approved on April 30, 1854, vesting more power in the executive, extending his term from two to four years, and providing more latitude for centrally governing the republic. Chamorro was named Chief Executive by the assembly for the first four-year term. He was thus, in effect, the last Chief of State under the Central America Federation and the first President of the revised Republic of Nicaragua.[5]

Aside from the Conservative dominance that the new constitution implied, the change from virtual political anarchy was perhaps too abrupt, causing restlessness among the citizens. Encouraged by these disorders and smarting from political subjugation, the Liberal exiles in Honduras began plotting to return. They were aided by Liberal Honduran President Jose Trinidad Cabanas, who furnished them with arms and money. On May 5, 1854, the political refugees sailed from Tigre Island in the Bay of Fonseca on a vessel commanded by an American, Gilbert Morton. They surprised and overwhelmed a small garrison at Realejo. Marching inland through the Occidental Department, they occupied the unresisting town of Chinandega, where new supporters adhered to their cause. At Chinandega, Jerez issued a proclamation outlining a five-point program.[6] The Liberal Party, the notice read,

(1) Declares the principal object for the army is to take power from Chamorro and return it to the people.

(2) Promises to respect and honor property.

(3) Names as traitors those who give service to the tyrant, Chamorro.

---

4   Guillermo Sofonias Salvatierra, Maximo Jerez Inmortal (Managua: Progresso, 1950), 40.

5   Rodrigo Sanchez, Panoramo Politico de Nicaragua, 1821-1940, (Managua: Perez, 1940), 3.

6   Sofonias Salvatierra, Maximo Jerez, 44

(4) Does not recognize the political parties that previously existed (constituting a call to all citizens).

(5) Invites all government employees, even those under arms, to join the crusade.

The Liberal contingent then proceeded to Leon, establishing its headquarters there and naming Castellon Provisional Director of the Republic. On May 10, 1854, Chamorro proclaimed a war to the death for the defense of "legitimacy," or legal succession to power. After two inconclusive battles, Chamorro's forces retired to Granada. The Liberal forces, or "Democrats" as they styled themselves, swelled their ranks with sympathizers and conscripts, and marched on Granada.

The Democrats (Liberals) laid siege to the city, occupying the suburban part, but were unable to penetrate the fortified plaza in the center of town. Withstanding the siege, the Legitimists had approximately one thousand men under arms. Guatemala was allied with them in their Conservative cause, but was unable to provide significant material assistance. At the height of the siege, the Democrats were able to muster one thousand five hundred men, including two hundred Hondurans. In addition, the Democrats recruited a dozen or so Americans in San Juan del Sur and Virgin Bay at the rate of $100 per month to pepper the Granada plaza with rifle shot.[7]

C.W. Doubleday, a British national and California pioneer on his way to the east coast of the United States, threw himself in company with the Democrats at San Juan del Sur. He recruited among the American passengers and took thirty of them to the siege at Granada. The Leonese were well-impressed with the quality of American soldiery.[8] The siege proved a stand-off and after nine months, in February, 1855, the Democrats gave up and retired toward Leon. At Masaya, Chamorro's forces, imbued with new spirit and encouraged by Conservative priests,[9] overtook the Democrats and three hundred men were killed in the ensuing battle. The Legitimists then captured San Carlos and refurbished their shot and powder stores with supplies from Jamaica. They regained Managua and Rivas and finally the whole state except Leon, Chinandega, and Realejo along with the Bay of Fonseca.

---

[7] "Nicaraguan Filibusters," Littell's Living Age, VIII (April 1856), 129-140 (reprint from Blackwood's Magazine).

[8] James Jeffrey Roche, By-Ways of War (Boston: Small, Maynard and Company, 1901), 91.

[9] Wells, Walker's Expedition, 49.

Nicaragua was now effectively divided between two fatigued and dissipated forces.

In the meantime, American relations with Nicaragua up to this point had been in the benign form of diplomatic and commercial activity. Now the seeds were planted for a far more disruptive element: American soldiers-of-fortune. The cumulative effect of the intrusions on that distressed country would prove almost fatal. Nicaragua was about to find itself squarely in the path of the steamroller of Manifest Destiny.

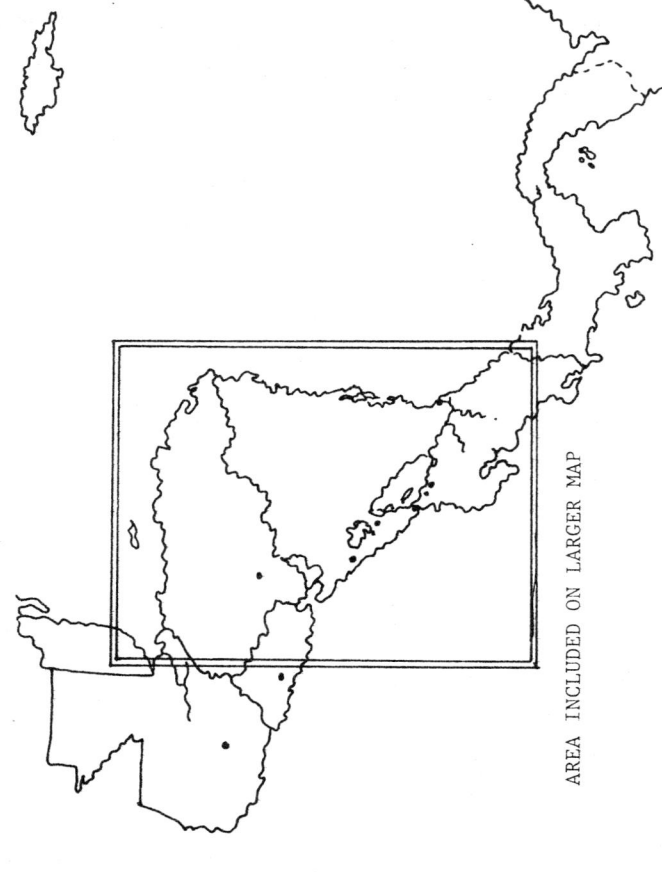

Figure 2. El Salvador, Honduras, Nicaragua, Costa Rica

CHAPTER I

MANIFEST DESTINY AND MIDDLE AMERICA

> We have a destiny to perform, a 'manifest destiny' over all Mexico, over South America, over the West Indies and Canada.[1]

This grandiose sentiment expressed by a New Orleans editor in 1850 reflected the attitude of a large portion of public opinion in the United States between the end of the Mexican War and the beginning of the Civil War. It was a crucial period in American history. Domestically, debate waxed over the extension of slavery into the territories. In foreign affairs, dreams abounded of a further enlargement of the American empire. These two issues were inextricably woven together. A major focus of these broader issues was Middle America, and a significant key to Middle America was the state of Nicaragua. The thoughts and actions of American citizens and their government with respect to Nicaragua were, in many ways, pivotal for U.S. relations with Central America as a whole during the nineteenth century.

A British magazine in 1856 referred to the role of Nicaragua in an editorial about the belief of the American people in their "manifest destiny" that they should "have the control of all the North American continent":

> The manner in which the State of Nicaragua has been reduced, or, it should rather be said, raised to her present position, by being occupied and governed by a large body of Americans, affords an instance of the truth of the statement. . . . Should the Americans in that country be able to maintain their position, of which, at present, there seems to be every probability, the successful filibustering of Nicaragua will be but the beginning; the end will be the occupation, by Americans, of all the Central American

---

[1] James D. B. DeBow, quoted in William H. Goetzmann, When the Eagle Screamed, The Romantic Horizon in American Diplomacy, 1800-1860 (New York: John Wiley & Sons, Inc., 1966), 75.

States, and, in due course of time, of Mexico and Cuba.[2]

The term "manifest destiny" was coined by John L. O'Sullivan who wrote in 1845 that "our manifest destiny !is1 to overspread the continent allotted by Providence for the free development of our yearly multiplying millions."[3] The attitude itself which the term characterized was a long-standing tradition in American history. This self-acknowledged right of continual expansion began as early as 1763, when loyal British subjects in America chafed at the Proclamation Line running along the crest of the Appalachians, beyond which the colonists were forbidden to venture. The subsequent surge to occupy and cultivate the Northwest and Louisiana territories was evidence of that sense of destiny. Finally, the acquisition by 1848 of the whole of the Mexican territory north of the Rio Grande and Gila rivers put America on the Pacific shore facing the Orient. At this juncture, still-restless Americans found themselves perplexed as to which direction they should next choose in order to expend their bursting energies.

The Treaty of Guadalupe-Hidalgo, which formally ended the Mexican War, was a compromise. While Nicholas P. Trist, the Chief Clerk of the State Department and President James K. Polk's agent for securing the peace treaty, feverishly negotiated with the remnants of the Mexican government, two contending forces in the United States pressured the President to alter the terms of Trist's instructions.[4] On the one hand, Whigs in Congress threatened to cut off appropriations for the prosecution of the war, and thereby forfeit the opportunity to seize art or all of the Mexican territory subsequently acquired. On the other hand, a growing group of American expansionists demanded that all of Mexico should be annexed, perhaps as a preparatory step to expansion through Central America to the Gulf of Darien.

---

[2] "Nicaragua and the Filibusters," Blackwood's Magazine, March, 1856, reprinted in Littell's Living Age, XIII, No. 621, April 19, 1856.

[3] John L. O'Sullivan, "Annexation," The United States Magazine and Democratic Review, July, 1845. O'Sullivan was more modest in his anticipation of the extension of our national patrimony than DeBow was five years later. His editorial had reference primarily to North America above the Rio Grande, but he envisioned this domain would encompass 250-300 million Americans by 1945.

[4] Polk's displeasure with Trist's apparent inability to expedite the negotiations induced the President to recall his envoy; Trist ignored the summons, and concluded the negotiations.

The terms of the treaty, signed on February 2, 1848, provided that Mexico cede to the United States the territory that includes the present-day states of New Mexico, California, Arizona, Nevada, Utah, and part of Colorado, and confirmed American title to Texas as far as the Rio Grande, in return for the payment of $15,000,000. The United States also assumed the claims of its citizens against the Mexican government to the value of $3,250,000. The acquisition of this new area served to inflame a smoldering social and political problem in the United States: the question of the extension of slavery to territories with aspirations toward statehood. The pattern had been established in 1820 that a "solution" to the problem would be worked out in Congress with each new incorporation. Thus, the Missouri Compromise of that year admitted Missouri as a slave state while free-soil Maine, formerly a part of Massachusetts, was admitted as a separate state. In addition, in the future slavery would be prohibited north of the line of 36° 30', the southern boundary of Missouri, in the area comprising the remainder of the Louisiana Territory.

Many anti-slavery Whigs in Congress had opposed the war against Mexico because a victory would ratify the admission of Texas as a slave state. Subsequently, the delicate balance between slave and free states was maintained, but the additional territories in the Southwest added a new dimension to the problem, and one that particularly concerned the South. California clamored for admission as a free state, and the popularity of the institution of slavery in the remaining area was dubious. Between 1848 and 1850, the South became increasingly disillusioned over their prospects in the Southwest, an area that southerners regarded as their heritage since the effort and the blood expended to acquire it had been largely southern. A new compromise was reached in 1850, one which provided for the admission of California as a free state with the remaining area—the territories of Utah and New Mexico—left open to "popular sovereignty," i.e., a territorial referendum.

Perhaps some southerners felt that an expected migration of slaveholders from Texas into the contiguous areas would assure the slavery-oriented future of the territories when time for admission arrived. Other southerners had witnessed the handwriting on the wall. Given the nature of the anticipated agricultural and commercial uses of the remaining territory within the Union, there seemed little hope that either popular sovereignty or Congress would concede these areas to the embattled institution. As a result, eyes were cast toward the tropics— where a type of plantation economy was already in existence—for land which could be annexed as territories and conditioned for statehood with slavery. This reorientation brought Central America and the Caribbean into the vortex of American domestic politics, and into the arena of projected American expansion.

Aside from those who were interested in the tangible practice of counting states, there was a large body of public opinion in the United

States that believed the ultimate destiny of the nation was continued expansion. Some of these limited their designs to specific targets such as Cuba. At the other end of the spectrum were those who dreamed of an American empire that stretched from the Arctic Circle to the Gulf of Panama, and perhaps even beyond. Many of these felt that it was America's manifest destiny and duty to carry the fruits of our civilization to the benighted inhabitants living beyond our borders. This attitude did not base itself on such mundane issues as slavery, commerce, or agriculture; rather it soared with such grandiose concepts as liberty, justice, and equality, all of which the United States was destined to purvey.

Expansion to the north had been sealed off by the 1846 treaty with Great Britain which had divided the Oregon territory between the two nations. Despite the cries in the Pacific Northwest, a hotbed of manifest destiny, for "Fifty-four forty or fight!", the existing demarcation line of 49° was extended westward to Puget Sound. In the south, Mexican territory had become diplomatically inviolable with the Guadalupe-Hidalgo line. All this meant that manifest destiny now had to consider lands elsewhere, and again Central America and the Caribbean came into the picture.

A third group of expansionists viewed intrusion into Central America as a necessity for reasons of communication and transportation. By 1849, gold had been discovered in California, and waves of Americans including prospectors, merchants, and general opportunists were seeking ways of going from one coast to the other without having to cross the almost trackless wilderness of the American interior. An alternative was to sail around Cape Horn at the tip of South America, but this was a long, arduous, and expensive passage. More to their liking was sailing from ports such as New York or New Orleans, crossing the Isthmus of Central America, and connecting with sailing ships or steamers which would carry them to San Francisco. A major problem was that the only reliable route across the Isthmus was a mule trail across Panama.

The ideal solution was a ship canal across the Isthmus, by which travelers and cargo could avoid the cost and inconvenience of debarkation or transshipment. The idea of a transoceanic canal was not a new one. It had been dreamed of as early as the reign of King Philip II in the last half of the sixteenth century. Spain, for reasons ranging from technological to xenophobic, had never undertaken the massive project. The time seemed appropriate to rectify that oversight, and possible routes were actively scouted by both American and European entrepreneurs. One possibility was Panama, then a part of Colombia; but a more attractive site was Nicaragua. Engineers and investors thought it possible to construct a route utilizing the San Juan River which flowed from Lake Nicaragua to the Caribbean Sea, cross over the upland lake, then dig a canal the rest of the way to the Pacific, a distance of less than twenty five miles.

The most aggressive of the American entrepreneurs was transportation magnate Cornelius Vanderbilt, who signed a contract with Nicaragua which provided for an interim land-water route across the Isthmus within the borders of that country, and ultimately for the construction of a ship canal. Although Vanderbilt was subsequently frustrated in his efforts to build the canal, his transit route employing river steamers, lake steamers, and carriages was the most popular route for crossing until closed in 1856 after being embroiled in the power struggle in Nicaragua. Nevertheless, other Americans continued to maintain—both before and after the Vanderbilt debacle—that ultimate American control of the country, whether by subterfuge or annexation, was the only viable hope for security for American capital.

At the same time, the U.S. government wanted to make sure that American capital was protected in the region generally, and with respect to transit and canal routes in particular. But Washington found itself in an awkward position. Although bound by the Neutrality Law of 1818 to prevent its citizens from making armed incursions into the sovereign domain of other nations,[5] the government could not turn a deaf ear to demands of its citizens for protection of their traditional rights to "colonize" if this colonization conformed to the laws of the recipient states. Therein lay the dilemma: with the introduction of filibusterism from the United States into Central America, adequately and definitively labeling these efforts was often difficult and sometimes impossible. In addition, the larger question of the "enforcement" of the Monroe Doctrine was inextricably interwoven with all the other problems facing the U. S. government in dealing with Central America.

The Monroe Doctrine was initially a statement of U.S. policy made by President James Monroe in his message to Congress on December 2, 1823. At that time, the United States was alarmed by the threat of French intervention, supported by the powers of the Holy Alliance, with the purpose either of restoring Spanish rule over the newly-liberated Spanish-American republics or of imposing some form of monarchical government. The original suggestion came from British Foreign Secretary George Canning, and was intended to be a joint British-American statement. Prophetically, Secretary of State John Quincy Adams persuaded the president to make the unilateral declaration with the thought that some time in the future it might be necessary to employ it against the encroachments of Great Britain.

In Europe, the proclamation prompted some resentment, and not a little amused disdain, and its "enforcement," if such it can be called, was probably a result of the superior British navy in the Atlantic and Caribbean protecting that nation's own commercial interests. The Doctrine was restated in 1845 by President Polk because of his concern

---

[5] U.S. Statutes, III, Chap. LXXXVIII, 447-50.

about English and French diplomatic activities in Texas and British interest in Oregon and California, and became a recognized principle of American foreign policy. With those issues settled either amicably or by force of arms, the United States turned its attention to the problem of apparent British expansion in Central America. It was clear to many, given the new American focus on this area, that the two nations were on a collision course over hegemony in the Isthmus.

The position of the United States in the Isthmus was not an enviable one. Despite repeated efforts, it had never really "normalized" relations with either the Central American federation or its successors, the five Central American nations. State Department envoys floundered around seeking out governments to which they could present their credentials. Transportation from the east coast of the United States to Central American capitals was always inconvenient and sometimes virtually non-existent. Somber instructions from the Department of State to its envoys often revealed an appalling ignorance of the geography of the area to which the diplomats were dispatched. One writer later characterized the situation in 1849 in almost dyspeptic terms:

> In the best of circumstances, there was little that any United States agent could do; for Central America had fallen under the dominion of Britain. Though it was almost at our doors, its approaches were guarded by the British outposts of Jamaica and Belize. Its flanks—Guatemala and Costa Rica—while American forces slept, had surrendered to British direction and control. Its Atlantic shore line, embracing the eastern terminus of the Nicaragua Canal route, had become in effect British territory under a thin Mosquito mask. Its Bay of Fonseca, dominating the western terminus of the route, lay under the guns of British warships. Its whole extent of land and waters was under the observation of British officials. Its very existence as a single state was subject to British whim. . . .
>
> Such was the Central American situation in 1849; such the result of a quarter of a century of diplomatic preparation on the part of Great Britain; such the result of a quarter of a

century of diplomatic futility on the part of
the United States.[6]

Although the situation was probably not as desperate as thus characterized, there was no question but that the British had a head start on the United States in this strategic area. British businessmen had been for years systematically deputized as consuls and commercial agents, and many had spent their entire adult lives in the region, marrying into local families and acquiring the confidence of native businessmen and politicians. Their reports to the Foreign Office were invaluable aids to the calculation of British policy in Central America. The British navy did roam the shores nearest the Pacific and Caribbean coastlines, and were ever ready to show the flag in protection of British commercial and diplomatic interests. But perhaps the most serious threat with respect to violation of the Monroe Doctrine were British neo-colonies on the Isthmus and the adjacent islands. Belize, or British Honduras, had been seized by the British at the end of the eighteenth century and it had remained under their rule, although the surrounding areas were fighting for their independence from Spain. Guatemala claimed the territory in vain, and in 1859 finally ceded the disputed area to Great Britain, albeit with a number of conditions attached to the agreement.

The history of the Mosquito Coast of Honduras and Nicaragua is even more complex. The basis for the earliest British claim was that English freebooters had utilized the corrugated shoreline of Cape Gracias a Dios on the frontier between Honduras and Nicaragua as a haven, and during the recurring colonial wars between Spain and England they had been commissioned as privateers by the Jamaican governors. Because the area did not fit into the scheme of Spanish colonial development, the Spanish had neglected it and had left its fortunes to the aboriginal Mosquito Indians. The British recorded a pseudo-protectorate status for the region with the "voluntary" submission in 1740 of the Mosquito king to the British crown.

The Spanish attempted to recover the area in the 1763 Treaty of Paris, in which Great Britain agreed to demolish all its fortifications on the "Spanish continent." The British, employing a pattern of diplomatic deviousness, interpreted this to mean South America, with, concomitantly, North America being the "American continent." The Spanish tried again in a supplementary treaty of 1786, but the British still retained the right to cut logwood, and thus preserved their foothold. After the decline of Spanish power in America, the British resumed transporting Mosquito "kings" to Belize for solemn but contrived coronation ceremonies. The British returned in force in 1848,

---

[6] Joseph B. Lockey, "Diplomatic Futility," Hispanic American Historical Review, X (1930), 294.

seizing the mouth of the San Juan River under the guise of preserving it for the Mosquito king, even though a Mosquito Indian had never dwelt within fifty miles of the river in any direction. Even so, the British claimed that it constituted "part of the proper dominions of his Mosquito Majesty of whom Great Britain was the lawful protector." In reality, British Foreign Secretary Lord Palmerston felt he had grasped "the key to the Central American Isthmus . . . the only feasible means of communication between the two seas."[7]

Far from retrenching or maintaining the status quo during the period, the British continued to press other claims. Shortly after occupying the mouth of the San Juan, Lord Palmerston attempted to seize the island of Tigre in the Bay of Fonseca, which he judged would be the western terminus of a canal route.[8] The British were also charged with quietly annexing Roatan Island and other nearby islands in the Gulf of Honduras.[9] It was clear to many in Washington that the pious platitudes of the Monroe Doctrine were not going to retain America for the Americans, and that positive and vigorous action was called for by the U.S. government. In spirit, and with the legacy of the expansionist Polk administration as a precedent, some of the succeeding administrations on the Potomac were not unwilling to act.

After his inauguration on March 4, 1849, Zachary Taylor, the Mexican War hero and political neophyte, had hoped to conduct a non-partisan administration. This non-partisanship would extend not only to

---

[7] Ephraim G. Squier, Adventures on the Mosquito Shore (Gainesville, 1965, orig. pub. 1855), 337-351. In an introduction, Daniel F. Alleger states that Squier had been sent in 1849 by President Zachary Taylor to Nicaragua as charge d'affaires as "one move in an effort to forestall a British dream of a Nicaragua canal up the San Juan River from the Caribbean to the Pacific." Ibid., ix.

[8] Ibid., 352.

[9] El Nicaraguense (Granada), July 12, 1856. John P. Heiss, who had been appointed by William Walker's Nicaraguan government as charge d'affaires in Washington, made the charge in an open letter to be read at a rally held in New York on May 24, 1856, in support of American filibusters in Nicaragua. Heiss also called on the United States government to revoke its "odious" neutrality laws and allow its citizens to aid anybody anywhere in obtaining a more liberal form of government. He charged that while the United States had interfered with "immigration" to Nicaragua, the British had aided the filibusters' opponents with arms and ammunition. Nevertheless, he maintained, Central America, along with Yucatan and the Bay Islands, would become Americanized and formed into one great republic.

patronage politics but to critical national issues as well. He would leave these issues to Congress to settle, and would content himself merely with implementation of the legislature's collective judgments. Unfortunately, he was unable to keep the office of the president above the battle that continued to rage over the question of the extension of slavery into the newly-acquired southwestern domain. When the territory of California petitioned for statehood, and indicated that it would enter sans slavery, a great hue and cry was raised in the South. Taylor adopted a stance of righteous indignation, feeling that sectional pressure was attempting to surrogate national law. His death in July, 1850, ended his opposition to the last compromise carefully pieced together by Henry Clay.

Taylor's successor and the last of the Whigs, Millard Fillmore, was, if anything, even more passionately opposed to the institution of slavery. He was however, more concerned with the preservation of the Union, and, rather than threatening to hang those who interfered with California's "popular sovereignty" as Taylor had done, he concurred with the Compromise of 1850. His acquiescence may have spelled doom for his own political career as well as that of his party, but it did allay the issue for the remainder of his term. It was the Franklin Pierce administration, taking over in March, 1853, that raised the spectre of new acquisitions and their corollary, new slavery extensions.

The Pierce administration, with its general program of southward expansion, was heir to the "Polk Doctrine" in both spirit and personnel. Pierce himself had been appointed to the rank of general by Polk in the Mexican War, and his cabinet included Secretary of State William L. Marcy, who had been Polk's Secretary of War. Key representatives abroad were also a legacy of the Polk administration. Polk's Secretary of State, James Buchanan, was minister to London, and Polk's second Secretary of the Navy, John Y. Mason, was minister to Paris. Perhaps the most curious appointment was Pierre Soule, a naturalized Frenchman and former Louisiana senator, as minister to Madrid.

> In rising to eminence in New Orleans [Soule] had fervently defended states' rights, the institution of slavery, Manifest Destiny, and expecially the acquisition of Cuba. He had campaigned for Cass in 1848 on the ground that Cass would annex Cuba. His appointment to the Madrid post, in view of this record, was near to being insulting.[10]

---

[10] Frederick Merk, The Monroe Doctrine and American Expansionism, 1843-1849 (New York, 1966), 271.

In his inaugural speech, Pierce made his position—previously intimated during the campaign—clear with reference to Middle America in general and Cuba in particular:

> The policy of my administration will not be controlled by any timid forebodings of evil from expansion. Indeed, it is not to be disguised that our attitude as a nation, and our position on the globe, render the acquisition of certain possessions, not within our jurisdiction, eminently important for our protection, if not, in the future, essential for the preservation of the rights of commerce and the peace of the world.[11]

The president also addressed the problem of British—and perhaps other European—encroachment in Middle America and the concomitant challenge to the Monroe Doctrine. European colonization upon "this side of the ocean," indeed any "idea" of interference or colonization, would be rejected as "utterly inadmissable [sic]."[12]

The most active foreign policy objective of the early Pierce administration was the acquisition of Cuba. Aside from its proximity to the U.S. mainland, other reasons attracted adherents to its incorporation into the American Union. First and foremost for many was the plantation economy which was well-suited to the employment of black slaves. Southerners concerned about the precarious balance in the Senate were heartened by the prospect of possibly carving up the island into two or more states. Others were interested in the strategic location of the island in terms of both naval and merchant marine activity. It was pointed out that Cuba commanded access to the mouth of the Mississippi River, the Gulf of Mexico, and future trans-Isthmian passages. Finally, there was the intriguing character of its ownership. The last great bastion of Spain's former empire in America, it was an anachronism. Secured by the unsteady hand of a depressed European state, its citizens were anxious to throw off the yoke of colonialism and to rise with the fortunes of the colossus to the north. The last two points—that Spain because of her weakness had forfeited the privilege of holding the colony, and that there was overwhelming support within the island for independence—were not universally accepted. Senator John P. Hale of New Hampshire spoke for those who felt there was something immoral about taking advantage of Spain's decrepitude. He wryly pointed out that if the administration was so concerned about the

---

[11] New York Evening Mirror, March 5, 1853.

[12] Ibid.

strategic position of Cuba that it was willing to attempt to bully Spain, then what about Canada, a British possession?

> I suppose that this country is not so low; or its patriotism is not of that doubtful character . . . . that it will take a position before a weak nation which it will not assume before a strong one. . . . I ask if the local position of Canada, in any aspect in which you may view it, whether in relation to the interests of peace or war, is not a thousand fold of more consequence than Cuba. . . ?[13]

This was logic, not realism, and the Pierce administration was early committed to southern expansion. In addition, Manifest Destiny tended to lose some of its fervor when directed at Anglo-Saxon lands and institutions, as in the case of Oregon.

With respect to the anticipated help from native Cubans, America was disabused of this expectation in the Taylor-Filmore years. A number of filibustering expeditions to Cuba sailed from American ports during this period, in spite of official efforts to discourage them. Their leader was Narciso Lopez, a Venezuelan who had long resided in Cuba. In 1848 he formed a revolutionary group on the island, but was defeated and fled to the United States the following year. In this country, he organized a group of Americans and mounted other expeditions to Cuba to fight for independence. In the course of these activities, he was arrested and prosecuted in the United States, but public sentiment was so much in his favor that a conviction could not be obtained, and he sailed again with another force. He was captured and executed in Havana in 1851.[14] The expected uprising in the island never occurred, and the Pierce administration determined to find alternative means of acquisition, either by purchase or by some ill-defined method of "detachment" from Spain.

This new orientation led to the ill-fated "Ostend Manifesto," drafted by Buchanan, Mason, and Soule. The project was one that was conceived by James Buchanan within days after Pierce took office. In a letter to Secretary Marcy, Buchanan advised, "If you desire to acquire Cuba in a peaceful manner, the President ought to select able and accomplished ministers to Naples, Spain, England, and France who would

---

[13] Congressional Globe, 32 Cong., 2 Sess., App. 97.

[14] Robert G. Caldwell, The Lopez Expeditions to Cuba, 1848-51 (Princeton, 1915), passim.

cordially work together."[15] Marcy acted on this suggestion, and appointed the expansionist trio to the operative posts. Marcy's instructions to Soule were revealing. He expressed concern over the possibility of aid by France or Great Britain to Spain to protect Spain's sovereignty in Cuba, thereby creating a virtual protectorate.

> We have recently learned in the instance of Central America what a protectorate means, and to what use it may be devoted. There is not a very great difference between the protector and the possessor of a territory, and when the possessor is weak and the protector strong, the distinction we apprehend would in effect be annihilated.[16]

Marcy observed that the minister to Madrid during the Polk administration had approached the Spanish government about purchase of the island. The secretary further pointed out that it had not been the policy of the American government to seek transfer of the island without the concurrence of the Cuban people. The United States might still be willing to purchase Cuba under certain conditions, but it was unlikely that the Spanish would be interested. Marcy believed that the Spanish government was under obligation to Great Britain and France

> not to transfer this island to the United States. . . . (Most likely) Spain will pertinaciously hold onto Cuba, and the separation, whenever it takes place, will be the work of violence. In the present aspect of the case the President does not deem it proper to authorize you to make any propositions for the purchase of that island.[17]

Marcy added that the United States would favor a "voluntary separation" of Cuba from Spain, with Spain perhaps retaining a principal commercial interest. Thus Cuba would fall into the "American Continental System and contribute to its stability instead of exposing it to danger." The United States would contribute more than just good will, Marcy

---

[15] Buchanan to Marcy, March 8, 1853, William L. Marcy Papers (Library of Congress).

[16] Marcy to Soule, July 23, 1853, ibid.

[17] Ibid.

intimated, but could not elaborate until Spain's position was better understood in Washington.[18]

Despite Marcy's admonition against purchase, hope of a spontaneous uprising on the island waned, and the secretary's subsequent instructions returned to the Polk-Buchanan procedure of trying to buy Cuba in the face of Spanish intransigence. Marcy directed his envoys to persuade financial interests in the European capitals to bring pressure on Spain for the sale so that Spain would have the money to pay some of its debts long due these financiers. The ministers held a series of meetings in the autumn of 1854 in Ostend, Belgium, and Aix-la-Chapelle, France, and forwarded their report to the Department of State on October 18. The report brought into intimate association the related ideas of American security, the importance of the Gulf of Mexico, the Isthmian routes, and the acquisition of Cuba in order to protect them. They also expressed concern about the "Africanization" of Cuba, fearing that a Haitian-type revolution and black seizure might encourage a similar movement in America's southern states. After again recommending purchase of the island, the ministers observed that should Spain refuse, "then, by every law, human and divine, we shall be justified in wresting it from Spain, if we possess the power"; and the trio left no doubt they believed the United States possessed that power.

Although the report was confidential, and accurately reflected the attitude of the administration, Pierce and Marcy disavowed it when newspapers in both the United States and Europe ferreted out the story. The vociferous and increasingly influential Republican press in the United States was especially critical, attaching the epithet "manifesto" to the report, and claiming that it was a pistol held to the head of Spain—a demand that Cuba be "sold or seized." After this disclosure, the Pierce administration was reluctant to press the case for acquisition. Ironically, Buchanan won the Democratic nomination and the presidential election in 1856 partly because he was not involved in the Kansas-Nebraska issue, having been out of the country, and because he was involved with the Ostend Manifesto.[19] Nonetheless, persistent efforts to acquire Cuba during his administration were not only unsuccessful but added to sectional bitterness over the issue of slavery extension and probably hastened the coming of the Civil War.[20]

With the hopelessness of a spontaneous uprising, the failure of purchase efforts, and the discrediting of official government efforts to

---

18 Ibid.

19 Roy F. Nichols, "James Buchanan," Encyclopedia Britannica (1970), IV, 341.

20 Merk, Monroe Doctrine, 275.

detach Cuba, the field was open to private adventurers. One of these was William Walker, an American soldier-of-fortune currently residing in California, whose primary interest seemed to be Nicaragua. Walker's grand design probably envisioned a Middle American superstate under his direction. With a small band of filibusters from California, Walker intervened in a Nicaraguan civil war in 1855, and almost miraculously, was successful in making himself master of that state for over a year. Though his motives and aspirations were never entirely clear to anyone but himself, many regarded his efforts as a forerunner to the extension of American control over Central America and the Caribbean.

One of those interested in Walker's success was Domingo de Goicouria, a cultured and highly regarded Cuban revolutionist. Goicouria's revolutionary credentials were respectable, as he had worked with Lopez in Mississippi on the 1849-51 Cuban invasions. Early in 1856, Goicouria, who was then living in New York, sent an emissary to Walker in Nicaragua to validate reports that the latter was preparing to use the Isthmus as a launching base for a Cuban invasion. Walker and the agent reached an agreement to pool their interests, first Nicaragua and then Cuba. Walker subsequently received aid from Cuba revolutionists, but it became increasingly clear to them that Walker's ambitions were not parallel to their aspirations. The break between the Nicaraguan filibusters and the Cuban revolutionists resulted in Goicouria's publication of Walker's letters indicating the filibuster's intent to annex Cuba in order to preclude the same action by the "barbarous Yankees."[21]

Walker's ultimate intentions were never disclosed because they were never realized, as his short-lived regime in Nicaragua was ended by armies from a coalition of Central American states. Speculation, then and subsequently, was rampant, and sectional interests in the United States tended to identify his plans with their own aspirations. There seems to be little question with respect to Walker's attitude toward slavery, for one of his first decrees after assuming power in Nicaragua was the repeal of the anti-slavery laws. Walker was from Nashville, Tennessee, but it appears he became a partisan of slavery during a sojourn in New Orleans and was obsessed with the idea of finding a territory for slavery expansion outside the reach of northern abolitionists. The Mexican War had proved the weakness of that country, and he determined to make it the "nucleus of a new slavery propaganda."[22]

---

[21] William O. Scroggs, "William Walker's Designs on Cuba," Mississippi Valley Historical Review, I (September 1914), 201-208.

[22] Theodore H. Hittell, "History of the Filibuster, William Walker," unpublished ms., ca. 1915, Sutro Library, San Francisco, 12.

When his efforts in 1853 to detach Baja California and Sonora from Mexico and to extablish an independent "Republic of Sonora" proved unsuccessful, Walker returned to San Francisco to await another opportunity to fulfill his ambition. The chance came with the offer by the Nicaraguan Liberals to hire a mercenary force led by Walker to aid them in their battle with the Nicaraguan Conservatives. Walker's subsequent meteoric rise to Commander-in-Chief of all Nicaraguan forces, and then President of Nicaragua, both startled and confused the Department of State, as well as those Americans who followed his fortunes. Some felt he was the emulator of Sam Houston, that he would Americanize Nicaragua, and then secure its admission to the American Union. Because of his identification with one side in a duel for control of the Isthmian transit, Walker was regarded as an agent of a coterie of American capitalists.[23] It seems probable, however, that his aims went beyond Nicaragua. He apparently planned to create a strong federated state out of the five Central American republics, organized and governed on military principles, and then to effect the conquest of Cuba. The introduction of an American population would serve to secure and regenerate the entire area. An interoceanic canal through Nicaragua would give the region an even greater strategic importance.[24]

In other words, Walker was bent on establishing a military slaveocracy in Middle America, with himself as its dictator. Reaction in the United States to this possibility was mixed. Some southerners were delighted, and hoped an alliance with Walker's "empire" might check northern opposition in the event of secession; some northern proponents of Manifest Destiny were alienated. Though they had taken slavery in the tropics for granted, they anticipated that action by Walker or the U.S. government would lead to opening up the area to trade or perhaps to annexation. They had not been expecting a competitive superstate with opposing ideas and institutions.[25] Initially, the ambivalence in the United States did not trouble Walker. His major concern was that equipment, supplies, and reinforcements arrive unimpeded from the northern republic, and for a time they continued to pour in without interruption. Ultimately, the pressure on the Pierce administration coming from opposition to official expansion and to the adventures of American citizens began to impinge. The government wavered, never entirely aware of the true situation in Nicaragua, and unable to decide whether to assign its imprimatur or to employ its naval forces to assure the failure of the filibusters. A contemporary editorial took the administration to task over its indecision.

---

23 New York Herald, November 29, 1856.

24 Scroggs, "Walker's Designs on Cuba," 199.

25 Ibid. 210.

> The general policy, aside from mere legal questions involved in this whole series of blunders of the Marcy-Pierce rule would seem to point to the encouragement, by every proper means, of the movement in Nicaragua. It is a mode of foreclosing the Central American controversy with England. It assures stability of government over the Transit route. It promises vastly increased growth in sugar, coffee and other tropical products. It binds California to the policy of the American Union. It stations a power to the southward of Mexico, and opens to that dissolving republic a means of renovation. It is an expression of American enterprise, precisely at the right point—indicative of the future of the whole of the North and Central American States. It raises up a rival in Cuba, where labor in freedom will be found vastly superior to that which is bound in the iron clamps of a military despotism. In short, the Nicaragua movement is wholly Anglo-American in character, orderly in administration, just in principle, and beneficial in results; and the sooner the government rectifies its mistakes the sooner will its errors be forgotten.[26]

If the administration's policy toward Walker, Vanderbilt, et al., seemed to lack continuity, there was even more confusion about the confrontation with Great Britain over the enforcement of the Monroe Doctrine and hegemony in Central America. President Polk, in his 1845 address which renewed the tenets of the Doctrine, had broadened the definition of "security" for this country, transforming the doctrine from a defensive statement to an expansionist statement. At the same time, there seemed to be a contraction in the zone of application. In 1823, the zone had embraced two continents—it was hemispheric; in 1845 it comprised only one continent—North America.[27] Taking the two together, the implication was either that the United States intended to make a more intensive effort to establish its fiat over Middle America or that this area was most vulnerable to British encroachment. State Department policy, however, was clouded by the fact that every British move seemed to be accompanied by diplomatic smoke screens and faits accomplis.

---

[26] Blackwood's Magazine, March, 1856.

[27] Merk, Monroe Doctrine, 281.

With the acquisition of California and the gold rush, the concomitant renewed interest in a transoceanic canal, and the British headstart toward exclusive influence in Central America, the Department initially strove to establish some degree of equality with the British. This effort resulted in a treaty between the United States and Great Britain signed in 1850 by the American secretary of state, John M. Clayton, and the British ambassador to Washington, Sir Henry Lytton Bulwer. It guaranteed the strict neutrality of an interoceanic canal opened across Central America. The countries agreed that neither would seek to control any canal that might be built, nor would they occupy or plant colonies in or exercise dominion over any part of Central America.

The ink was hardly dry on the agreement before the Clayton-Bulwer Treaty became the subject of conflicting interpretations. The U.S. government understood it to mean that the British process of establishing new colonies in Central America would now be reversed and, at the very least, they would withdraw from their occupation of the Mosquito Territory. The British foreign office pointed out that the treaty did not apply to that portion of Nicaragua's coast as it was not a colony but a protectorate, therefore not included in the agreement, and that the treaty was not retroactive. British intransigence complicated Washington's diplomacy with respect to Nicaragua and Central America.

Fully confident that American capital would build the canal, thereby enhancing American prestige, security, and commerce, the State Department attempted to establish the proper milieu for such an eventuality. The task included providing its good offices in settling the Nicaraguan-Costa Rican border dispute, for the canal route would pass through part of the contested area and hostilities might seriously impair transit operations. In addition, the Department also wanted to make it possible for the operating company to contract with only one sovereign state, rather than risk the confusion of having to deal with two or even more. A basic problem was the negotiation of a treaty of peace, amity, and commerce with Nicaragua; the treaty would be necessary to ensure the safety of U.S. citizens and their investments. Due to British interference and the actions of its own private citizens, the United States failed to exchange treaty ratifications with Nicaragua during the entire period. The border dispute was finally settled, but without U.S. help or arbitration.

The advent of the Civil War curtailed American interest in southward expansion until the close of the century. When Confederate guns fired on Fort Sumter on April 12, 1861, all eyes turned inward at the coming holocaust. Little thought and less attention was given to what had recently been a pressing and formidable issue. In many ways, a short-lived era had passed. It was an era in which there was much agreement in the United States on something called Manifest Destiny, but much disagreement on its implementation and its implications. The nation's leaders at times seemed to be committed to expansion; indeed, many were elected on expansionist platforms, but their erratic courses left little in concrete achievement. A few intrepid individuals launched expansionist programs of their own, but by the end of the decade, these had borne little fruit. Nevertheless, governmental, entrepreneurial, and filibuster efforts in Nicaragua during the era provided an insight into United States relations with all of Central America during the nineteenth century.

Figure 3. Nicaragua

CHAPTER II

DIPLOMATIC FRUSTRATION

> The United States government's interest is in keeping the transit route under one authority (i.e.: Nicaragua), and that conflicts arising from grants should be adjudicated by the judicial authorities, that all parties should act in good faith.[1]

These instructions from the Secretary of State to his envoy in Nicaragua pinpoint America's primary concerns while trying to negotiate a satisfactory treaty with Nicaragua during the decade of the 1850's. The task was not a simple one. After independence from Spain, Nicaragua had spent a 15-year apprenticeship as a state in the Federation of Central America. By 1838, the Federation was moribund, and its members began launching careers of separate nationhood punctuated by regional strife. Nonetheless, the United States was anxious to "normalize" relations with the five new republics, especially Nicaragua.

Nicaragua was the focal point because its geographical and topographical advantages made it a likely site for an interoceanic canal or a transisthmian transit route. A further concern of the United States was that Nicaragua was one of the areas where the British were making not only commercial, but apparently neo-colonial inroads. The Mosquito Coast of Nicaragua had been occupied by the British since January 1, 1848, and this area included San Juan del Norte, which was expected to be the eastern terminus for either a canal or a transit route. In addition, the British were giving evidence of coveting naval bases in the Bay of Fonseca, shared by Nicaragua, El Salvador, and Honduras, and of establishing a pre-eminent sphere of influence in central America as a whole.

Early U.S. efforts to negotiate a bilateral treaty were frustrated by a number of events and circumstances. One problem was identifying a legitimate government with which to do business. Even after the breakup of the Central American Federation, numerous efforts were made in various states to bind the union together again. On occasion, these efforts were nominally successful, but more often they resulted in temporary arrangements made by caudillo leaders of similar ideological

---

[1] Lewis Cass to Mirabeau B. Lamar, January 2, 1858, Diplomatic Instructions of the Department of State, 1801-1906, National Archives Microfilm Publication M99, roll 27, frame 288.

proclivities. However, the problem was not limited to the international level. Internally in Nicaragua there were two principal parties, the conservatives (Legitimists or Serviles) and the liberals (Democrats). Actually, this ideological demarcation was a legacy from the era of the federation, and continued well into Nicaragua's national period, being in many cases more important than the fact of international frontiers. Civil war was endemic in that Isthmian country, causing precipitous changes in government and shifts in the location of the capital, with Leon, Masaya, Managua, and Granada all vying for the distinction at one time or another.

British efforts to frustrate American diplomacy in order to enhance their own commercial and strategic interests were largely in the domain of Frederick Chatfield, the consul-general to Central America. During Chatfield's seventeen years on the Isthmus, from 1834 until 1851, he was indefatigable in his efforts to establish British predominance, even if it meant a rather undiplomatic subversion of American attempts to negotiate satisfactory international accords with the Central American republics. The first consequential American representative to feel the sting of Chatfield's interference was Elijah Hise, named by President James K. Polk as United States charge d'affaires to Central America in October, 1848.[2] Hise's primary mission was to negotiate treaties of friendship and commerce with Guatemala and El Salvador, but a secondary responsibility was to keep an eye on Chatfield and report the British agent's activities. Hise was also assigned the task of urging a reunification of the republics of Central America. It was felt in Washington that a renewed federation, or even a confederation, would be strong enough to effectively blunt British imperial encroachments upon the Isthmus. There was a certain contradiction in Hise's instructions. Separate treaties negotiated with the various Central American states would imply recognition and encouragement by the United States of the individual character of each republic, and would therefore undermine the secondary goal of aiding in the achievement of reunion. Inasmuch as part of Chatfield's overall plan was to prevent a resumption of the federation, the British agent was pleased with Hise's progress in formulating separate accords.[3]

---

[2] Before his appointment, Hise, 47, had a large and lucrative law practice in his native Russellville, Kentucky, and had served in the Kentucky legislature. Subsequent to his diplomatic mission, he was twice elected to Congress. Hise committed suicide in 1867 because of despondency over post-Civil War conditions. National Cyclopedia of American Biography (New York: James T. White & Company, 1904), VII, 55.

[3] Mario Rodriguez, A Palmerstonian Diplomat in Central America (Tucson: The University of Arizona Press, 1964), 300.

-21-

Although no match for the intriguing Briton, Hise did recognize the importance of the projected canal and felt a special sense of urgency about coming to terms with the Nicaraguans on this crucial issue. Accordingly, he signed a treaty with Nicaraguan Foreign Minister Buenaventura Selva on May 31, 1849, even though the administration which had appointed him was now out of office and a new charge had already been appointed.[4] The treaty provided for a right-of-way for a canal, road, or railroad, in perpetuity and under American auspices, permitted fortifications if necessary, and guaranteed the territorial integrity of Nicaragua by the United States. The provisions giving the American government, or a company endorsed by it, an exclusive franchise, and making Nicaragua a virtual protectorate of the United States, were greater commitments than those in any subsequent treaty which came under consideration.

The Hise-Selva Treaty was hardly written when Hise's replacement, Ephraim George Squier, arrived at San Juan del Norte.[5] The treaty was rejected by the new administration of Zachary Taylor on three counts: Hise had never been authorized to negotiate a treaty with Nicaragua (though he had requested permission and had received no response from the Department of State), his commission had expired and he had already been replaced by Squier, and the administration had no intention of assuming a protectorate over Nicaragua. When Squier arrived, American financiers were already engaged in trying to secure a franchise for either a canal or transit route. Consequently, his instructions were to make a treaty of commerce in the interests of the American Atlantic and Pacific Ship Canal Company and to secure a right-of-way for a canal open to all nations. Squier could assure the Nicaraguans of moral support in their struggle to recover the alienated

---

[4] Miles P. DuVal, Jr., Cadiz to Cathay (Stanford University Press, 1940), 52. Rodriguez fixes the date of the treaty as June 21.

[5] Squier had been a precocious youth who taught school in his native New York State while still a teenager and despite limited formal education. Early efforts at journalism brought mixed success, but his published works on the archeology of New York and Ohio were regarded as authoritative. In 1848 he served as clerk of the Ohio House of Representatives. Squier's appointment as charge when he was only 28 was largely through the influence of W. H. Prescott. After his stint in Nicaragua, he returned to Central America in behalf of the unsuccessful Honduras Interoceanic Railway Company. Later he served as U.S. commissioner to Peru and Honduran consul-general in New York City. He capitalized on his residence in Latin America by publishing a number of archeological works on the area. Squier died in Brooklyn in 1888 after a long illness. Dictionary of American Biography (New York: Charles Scribner's Sons, 1935), IX, 488-9.

Mosquito Territory, but under no circumstances was he to guarantee the territorial integrity of Nicaragua, or to commit the American government to any alliances, controversies, or speculative schemes.[6]

On September 3, less than a week after the Ship Canal Company headed by Cornelius Vanderbilt had signed a contract with the government of Nicaragua for canal and transit rights, Squier reached an accord with the Nicaraguan foreign ministry. Sensitive to Chatfield's intrigues and diplomatic maneuvering, the American minister went beyond his instructions, conceding a limited guarantee of Nicaragua's territory. Article 35 of the treaty reaffirmed the Vanderbilt company's transit franchise. It required, however, that the United States recognize the rights of sovereignty and property which Nicaragua possessed over the line of the canal and guaranteed the neutrality of the strip as long as it remained under the control of American citizens.[7] Perhaps at the behest of the company, Secretary of State John M. Clayton indicated that if the United States were committed to undertaking the defense of the canal, some extra-territorial provision, or at least a provision for exclusivity, should be included. In addition, Clayton pointed out to Squier that the treaty had only a twenty-year duration, with a provision for annulment on twelve-months' notice, whereas Vanderbilt's franchise had a life of eighty-five years. Clayton did not feel that this gave the entrepreneurs sufficient protection, so he advised Squier to refrain from further bargaining pending an anticipated treaty with Great Britain encompassing the whole Isthmian issue.[8] The result of these latter negotiations was the Clayton-Bulwer Treaty, signed on April 19, 1850, in which the United States and Great Britain agreed that neither would obtain or maintain any exclusive control over a canal, nor would they erect or maintain any fortifications commanding a canal.[9]

In the meantime, at the urging of Eduardo Carcache, Nicaraguan Charge d'Affaires in Washington, Clayton agreed to submit the Squier treaty to the Senate. The Secretary advised Carcache, however, that even if the Senate approved it, the President would sign only with the understanding that other provisions might be agreed upon later between the two governments for "more effectually securing the objects contemplated by the 35th article." Apparently the canal company had requested the delay in submission of the treaty until it could send agents

---

[6] House Ex. Doc. No. 75, 119-130.

[7] Daniel Webster (Secretary of State) to J. Bozman Kerr (Charge d'Affaires to Central America), June 6, 1851, Diplomatic Instructions, National Archives, M77, 27/113.

[8] Clayton to Squier, November 20, 1849, ibid., 27/101.

[9] Ibid., May 7, 1850, 27/104

-23-

to Nicaragua to discuss the import of Article 35. Clayton also thought that the article "might be changed so as to inspire greater confidence in capitalists who might be disposed to invest their funds in the construction of the ship canal and at the same time, extend the benefits of protection to the canal." To facilitate this modification, Clayton recommended that Carcache return to Leon and get full powers to negotiate a new treaty.[10]

There the issue languished during the remainder of the Fillmore administration and Secretary Clayton's tenure in office. But the gauntlet was seized with a vengeance by William L. Marcy, Secretary of State under the new president, Franklin Pierce. One of the best-prepared men in U.S. history to assume the responsibilities of that office, Marcy had both the antecedents and the credentials for the job. Born of a pioneer Massachusetts family, he graduated with honors from Brown University in 1806. Like so many others, he then proceeded to learn a trade, reading law and receiving admission to the bar in New York state within three years. His initiation into New York politics came when he delivered a scholarly oration defending Jeffersonianism before the Tammany Society in New York City in 1809.

Adding to his eclectic credentials, he rose through the ranks of New York's 155th Regiment, eventually assuming the post of state adjutant-general. Thereafter, he was often addressed as "General" Marcy. After participation in the War of 1812, Marcy began a fruitful relationship as a protege of Martin Van Buren. In 1829, Governor Van Buren appointed him associate justice of the state supreme court, for which he wrote several learned and celebrated opinions. Resigning from the bench in 1831, he reluctantly accepted an election to the United States Senate. His short stint in that chamber is best remembered for his observation that he could see "nothing wrong in the rule that to the victor belong the spoils of the enemy," an expression that quickly found its way into the American political lexicon.

Marcy's resignation from the Senate was prompted by his election in 1832 to the first of three consecutive terms as New York's governor. Among other accomplishments, Governor Marcy organized the state's first geological survey, for which he was honored by having the highest peak in the Adirondacks christened "Mount Marcy." Also as governor, Marcy inveighed against the zeal of the Abolitionists as likely to destroy

---

[10] Clayton to Carcache, January 2, 1850, Notes to Foreign Legations in the United States from the Department of State, 1834-1906, National Archives Microfilm Publication M99, roll 10, frame 2. An extraordinary error was made by Clayton in this communication. He continually referred to the "Heisse" special convention of September 3, 1849. Presumably this meant "Hise," but it was Squier, Clayton's own representative, who signed it.

the Union, and suggested that states might employ penal laws against activities tending to promote insurrection in another state.

Marcy received a few votes for the vice-presidency at the 1844 Democratic Convention in Baltimore, and was subsequently named Secretary of War in the Polk administration. As Secretary, he repeatedly clashed with the imperious Winfield Scott, U.S. Army Commanding General, over Mexican War policies. Weathering Scott's clear insubordination, Marcy emerged with greater stature and an addition to his record of administrative competence.

Disappointed at not receiving the Democratic nomination in 1852, he settled for the office of Secretary of State under President Pierce. During the next four years, Marcy was chiefly responsible for the negotiation of 24 treaties, the largest number ratified within an administration up to that time. Unhappily, a treaty with Nicaragua was not among them.

Aside from the Canal Company's interests, Marcy had other substantial reasons for wanting to conclude an agreement with Nicaragua. William F. Boone, the U.S. Consul at the small Pacific port of San Juan del Sur, pointed out some of the problems inherent in the non-treaty status. In contrast to Britons who were residing and doing business there, Americans contended that no protection was provided by the U.S. government. American sailors complained that this situation was unlike that of any other port-of-call which they had visited. In addition, for the six-hundred Americans resident in Nicaragua, there was no postal arrangement unless twenty-five cents were prepaid in New York to the purser of the Vanderbilt line.

One key to the lethargic state of the treaty was another change in the juridical status of Nicaragua. On December 15, 1851, Boone was informed by Foreign Minister Pedro Zeledon that his country no longer existed as a sovereign state. Zeledon contended that a confederation of Honduras, El Salvador, and Nicaragua had been formed some two years earlier, and that the seat of this government was in Tegucigalpa. Apparently the Granada-Leon rivalry played a role in what appeared to be disingenuousness on Zeledon's part. The latter official was aligned with the Granada faction in Nicaraguan politics, while J. Bozman Kerr, nominated by the State Department as Charge' d'Affaires, was in Leon. Kerr had given Boone his commission, but even Kerr had yet to be accredited. Zeledon told Boone that in order to receive official recognition, he would have to "apply to the Central Confederation, located some place in the mountains of Honduras, some five hundred miles off." In later conversation, Zeledon conceded that he did not really expect Boone to find a government there.[11]

A problem for American citizens similar to that in San Juan del Sur arose on the opposite side of the Isthmus at San Juan del Norte, where the United States was compelled to give a temporary countenance to the de-facto government installed by Great Britain in order to provide protection for its citizens congregating there. Far from resolving the difficulties between the United States and Great Britain, the Clayton-Bulwer Treaty seemed to compound them because of the different interpretations put on its provisions. Although the United States never acknowledged the Greytown (San Juan del Norte) authorities as a legitimate government to be sustained against the claims of Nicaragua, the British continued to deny that Clayton-Bulwer was retrospective, or that they had yielded their protectorate over the Mosquito Indians. In his instructions to Solon Borland, newly appointed envoy to the Central American states, Secretary Marcy complained that a copy of the instructions from British Foreign Secretary Lord Clarendon to British Minister to the United States John F. T. Crampton showed that Great Britain maintained the same right to "intermeddle" in Central American affairs as before the signing of the Clayton-Bulwer accord, and "continued to manifest an equally forward disposition to do so." Marcy observed, however, that the British appeared to be willing to relinquish their protectorate if Nicaragua would give assurances of good treatment of the Indians and would pay the Indians some compensation. Borland should therefore urge on Nicaragua the same type of settlement that the United States had made with her Indians! Marcy noted that the Indian question might be a subterfuge, and the real issue was Britain's concern about protecting the commerce in British manufactures and Costa Rican coffee.[12]

Costa Rica was dependent upon the port of San Juan del Norte as the Serapiqui-San Juan River system provided the major outlet from Costa Rica's heartland to the Caribbean and thence to Europe. As long as the Central American "confederation" existed, there seemed to be no problem, but when it broke up and the independent state of Nicaragua purported to possess sovereign rights at San Juan del Norte, the British felt compelled to move in. Perhaps, Marcy told Borland, the best course

---

[11] Boone to Webster, December 27, 1851, Consular Despatches from San Juan del Sur, National Archives Microfilm Publication T-152, roll 1, frame 38. John Bozman Kerr served as Charge d'Affaires to Nicaragua from March 24, 1851 until July 30, 1852.

[12] Marcy to Borland, June 17, 1853, M77, 27/177. Borland served as Minister to Central America from April 30, 1853, until June 28, 1854.

for the U.S. government would be to urge the reconstitution of the confederation.[13]

The minister was also directed to negotiate another treaty with Nicaragua, and to try to include a provision that Americans could buy and hold property for any purpose. Marcy pointed out what he considered to be the benefits of such a program:

> The residence of our citizens in these states would import strength and stability to the political and commercial relations which for the mutual interest of both countries, should be maintained. Our citizens, should they find sufficient inducements to settle in any of these states would carry with them their capital and that enterprise, for which they are so much distinguished. Coming from a country of similar political institutions, imbued with the principles of a free government harmonizing with their own, such residents could not excite jealousies, or create any apprehensions of disturbing influences.

Borland was warned not to give reciprocity for this concession, as the treaty might not pass the Senate. Moreover, Marcy contended, such a reciprocal provision was probably unnecessary, considering the openness of the various American states in granting these rights.[14]

Borland concluded "A General Treaty of Peace, Amity, Commerce, Navigation, and Protection between the United States and Nicaragua" on February 14, 1854, but the treaty was amended in Washington and returned to his successor for acceptance in its new form by the Nicaraguan government.[15] By the time it was returned, other dramatic events had occured and the Borland treaty, like its predecessors, miscarried. The first impasse was the bombardment of San Juan del Norte by the United States Sloop-of-War <u>Cyane</u> on July 13, 1854, as punishment for alleged depredations against the Vanderbilt Transit Company property.[16] Carcache's successor in Washington, Jose de Marcoleta, protested vigorously to the Department of State and

---

13 Ibid.

14 Ibid.

15 Marcy to John H. Wheeler (Minister-Resident in Nicaragua), October 23, 1854, M77, 27/228.

16 Ibid., 231.

-27-

demanded reparations "to those respectable citizens of Nicaragua who suffered . . . grievous losses of property . . . and also, to the Government of Nicaragua." Marcy's rejection of this protest clearly showed the depth of resentment and misunderstanding between the two governments engendered by the confused and complex situation in Nicaragua:

> I beg to submit that it is scarcely credible, as your note seems to imply, that any considerable number of respectable citizens of the Republic of Nicaragua had taken up residence or placed their property among those whom you properly characterize as "the pseudo-sovereigns" [i.e., the British]—San Juan —a place as you admit, held by usurpation against the sovereign authority of their own government. These citizens for whom you make reclamation, must have lived in treasonable association with the open and avowed enemies of your country, and if engaged there in business they must have been incorporated with that community which you describe in such severe but probably just terms.

Marcy pointed out that the residents had been given notice "that the town would be punished for its misdeeds" and could have evacuated the area. Furthermore, they had time to persuade the Cyane's commander, Captain Hollins, to make a distinction between them and those implicated in the destruction of American property. They chose instead to cast their lot with "the abandoned and lawless dwellers at that place." Marcy concludes,

> Nicaragua may think herself kindly treated if she is not held responsible for the acts of those who were permitted by her to occupy her territory and perpetuate deeds injurious to friendly powers while within her jurisdiction. She owed it alike to herself and to these powers to have driven the band of marauders settled at San Juan from her acknowledged soil. If she had the indiscretion to open an account with the United States upon this matter this Government will be at liberty to make her responsible for all the injuries its

citizens have suffered from those occupying her territory.[17]

The second incident to disturb the relations between the two countries was the organization of a colonizing expedition by an American, Colonel Henry L. Kinney. Kinney and his associates had acquired title to a grant originally made by the Mosquito Indian "King," the grant being a tract of land on the Mosquito Coast which included San Juan del Norte. These American entrepreneurs formed the "Central American Land and Mining Company" to exploit the tract, and began advertising for stockholders in the fall of 1854 in American east coast newspapers. Marcoleta, as well as Pedro Molina, the Costa Rican representative in Washington, objected to the anticipated occupation. The Costa Rican concern stemmed from a claim to the south bank of the San Juan River and to rights in the Bay of San Juan. Molina vigorously protested against the validity of "any title or grant made by the Kings or Chiefs of the Mosquito Indians," and avowed that his government would

> not allow any colonist or party of colonists from whatever country they may proceed to occupy, locate or take possession of lands belonging to Costa Rica for the purposes of agriculture, mining or any other, unless he or they shall have previously applied to the government of Costa Rica, and duly obtained a permission and legal title to that effect.[18]

Marcy replied that the expedition appeared to be peaceable, so was not subject to U.S. neutrality laws. The Secretary said that he presumed Costa Rica's concern was about the land title, but that this was the exclusive jurisdiction of Costa Rica and not the responsibility of the United States.[19] Subsequently, the State Department did develop misgivings about the nature of the Kinney expedition, and introduced strategies to prevent it.[20] Despite the concerted efforts of the courts and the New York port authorities, Kinney managed to make his way to San Juan del Norte with a reduced contingent by early September, 1855.

---

[17] Marcy to Marcoleta, August 2, 1854, National Archives, M99, 10/62.

[18] Molina to Marcy, December 13, 1854, ibid. , M99, 10/72

[19] Marcy to Molina, December 19, 1854, Ibid., M99 10/73.

[20] At the direction of the District Attorney, the New York port authorities seized Kinney's ship. Kinney was arrested and subsequently released without trial.

While Kinney was enroute, Marcoleta's importunities became more strident, and he finally demanded that the State Department issue orders for the U.S. Navy to intervene to prevent the disembarkation of the colonists on Nicaraguan soil. Again Marcy lectured Marcoleta, this time taking the Nicaraguan agent to task for not recognizing the limitations of sovereignty and jurisdiction:

> Mr. Marcoleta is . . . fully aware that unassociated individuals have a right to leave the United States, and go whither they please, and that this government has no right to enquire into the motive for such a removal. They can be dealt with only as members of an expedition fitted out within our limits, against a friendly state and while they are within our jurisdiction. If such an expedition escapes the vigilance of officers and arrives within the territories of a foreign state, they cannot be pursued and seized while within such territories by the authorities of the United States.

Marcy advised Marcoleta that an American naval vessel "could not, without assuming illegal power and involving the sovereign rights of that state, interpose to prevent the disembarkation of arms, ammunition, or other articles to which reasonable suspicions are attached."[21]

The third interruption of normal relations between the United States and Nicaragua, and one that might be termed a catastrophe, may have been referred to in Marcoleta's request. The Nicaraguan Minister's allusion to "the meeting of suspicious persons in that locality" may have been a reference not only to Kinney, but also to the filibuster William Walker. Walker from Nashville, Tennessee, via New Orleans and California, had acceded to the Liberal Party's request to bring down an army of mercenaries to strengthen the Democratas' cause. By August, 1855, Walker and his band of 58 men had landed in Nicaragua and were conducting independent military operations against the government at Granada which Marcoleta represented, ostensibly on behalf of the Democratas headquartered at Leon. It was widely believed at that time, particularly on the American east coast, that Kinney and Walker were acting in concert rather than as rivals, as subsequent events were to prove. Marcoleta may have been alarmed at the possibility of a filibuster pincer movement operating from opposite littorals of the Nicaraguan Isthmus.

---

[21] Marcy to Marcoleta, August 22, 1855, ibid., M99, 10/85.

At this juncture, a whole new twist was added to the diplomatic conundrum. Walker not only succeeded in seizing power in Nicaragua, but proceeded to dispatch a series of his own envoys to Washington to continue seeking recognition—their own and Nicaragua's. In the meantime, Kinney was attempting to carve out a fiefdom on the Caribbean side, Vanderbilt's transit route was throttled, and the Nicaraguans wrestled with Costa Rica over the location of their joint boundary as the State Department wrung its hands and tried to mediate, but mostly just wrung its hands.

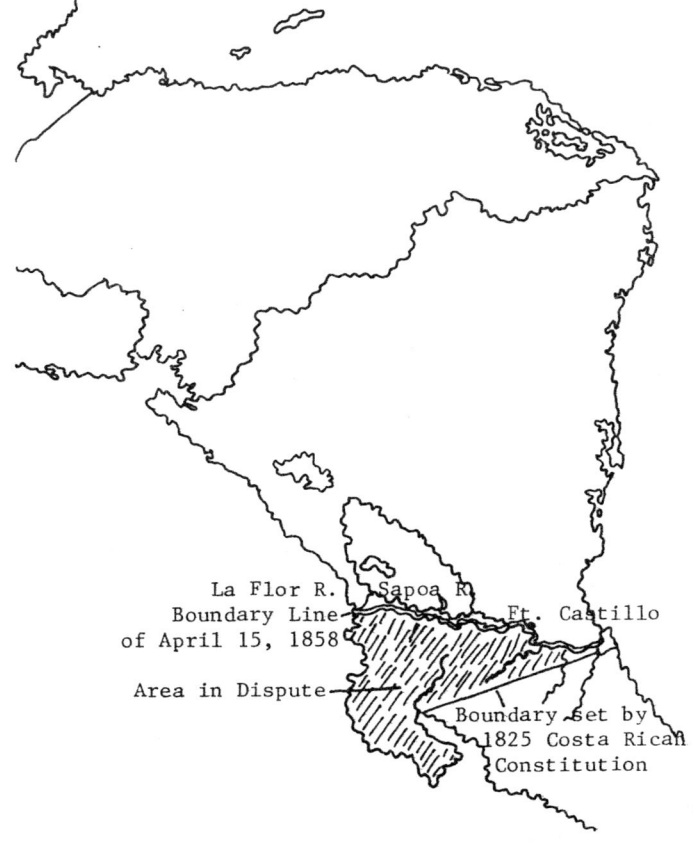

Figure 4. Area Disputed between Nicaragua and Costa Rica

CHAPTER III

THE SAN JUAN AND NICOYA FRONTIER

The government of the United States would see with great pain the prevalence of hostilities in the states of Central America either between themselves or between any of them and a foreign power. Recent events, the increase of commerce on both shores bounding this country, the plans for various lines of communication across it by railroads and canals from sea to sea have given to the whole region a new importance. All must desire that the Republics of Central America should now come into the enjoyment of peace and the pursuits of industry so that they might commence that career of prosperity and progress to which their climate, soil and position seem to invite.[1]

Thus Secretary of State Daniel Webster summarized the ambivalent attitude of America officialdom toward Nicaragua during this period. Couching his language in the rhetoric of diplomatic communication, Webster advised a Nicaraguan envoy that hostilities in Central America, particularly around the transit route, would seriously inconvenience American business enterprise. Fostering the efforts of private American capital on the Isthmus was probably the first—and most practical—policy of the Department of State. But other motives for interference in Nicaraguan domestic affairs, such as colonization and filibusterism, were entertained by Americans as groups or individuals, and tended to cloud the issues for the State Department. In addition, it was not clear what the aims of British policy were, or what degree of posture of defiance or belligerence the United States should adopt vis-a-vis this policy. Nonetheless, there was a high degree of altruism in the efforts of the State Department to help settle the long-standing dispute between Nicaragua and Costa Rica over their mutual frontier.

The question of borders among the various Latin American states was probably the most difficult and enigmatic that had faced the republics in the national period. The problem was largely inherited from colonial times, when Spain—considering that the territories in the new world would be under Spanish sovereignty in perpetuity—established a

---

[1] Daniel Webster to Ignatius Gomez, February 7, 1851, National Archives, M99, 10/6. In the same message, Webster advised Gomez that his accreditation would be delayed until he received fresh instructions since his commission was relatively old.

-33-

conglomeration of overlapping jurisdictions. Lines were drawn according to juridical, administrative, and canonical dictates, and were juggled regularly, often superimposed rather than readjusted. The system gave rise to friction between—among others—these two Central American states.

The major areas in question were the San Juan River and the province of Nicoya (called Guanacaste by Nicaragua), which lies on the Pacific side directly south of Lake Nicaragua. The influx of American travelers crossing the Isthmus after the discovery of gold in California exacerbated the issue. In its initial contracts with American transit entrepreneurs, Nicaragua seized the initiative, but by 1852 the Costa Ricans were clamoring for their "legitimate" rights, along with participation in the proposed commercial ventures. In addition, economic reverses had caused Costa Rica to desperately need the San Juan port if its coffee was to compete in the European market, freight costs via Cape Horn having become prohibitive. The disagreement spanned the national period to that time, and both sides marshalled historical evidence to support their claims.

As an example, a Costa Rican apologist demonstrated the antiquity of that country's claim to Nicoya (Guanacaste) by quoting an eighteenth century engineer:

> On the 19th of January, 1744, I reached the mountain of Nicaragua, a very rough one, which marks the end of the province of that name . . . and I entered the jurisdiction of Nicoya, which although an "alcaldia mayor," separate from the Government of Costa Rica, is reputed to belong to this province.[2]

This vague colonial proprietorship led directly to the issue of ownership in the national period. The same disputant claimed that after the constitution of the Federal Republic of Central America was promulgated in 1824, Nicoya "by an act of its free and spontaneous will, asked for its annexation to Costa Rica."[3] Nevertheless, it appears that Costa Rica may have drawn its state lines in 1825 without including

---

[2] Pedro Perez Zeledon, <u>Argument on the Question of the Validity of the Treaty of Limits between Costa Rica and Nicaragua,</u> Translated by J.I. Rodrigueqz (Washington: Gibson Brothers, 1887), 26.

[3] Ibid., 27.

-34-

either the San Juan River or Nicoya.[4] Its first constitution, that of 1825, provided that:

> The territory of the State extends, for the present, from west to east, from the river Salto which divides it from the State of Nicaragua, to the river Chiriqui, bounding the Republic of Colombia; and from north to south from one sea to the other; its limits on the North Sea being from the mouth of the river San Juan to the Escudo de Veragua; and on the Pacific from the mouth of the river Alvarado to that of Chiriqui.[5]

The reference to the Alvarado River is unclear, but the designation of the Salto River as the boundary between Costa Rica and Nicaragua clearly concedes Guanacaste to the latter, at least "for the present." After the breakup of the Federal Republic in 1838, "the Province of Nicoya or Guanacaste felt once more the necessity of again emphatically expressing its desire to remain united to Costa Rica and, by new acts, it renewed its annexation."[6] What may be regarded as Nicoya's second secession from Nicaragua was formalized in the language of Costa Rica's second constitution, promulgated in January, 1847. This document designated the frontier as the San Juan River, Lake Nicaragua, and the Rio de la Flor.[7]

The selection of the La Flor River boundary unquestionably incorporated the entire province of Guanacaste and, if anything, encroached upon territory indisputably Nicaraguan; however, the

---

[4] David I. Folkman, Jr., The Nicaragua Route (Salt Lake City: University of Utah Press, 1972), frontispiece map drawn by Ephraim George Squier, United States Charge d'Affaires to Guatemala, in 1851.

[5] Gordon Ireland, Boundaries, Possessions, and Conflicts in Central and North America and the Caribbean (Cambridge: Harvard University Press, 1941), 3.

[6] Zeledon, Treaty of Limits, 28.

[7] Ireland, Boundaries, 3, 4.

-35-

language appeared to anticipate a Nicaraguan challenge, and provided that the issue might be settled by arbitration.[8] During the period of the Federal Republic, Nicaragua had made gestures toward incorporating the province, but failed to press its claim when Costa Rica threatened hostilities.[9] Actually, it appears that Nicaragua, aside from being distracted by domestic quarrels, was acting in a somewhat pragmatic fashion. Nicoya was not at the moment as important as the San Juan River, particularly after the establishment of the transit route in 1849. From this point on, it seems that Nicaragua acted with a cavalier disregard for the presumed rights of Costa Rica in that area.

The issue again goes back to the colonial era. Most of the references in colonial documents refer to the "desaguadero" (outlet) as the dividing line between the two jurisdictions. To what did the "desaguadero" refer? Costa Rica claimed that it meant the outlet to the sea for Lake Nicaragua via the San Juan River. (This posed another question: as the San Juan River has three mouths—the San Juan, the Taura, and the Colorado Rivers—to which did it refer?) The Nicaraguans claimed that the "desaguadero" meant the valley—or port—of Matina, some sixty miles to the south.[10]

The issue was brought to Washington with the nomination of Jose de Marcoleta as Nicaraguan Envoy in February, 1851.[11] Although the State Department was already embroiled in the question of a United States-Nicaraguan treaty which would serve to protect the rights of the transit entrepreneurs, Webster was called upon to mediate between

---

[8] Article 25 stated that "the frontier boundary line between this State and that of Nicaragua shall be definitively fixed when Costa Rica shall be heard in the national representation, or failing this, the matter shall be submitted to the impartial decision of one or more States of the Republic."

[9] In 1838, the Costa Rican representative to Nicaragua said his country would defend her frontiers of the San Juan River, the Lake, and the La Flor River. Zeledon, Treaty of Limits, 46. The first three constitutions of Nicaragua (1826, 1838, 1850) did not establish definitive boundaries, but merely referred to the boundary with Costa Rica as being Nicaragua's southern limits. Ireland, Boundaries, 8, 9.

[10] Zeledon, Treaty of Limits, 28-43, passim.

[11] Webster to Marcoleta, February 21, 1851, National Archives, M99, 10/8.

Marcoleta and Felipe Molina, Marcoleta's Costa Rican counterpart.[12] Even though the State Department initially acceded to a request by Molina to lend its good offices in a different but allied dispute,[13] it hesitated about assuming the responsibility for ensuring that an equitable treaty between Nicaragua and Costa Rica should be drafted on Marcoleta's request.[14] This reluctance was due, according to the Department, to the fact that the U.S. charge' d'affaires had not been, even after three months, recognized by Nicaragua, and to the rumor that a treaty was being drafted among Nicaragua, Salvador, and Honduras, which might nullify any efforts toward a bilateral accord. As in the case of many previous plans to reestablish all or part of the Central American federation, the latter treaty proved to be a will-of-the-wisp.

By early the next year, however, the State Department realized that the claims of Costa Rica would have to be taken into consideration before the contract between Nicaragua and the transit company could be considered secure, and before a definitive treaty between the United States and Nicaragua could be formalized.[15] In April Webster conceded to Molina that the President would hesitate to sign a treaty with Nicaragua without the cooperation and consent of Costa Rica, in view of

---

[12] There was initial hesitancy over even recognizing Molina. To try to keep things untangled among the ubiquitous Central American representatives, who had a penchant for representing different republics in various categories, the State Department appeared to delay in the reception of Molina, the representative of both Costa Rica and El Salvador. The required interview with the President for Molina to present his credentials was postponed the first time due to "unforeseen causes," and on the second scheduled occasion because the President had to accompany some army officers to Mount Vernon. (Webster to Molina, March 20 and 21, 1851, ibid.) The problem was further confused when Ignacio Gomez claimed a commission from El Salvador.

[13] W.S. Derrick (Acting Secretary) to Molina, August 14, 1851, ibid., 10/14. Derrick promised to instruct the newly-appointed Charge to Central America, J. Bozman Kerr, to use his good offices—within the bounds of propriety—between Guatemala and other Central American states.

[14] Webster to Marcoleta, November 11, 1851, ibid., 10/15.

[15] Webster to Molina, November 25, 1851, ibid., 10/17. Webster acknowledged receipt of a copy of Molina's letter to Joseph L. White, agent of the Atlantic and Pacific Ship Canal Company, protesting projected plans of the company to occupy lands claimed by Costa Rica.

the latter's claims. But he also pointed out that Nicaragua had already granted the transit company land on either side of the San Juan River, so if Nicaragua should—by treaty with Costa Rica—cede the south bank, Nicaragua should simply stipulate the rights of the company, thereby expediting the matter.[16]

In view of the positions of the two nations and the personalities of the emissaries, the State Department's decision to accept the role of honest broker put it in an almost untenable position. The first response from Marcoleta was not encouraging:

> Costa Rica should sacrifice either the district of Nicoya, or the right bank of the San Juan River, and the river itself, which since the foundation of the colony [Nicaragua] had been, and is, one of its principal exits to the Atlantic, and which will afford to it a proper communication with both seas when the work of the Interoceanic Canal shall be accomplished.[17]

But it was Molina's reply that most irritated Webster. Costa Rica would concede two sections of land on the south bank to the transit company if Nicaragua would pay Costa Rica $100,000 from revenues from the company, along with other conditions. Webster's annoyance at the presumption of Molina's proposition was evident:

> It is to be regretted that the expectations of your government should be so high in regard to its differences with the Nicaraguan government. I had indulged the hope that the proposition contained in my note of the 8th instant would under the circumstances, have been considered by you so moderate and reasonable that you would not, by rejecting it, lose the opportunity which it afforded Costa Rica to avail herself of the good offices of the United States and Great Britain towards accommodating the disputes between her and Nicaragua.[18]

---

[16] Webster to Molina, April 8, 1852, ibid., 10/20.

[17] Zeledon, Treaty of Limits, 48.

[18] Webster to Molina, April 15, 1852, National Archives, M99, 10/21.

Because of the Costa Rican attitude, Webster said, he and British Minister John F.T. Crampton would resolve the Mosquito question (as the British protectorate encompassed the San Juan area), and would merely communicate this settlement to the governments of Costa Rica and Nicaragua.[19]

Aside from the request that the United States take a role in the mediation of the Costa Rican-Nicaraguan treaty, there were other distinct reasons why the agreement should be virtually quadripartite. The major interest of the United States was to settle the question of conflicting claims along the existing transit route (and the proposed canal route) in order to guard against confusion for American companies which might secure the transit concession by contract with—preferably— only one of the contending states. Great Britain's interest lay in the fact that she claimed a protectorate over the Mosquito Kingdom, a strip of land lying on Nicaragua's Caribbean coast, and had occupied the area (which included the Atlantic terminus of the transit route) since January 1, 1848. Conversely, it was the hope and the continuing policy of the United States to try to remove British influence from the area, something the State Department mistakenly thought it had achieved with signing of the Clayton-Bulwer agreement.

After Webster and Crampton worked out a tentative solution, Webster dispatched Robert M. Walsh as commissioner to Costa Rica to circumvent the Molina-Marcoleta bottleneck, and to persuade the Costa Rican government to accept the arbitration treaty. As background information for Walsh's mission, Webster explained that the Costa Rican claims to the south bank of the San Juan River were sound, but not those to Guanacaste. Costa Rica probably calculated that if its claims were upheld, and if the Pacific terminus of the canal were the Bay of Salinas in Guanacaste, it would have virtually exclusive control of the canal. Conversely, Webster continued, the Webster-Crampton arbitration actually did just the opposite, giving Nicaragua effective control. Costa Rica would get Guanacaste, but that would be immaterial, since the engineers indicated that the most feasible Pacific terminal would be at Brito (north of Guanacaste), and thus wholly within Nicaraguan territory. On the Atlantic side, Costa Rica would be awarded only the right bank of the Colorado River (the southernmost mouth of the San Juan River), well below the Atlantic terminus of San Juan del Norte (British Greytown). The negotiators felt it preferable to have the entire route in Nicaraguan territory to avoid possible conflicting grants to other companies by Costa Rica, and because of the history of negotiations between Nicaragua and American companies (as well as the money already spent by the latter) under the assumption that the area was indeed Nicaraguan territory. Webster advised Walsh that if Costa Rica did not agree—and it appeared from Molina's representation in

---

[19] Ibid.

Washington that it might not—the United States and Great Britain would simply impose settlement by means other than persuasion.[20]

At the same time, Webster sent instructions to John Bozman Kerr, his charge' d'affaires in Nicaragua, to obtain that government's adherence to the mediation. He first explained why Marcoleta and Molina had been bypassed: Marcoleta had not been invited to join the negotiations because it initially appeared that Kerr had not been received in the Nicaraguan capital, and when that was resolved it seemed Marcoleta's instructions from his government were inadequate. As for Molina, he was merely written off as uncooperative, and Webster and Crampton had proceeded to sign the agreement, which restored the Mosquito Territory to Nicaragua on the payment of a stipulated amount to the British-protected Mosquito Indians. If Nicaragua objected, Kerr was to point out that the payment did not concede the validity of the British occupation, even though that occupation had never been contested. In addition, the amount was small and the terms reasonable. If Nicaragua should think that by being obstinate it could wait out the administration in Washington until a new one would allow them to take the area by force of arms, the proposition would be self-negating, as potential investors of capital simply wouldn't risk their money. Kerr was to ask the Nicaraguan president and senate to ratify the quadripartite treaty and empower Marcoleta to sign, and it would be submitted to the United States Senate at the current session. Finally, Kerr was to point out that this was probably Nicaragua's last chance to settle amicably and peaceably, and as the canal would probably use the San Juan River bed, along with locks and dams, it would presumably be entirely in Nicaraguan territory.[21]

After the message advising the U.S. representatives of the situation and of their responsibilities was dispatched, Molina was informed of the contents of the settlement. The Department explained to him that the major difference from Webster's previous "recommendation" was that it now required that four sections rather than two be stipulated for the transit companies' use on the south, or Costa Rican, bank of the San Juan River. To soften the impact, the Department observed that the company might not want to use all four sections. In addition, the area now had no appreciable value, but that would come if the company "should apply capital and skill to the cultivation of the sections allotted to them. . . . Besides raising the value of the lands reserved by Costa Rica this will give her an important

---

[20] Webster to Robert M. Walsh (United States Special Commissioner to Central America), April 29, 1852, ibid., M77, 27/123.

[21] Webster to John Bozman Kerr, April 29, 1852, ibid., 27/129.

source of direct revenue and other incidental advantages."[22] In a subsequent note to Molina, the Department acknowledged his concern about losing steam navigation rights on Lake Nicaragua and the San Juan River in perpetuity, but felt that Costa Rica should not mind a stipulation that it be ceded only for the life of the contract—that is, until its normal expiration or legal forfeiture.[23]

Considering all the groundwork laid by the State Department, the response from Nicaragua was unexpected. The legislature not only rejected the treaty but also castigated the United States for "interference." On this occasion, it was Marcoleta who sustained the brunt of State Department anger. A department spokesman explained to him that the United States government had interceded with Great Britain at the "solicitation" of Nicaragua. The State Department had not gotten all that Nicaragua wanted, but certainly more than Great Britain had heretofore conceded. The Department had also presented the recommendation to the Government of Nicaragua for "consideration" only, and the latter had a perfect right to reject it. Unfortunately, "the Legislative Assembly of Nicaragua saw fit 'solemnly to protest against all foreign interference in the affairs of their government'." The response was "unfair and unexpected." Had it been made by a "more powerful nation," Washington would simply have declined further communications.[24]

Hard on the heels of this impasse, Marcoleta got into personal trouble with the Department of State. Previously, in spite of the fact that the treaty was being negotiated on a tripartite basis (due to his lack of credentials), the Department had endeavored to keep him informed, allowing him to read the draft negotiations. The chief clerk had given Marcoleta the treaty to read in the anteroom of the clerk's office, and he seemed to have taken an inordinate amount of time to peruse it. On July 25, 1852, a Senate resolution calling for a copy of the propositions to be sent by the President to Congress indicated that the Senator who had framed the resolution had actually seen the document itself. The executive branch did not comply, but on July 1, the draft proposals were published in the New York *Courier & Enquirer* over the byline of its Washington correspondent who, incidentally, was known to be an intimate of Marcoleta. In describing the incident to Kerr, the Secretary of State noted that Marcoleta's hostility to the canal and particularly to

---

[22] William Hunter (Acting Secretary) to Molina, May 5, 1852, ibid., M99, 10/23.

[23] Hunter to Molina, May 19, 1852, ibid., 10/24.

[24] C.M. Conrad (Acting Secretary of State) to Marcoleta, October 28, 1852, ibid., 10/28.

the transit company were "known to any reasonably informed man in Washington." Continued the Secretary,

> It was impossible for any person, living in the society of Washington, to remain ignorant of the boasts which he made of his influence with Senators, and of his menaces to use it. The executive might have been destitute of every feeling of self respect, if it had continued to place confidence in a man who was daily threatening that he would baffle their measures in the Senate.[25]

This episode resulted in Washington's efforts to get Marcoleta recalled.[26] Again there was frustration on the Potomac when the Nicaraguan government virtually ignored the request, inquiring only as to the reason for it. Subsequently the Department's position was that Nicaragua's reluctance to replace Marcoleta amounted to a rupture of relations. In any event, Washington felt that unless the Nicaraguan government gave an explanation for the rejection of the quadripartite treaty, no further discussion could take place.[27] Marcoleta continued to reside in Washington, and with the change in administration was subsequently recognized as Nicaragua's Envoy Extraordinary and Minister Plenipotentiary;[28] thus his previous problem with the Department of State did not permanently impair chances for a settlement.

At the same time that Marcoleta was under a cloud, Molina's star was rising. The Department notified him that it was pleased that Costa Rica had accepted the Anglo-American proposal in direct proportion to the displeasure it felt with Nicaragua for rejecting it. The State

---

[25] Edward Everett (Secretary of State) to Kerr, January 5, 1853, ibid., M77, 27/152.

[26] The New York Times added that because Marcoleta was afraid that Nicaragua's interests were being sacrificed to England and her "protege" Costa Rica, he had "indulged in some rather undiplomatic language with respect to Mr. Webster and the Administration." Also, "there is no doubt that the influence of the Canal and Transit Company . . . has been actively employed against him." Times, January 4, 1853.

[27] Everett to Kerr, December 30, 1852, National Archives, M77, 27/147.

[28] William L. Marcy (Secretary of State) to Marcoleta, November 16, 1853, ibid., M99, 10/47.

Department also indicated it would study the Costa Rican suggestions for modifications, but could not treat separately with that country yet (and hoped it would not become necessary at all). In order to expedite matters, Washington would send a minister to Central America to reside alternately in the various capitals to try to arrange some sort of settlement of the problems existing between the several governments.[29] In the meantime, Secretary William L. Marcy assured Molina that the United States and Great Britain would not prejudice the rights of Costa Rica with respect to the borders claimed by that country.[30]

Molina's apparent effort to enlist the United States in backing the Costa Rican position to the exclusion of Nicaragua was soon matched by a similar maneuver on Marcoleta's part. Marcy declined to cooperate with Nicaragua in making a tripartite treaty with Great Britain with respect to territory and jurisdiction on the grounds that (1) the issue was between Nicaragua and Costa Rica and no treaty could be made without Costa Rican participation or at least its assent, and (2) as the United States denied that Great Britain had any territorial rights in Central America, such negotiations might be misinterpreted as tacit acknowledgment of British claims. Marcy did suggest that it might be acceptable to submit the provisions of a Costa Rican-Nicaraguan treaty to Great Britain for acquiescence to the provisions for the Mosquito Indians.[31]

This was the last effort of the United States to negotiate a multilateral convention in association with Great Britain in order to resolve the confusing and conflicting claims. Subsequent initiatives were now the responsibility of the Central American states. Henceforth, both the United States and Great Britain would fall back on the provisions of the Clayton-Bulwer treaty, which provided for each to negotiate bilateral treaties with the various Central American republics to implement fully the intent of that treaty.

Marcoleta and Molina finally broke the impasse the next year and, on January 28, 1854, signed at Washington a preliminary convention upon

---

[29] Everett to Molina, February 23, 1853, ibid., 10/40.

[30] Marcy to Molina, October 14, 1853, ibid., 10/45. Solon Borland had been dispatched on April 30 with instructions to "use his good offices in regard to any controversies that may exist among the Central American states." He was "cautioned against any interference in these matters which may be objectionable to any one of them." Ibid.

[31] Marcy to Molina, February 21, 1854, ibid., 10/53.

boundaries and interior navigation.[32] In Article 1, it was agreed that unfortunate differences should be terminated as soon as possible by direct agreement or by arbitration of a friendly power. Article 2 provided that if pending negotiations failed, the questions should be submitted without reservation to the arbitral judgment of the French emperor or any other government agreed on at the exchange of ratifications. Article 4 stipulated that in the meantime the status quo should be strictly maintained, with no concession of land or navigation privileges on the disputed rivers and lakes. In Article 5, Costa Rica conceded that althought Nicaragua had made contracts for the opening of an interoceanic canal, with privileges which Cost Rica considered affected her rights, she would not oppose Nicaragua's fulfilling her obligations in case of the execution of the projected canal works. On the other hand, Nicaragua agreed to put no obstacle in the way of the execution of the contracts which Costa Rica might have made for the navigation of the Serapiqui River, a southern tributary of the San Juan River and Costa Rica's principal outlet to the latter river and the port of San Juan del Norte.

Unfortunately for the troubled San Juan frontier area, this Marcoleta-Molina preliminary agreement was not brought to fruition for four more years. The major distraction was the interference of American adventurers Henry L. Kinney and William Walker. Walker's government sent its own representatives to Washington, thus putting the Department of State in a quandary with respect to recognition and negotiation. At the same time, there was little hope of reaching any understanding over frontiers or any other mutual problems with Costa Rica since the latter country never recognized the legitimacy of the Walker regime.

Costa Rica emerged from the Walker era both stronger and more prestigious than Nicaragua, and generally set the tone for boundary negotiations that followed. General Jose Maria Canas for Costa Rica and Gregorio Juarez for Nicaragua signed at Managua on July 6, 1857, an agreement setting out the proposed boundary between the two countries. On December 8, General Canas and Emiliano Quadra for Costa Rica and President General Tomas Martinez for Nicaragua signed at Rivas, Nicaragua, a treaty of peace.[33] There were two major reasons for this new and—in the context of recent relations among Central American states—enlightened convention. The first was that both

---

[32] Ireland, Boundaries, 12, 13.

[33] Ibid., 13.

countries were now governed by moderate and progressive presidents,[34] Martinez for Nicaragua and Juan Rafael Mora, brother of General Jose Joaquin Mora, for Costa Rica. The second was a certain sense of urgency, and a feeling of commonality of fate and inter-dependence. Walker had landed on the San Juan River with a new collection of filibusters, and though the invasion failed due to the intervention of American Navy Commodore Hiram Paulding, feelings of Yankeephobia again ran high.

The Canas-Martinez agreement provided that Costa Rica should return to Nicaragua El Castillo Viejo and Tortuga Point, that the countries should mutually forego their claims against each other, and that the boundaries should be either those of the Canas-Juarez treaty of July, 1857, or the ancient lines of the Partido de Nicoya, as Costa Rica should prefer. If Nicaragua should cease to be bound by the transit convention made for her by Antonio Jose de Irisarri in the United States with the canal company, Nicaragua would make no further contract concerning transit without first hearing the opinion of the other Central American governments. A boundary treaty was signed at San Jose, Costa Rica, on April 15, 1858, with the second article[35] establishing the frontier as the San Juan River upstream to Castillo Viejo, then two miles south of the San Juan, Lake Nicaragua, and the Sapoa River, to the Pacific.

---

[34] Thomas L. Karnes, The Failure of Union, Central America, 1824-1960 (Chapel Hill: The University of North Carolina Press, 1961), 142.

[35] The dividing line of the two Republics, starting from the North Sea, shall begin at the extremity of Castilla Point, at the mouth of the San Juan river, in Nicaragua, and shall continue along the right bank of said River to a point three English miles from El Castillo Viejo, measured from the exterior fortifications; thence in a curve, with center in the works of El Castillo and distant three English miles therefrom to a point two miles from the river bank at the waters above El Castillo; thence towards the Sapoa river, which empties into Lake Nicaragua, in a course distant always two miles from the right bank of the San Juan river, with its turnings, to its origin in the Lake and along the right shore of said Lake to the aforesaid Sapoa river, where this line parallel to the said banks terminates; from the point where it meets the Sapoa river, which as stated should be two miles from the Lake, in an astronomically straight line to the center point of Salinas Bay in the South Sea, where the demarcation of territory of the two Republics terminates. Ireland, Boundaries, 14; Coleccion de Tratados Internacionales de Nicaragua (Managua, 1909), 335.

It was also agreed to mark this line, with power vested in the commissioners to deviate slightly from the described lines in case of natural landmarks. The bays of San Juan del Norte and Salinas were to be common to both republics, who consequently were bound to their defense. Until Nicaragua should recover full possession of the port of San Juan del Norte from the British protectorate of Mosquito, Castilla Point was to be for equal use, and without collection of port taxes by Costa Rica from Nicaragua. Nicaragua was to have exclusive dominion and full power over the waters of the San Juan, from the lake to the Atlantic, but Costa Rica was to have perpetual rights of free navigation in those waters. It was further agreed that this territorial division was not to prejudice any obligations previously contracted by Nicaragua in political treaties or in canalization or transit contracts. If for any reason the canalization or transit contracts previously made by Nicaragua ceased to be in force, she was not to make any new ones without consultation with Costa Rican rights, although the latter's opinion would be merely advisory. As in the Marcoleta-Molina agreement, all claims by both countries were to be permanently suspended. Finally, with El Salvador acting as both mediator of the treaty and special guarantor of this particular clause, no act of hostility was to be permitted in the port of San Juan del Norte nor in the San Juan River or Lake Nicaragua.[36]

If at the beginning of the negotiations, Costa Rica claimed both Guanacaste and the right bank of the San Juan as bargaining chips, she achieved more than expected. Except for a two-mile buffer zone from the shores of the San Juan River and Lake Nicaragua running from Castillo (about three-quarters of the way up the San Juan from San Juan del Norte to the lake) to the Sapoa River on the Pacific side, Costa Rica got both of the major areas she claimed. It may well have been that Nicaragua made these concessions because she was still fearful of a return of Walker or some other North American filibuster, and wanted a defensive alliance to ensure against this eventuality.[37] A Nicaraguan government official later maintained that Nicaragua was still obsessed with gratitude for Costa Rica's earlier deliverance from the hands of Walker, and that she was also intimidated in the negotiations by Juan Rafael Mora's superior army.[38]

Nevertheless, the boundary agreement, if not the treaty itself, proved remarkably resilient. The first challenge was by Nicaragua, which doubted the validity of the treaty considering the circumstances under which it was negotiated. The issue was submitted to President

---

[36] Ibid.

[37] Zeledon, Treaty of Limits, 62,63.

[38] Ireland, Boundaries, 15; Tratados de Nicaragua, 437.

Chester A. Arthur, who found generally in favor of Costa Rica. On February 5, 1883, the two governments involved signed a new accord in Granada, Nicaragua, resolving some of their conflicting interpretations based on the Arthur judgment.[39] Though slight modifications have subsequently been made and remade, the present Nicaraguan-Costa Rican frontier remains substantially the one fixed in the treaty of 1858.

---

[39] Ireland, Boundaries, 15; Tratados de Nicaragua, 437.

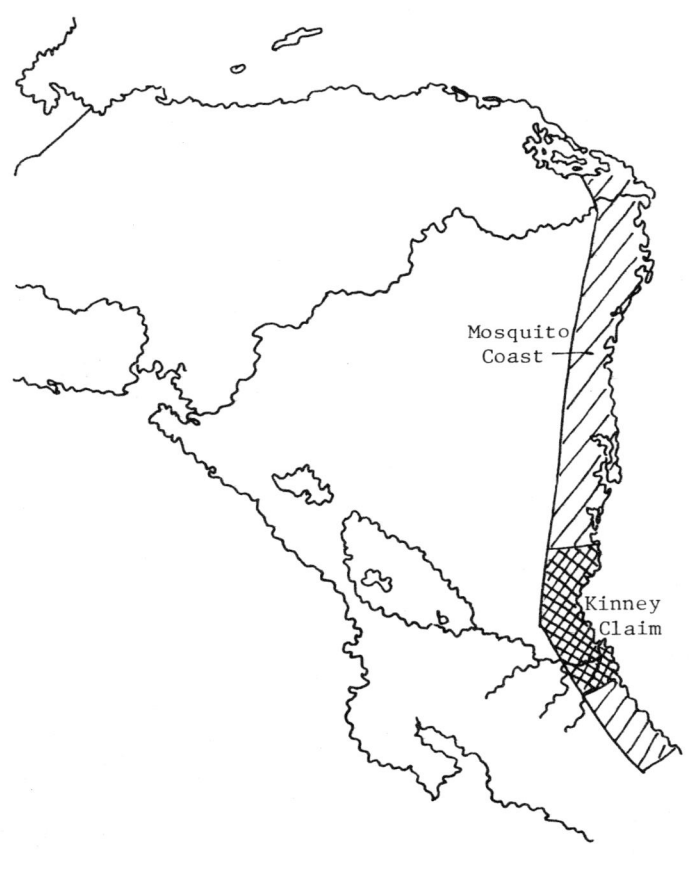

Figure 5. Mosquito Coast

CHAPTER IV

KINNEY AND THE MOSQUITO COLONY

"I have entered upon one of the noblest
enterprises of the present century."[1]

This was Henry L. Kinney's modest characterization of his efforts in 1855 to establish an American colony on Nicaragua's Mosquito Coast. Kinney had already made a name for himself as a swashbuckling warrior and adventurer in the Black Hawk War in Illinois, the Seminole rout in Florida, and the Mexican War in Texas (in which he earned the rank of colonel). During the years after the war, Kinney maintained a small private army of eighty to one hundred men whom he employed against both the Indians and the Mexicans, and this may have been the genesis of the famed Texas Rangers.[2] At any rate Kinney did serve in the Texas legislature, and somehow accumulated nearly one-million acres of land in the state,[3] but he nonetheless clearly regarded his Mosquito project as his most ambitious undertaking to date.

The fringe area of Nicaragua coveted by Kinney, the Mosquito Coast, had already undergone a turbulent history quite apart from that of the Pacific Ocean side of the Republic. Geographically, it is a strip along the Caribbean coast of Nicaragua (and a portion of Honduras) about 40 miles wide and 225 miles long. The name is derived from its early Indian inhabitants, the Miskito or Mosquito Indians. While the term "Miskito" can still be used to refer to an identifiable Indian population, a large percentage have long been mixed with Negroes from Jamaica and especially from the Lesser Antilles. Although the Mosquito Coast was first discovered by Columbus in 1502, the Spanish made only a few tentative efforts at colonization, and for practical purposes it did not

---

[1] Henry L. Kinney, "Pronunciamento," New York Weekly Post, September 6, 1855.

[2] New York Times, December 15, 1854. This last attribution may have been fanciful, perhaps on the part of Kinney himself. One historian points out that Stephen F. Austin formed a company of ten men at his own expense to serve as "rangers" against hostile Indians. Joseph Chadwick, The Texas Rangers (Derby, Connecticut: Monarch Books, 1963) 5-40, passim.

[3] Interview with Kinney, The Royal Standard and Gazette of the Turks and Caicos Islands, July 7, 1855.

come into contact with Europeans until the era of the buccaneers in the seventeenth century.[4]

A British claim to the area dates from the colonial period when, between 1741 and 1786, the British actually occupied the coast with a small contingent and the Spanish permitted the Mosquitos "to consider themselves under the protection of Great Britain." Britain never relinquished this precarious authority. She continued to crown Mosquito kings in farcical pomp and circumstance, but more practical aid and control came from the supplies of money and goods given by the British to the somewhat unindustrious and apathetic Mosquitos.[5]

The land which Kinney proposed to colonize was known as the Shepherd Grant. It was originally a cession made to commercial traders Peter and Samuel Shepherd by the Mosquito King, Robert Charles Frederick I (the king and his chiefs were required to adopt Christian names). In 1839, His Majesty cancelled a debt for "sundry liquors and other royal supplies" by making a grant of territory on Nicaragua's Caribbean coast encompassing the area around the mouth of the San Juan River and amounting to about 22,500,000 acres. The land was to be subject to colonization, and free from taxation and other "burdens usually incident to citizens and subject."[6] It could be—and was—argued that the land was not really theirs to alienate and that they did not have an inkling as to what they were doing. The most serious economic crisis they had heretofore faced was when the turtle shell harvest was bad, so their naivete probably knew no bounds. At the instigation of the British, who exercised their shadowy protectorship over Mosquitia, Robert Charles Frederick's successor, King George William Clarence, revoked the grant two years later on the grounds that (1) the consideration was insufficient, and (2) the grant had been fraudulently obtained inasmuch

---

[4] Mariano Faillos-Gil, "Mosquito Coast," Encyclopaedia Britannica (Chicago: William Benton, 1970), XV, 887.

[5] Peter F. Stout, Nicaragua: Past, Present and Future (Philadelphia: J. E. Potter, 1859), 168-71. In a letter informing the heir apparent of inaugural arrangements, a British official remarked: "I sincerely trust you will not be disappointed in the advantage you expect to derive by its being understood by your subjects, that you are in a particular manner under the protection of the British Government." Sir George Arthur (Superintendent of Honduras) to Prince George, January 14, 1816, British and Foreign State Papers, 1848-1849, XXXVII, 679.

[6] Peter F. Stout, Nicaragua: Past, Present and Future (Philadelphia: J.E. Potter, 1859), 172.

as the king and his court were drunk.[7] According to the Nicaraguan minister in Washington, the grant was "a concession extorted . . . by various individuals . . . amid the delirium and excesses of a disgusting orgy, from the brutal intoxication of the chief of a savage tribe."[8]

The British position vis-a-vis the Mosquitos was outlined in a letter of May 2, 1854, from Foreign Secretary Lord Clarendon to Secretary of State William L. Marcy. Britain, Clarendon averred, had never claimed sovereignty over Mosquito, but her protectorate had not been extinguished by the Clayton-Bulwer Treaty. He conceded that a British consul might "be called upon to give his opinion or advice to the Mosquito government, as is usual when weak governments are in alliance with strong ones." The Foreign Secretary also observed that

> Englishmen may thus be in the councils of the king of Mosquitos, acting as his ministers. . .
> . .To alter this state of things might, at the present moment, be impossible, but her Majesty's government would be ready and willing to enter into such engagements as should prevent Great Britain from receiving any privileges or advantages from the Mosquito government, not granted to other States.[9]

Although Nicaragua had largely ignored her Caribbean coast throughout the colonial and early national period, in recent years she had hesitantly begun to lay claim to the area. This Nicaraguan action, plus the fact that there seemed to be a movement underway in the United States to utilize the Shepherd Grant, prompted Great Britain to reoccupy the area on January 1, 1848, after a hiatus of several years. The territory in question centered around San Juan del Norte (renamed Greytown by the British in honor of the governor of Jamaica) situated at the mouth of the San Juan River. San Juan del Norte was the expected eastern terminus of an interoceanic canal which Cornelius Vanderbilt and his Accessory Transit Company had contracted with the Nicaraguan government to build. It was also the terminus of an existing land and water route across the Isthmus operated by the transit company.

---

[7] Ibid., 175.

[8] Jose de Marcoleta to William L. Marcy, Secretary of State, December 11, 1854, in William B. Manning, Diplomatic Correspondence of the United States: Inter-American Affairs, 1831-1860, IV, Central America, 1851-1860 (Washington: Carnegie Endowment for International Peace, 1934), 429.

[9] Boston Daily Advertiser, January 30, 1856.

Along with eighteen other capitalists from New York and other cities, Kinney obtained the Shepherd Grant and organized the Central American Colonization Company to exploit it. In order to pave the way diplomatically for the venture, Kinney went to Washington in December, 1854, and "had interviews with the President and other members of the Government, and . . . satisfied them entirely that the enterprise is not a filibustering one in any sense, and contemplates neither a violation or evasion of our neutrality laws."[10] The company issued 225,000 shares at twenty-five dollars each, a share representing 100 acres, and offices were opened in New York and Philadelphia to promote the sale of the stock. The company's stated objectives were the colonization of the land and the development of its resources.[11] Kinney himself spent more than $52,000 of his own funds in fitting out a party of colonists to carry out this design.[12]

Sympathy among both the press and the public in the United States depended—though by no means exclusively—on one's position vis-a-vis slavery. Those who condoned the institution hoped that the private incursions into Nicaragua would be the opening wedge of Anglo-Saxon domination, turning the Central American Isthmus into another Texas. They assumed that Mosquitia, given the putative nature of its plantation economy, would be a new slave-holding region. Supporters also were motivated by the fashionable creed of Manifest Destiny. Those opposing the expedition did so out of a fear of slavery extension, as well as a legal and moral concern about the flouting of American neutrality laws. Whatever their sentiments respecting the success or failure of the expedition, the public generally agreed with the British news-magazine Blackwood's about Kinney's goals:

> A great deal was said about the promotion of agriculture on the Mosquito coast; but it was pretty generally understood by the public, that the real object in view was to filibuster the State of Nicaragua, or at all events to establish a depot in that part of the world, from which, when all should be ready, a descent upon Cuba might be conveniently made.[13]

---

[10] New York Times, December 15, 1854.

[11] William O. Scroggs, Filibusters and Financiers (New York: Russell & Russell, 1916), 100.

[12] The Royal Standard and Gazette, July 7, 1855.

[13] Blackwood's Magazine. March, 1856, reprinted in Littell's Living Age, XIII, No. 621, April 19, 1856.

An indication of the interest and indignation aroused in the United States can be found in family letters to William Sidney Thayer, a journalist who subsequently accompanied and aided Colonel Kinney. Thayer was of a prominent New England family, a Harvard graduate in the class of 1850, a sensitive if unpolished poet, and an admirer of Charles Sumner, the abolitionist senator from Massachusetts; hardly, it would seem, a likely candidate for an expedition reputed to have filibustering designs. Nonetheless, when Thayer moved to Washington to become a correspondent for the New York Evening Post and to launch his journalistic career, mutual friends led him into association with the controversial Kinney. Thayer's father wrote him in May, 1855, that the New York Tribune had charged the expedition was designed to establish slavery in Central America.[14] In June the elder Thayer wrote that he had read in the newspaper that his son had "taken stock in the Kinney Expedition." It was bad enough, he said, that Thayer should associate with Kinney, and write articles and make speeches in the colonel's behalf, but this was too much. Apparently Thayer's father had never been satisfied with the legality and morality of Kinney's activities in Texas.[15]

Thayer's brother wrote him in August that he was having trouble explaining to their friends (who read the Tribune and other New York papers) just what "Bill" was doing on a filibuster expedition. "I am always careful," he said, "to state first what I believe to be the nature of the expedition, which is simply praiseworthy, and second that you go out not as a member of the concern but for the sake of the trip and to see the country."[16] Two days later, Thayer's father wrote:

> The government prosecutions of Col. K. and his partner, together with the printed condemnation of the expedition by the New York Tribune, identifying it with the brigand troop of Walker & Co. and also alluding to it in connection with the Cuban Filibusters [presumably a reference to the landings in Cuba of former Venezuelan Narcisco Lopez], have created a strong public sentiment against the whole enterprize; and everyone in any way

---

[14] Abijah W. Thayer to William Sidney Thayer, May 2, 1855, William Sidney Thayer Papers, Library of Congress.

[15] Ibid., June 8, 1855.

[16] James B. Thayer to W.S. Thayer, August 3, 1855. The word "concern" is a reference to the Central American Colonization Company.

connected with it is regarded as more or less of a fillibuster—an outlaw.[17]

Nicaragua reacted on June 1, 1855, when President Jose Maria Estrada issued a proclamation stating that the government had information that the "filibusters Kinney and Fabens" (Joseph W. Fabens, former consul in San Juan del Norte and an associate of Kinney's) were mounting an expedition in the United States and called for war to the death against them. All able-bodied men were subject to mobilization. All foreigners (except long residents and transients on the transit route across Nicaragua) were to be moved away from the frontiers. Anyone caught helping the filibusters would be considered a traitor. Any area occupied by the filibusters should be abandoned, and those not complying would suffer the consequences.[18] Despite the apparent determination voiced in this decree, the probability of enforcement was remote, as Nicaragua was engaged in a sanguinary Conservative-Liberal civil war.

Nonetheless, a protest was made to the United States government by Jose de Marcoleta, Nicaraguan minister to Washington. Marcoleta was paid no salary by the Nicaraguan government, and his personal disinterest became suspect when it was revealed that his legal counsel was Joseph L. White, a director of the Accessory Transit Company. The extinguishing of any authority in San Juan del Norte (including Nicaraguan and British) other than that of the transit company was a goal of White and his colleagues. The Kinney expedition could not be regarded as anything but a threat to that goal.[19]

The U.S. Government was hesitant about intervening, perhaps partly because it was alleged that President Franklin Pierce was somehow involved in the Kinney enterprise through Daniel Webster's son, Fletcher, a sometime counsel for the expedition. (Fabens observed that "Pierce poor devil is frightened half out of his boots" for fear of a scandal.)[20] But the government was finally prodded into action by the public clamor and by the remonstrances of the Nicaraguan minister. A proclamation was issued by New York District Attorney John McKeon warning people "not to take part in the hostile invasion of a friendly

---

[17] A.W. Thayer to W.S. Thayer, August 5, 1855.

[18] John Priest (United States consul in San Juan del Sur) to Marcy, June 1, 1855, National Archives, T172, 1; John H. Wheeler (United States minister to Nicaragua) to Marcy, July 1, 1855, ibid., M219, 11/19.

[19] Scroggs, Filibusters, 102.

[20] Fabens to Kinney, July 3, 1855, Foreign Office Archives, Public Record Office (London) 5/622, f. 215.

state."[21] In the meantime, a federal grand jury returned indictments against Kinney and Fabens, charging them with violation of the neutrality law of 1818, to wit: "Setting on foot a military expedition." A U.S. marshal brought the defendants to court on April 28, 1855, and, on McKeon's recommendation, bail was set at $10,000. Trial date was set for May 7.[22]

Kinney and Fabens had chartered a large steamer, the United States, to take several hundred colonists to Nicaragua. On May 24, the government stationed three steamers and a revenue cutter in New York harbor to prevent a surprise departure by the emigrants. Government litigation against Kinney was introduced in Philadelphia, and he was compelled to travel there to post another substantial bond. It became clear that the strategy of White and Marcoleta, aided and abetted by McKeon, was to delay the expedition while Kinney's funds dwindled and his supporters became demoralized.[23]

At the May 7 trial, the attorney for the defendants contended that the district attorney was deliberately inconveniencing his clients. The expedition was scheduled to sail that very day, and in anticipation a ship of 1,600 tons was waiting at dockside with coal and provisions on board. The charter cost for the vessel was $21,000, and daily demurrage of $1,500 had to be defrayed by the company. In addition, four to five hundred colonists were being quartered at New York hotels at a cost to the company of $1,000 a day. The New York Times reasoned, "The proposition of the District Attorney was to plant the colony here temporarily—to detain all these men in the City of New York through the dog days."[24]

Marcoleta's attorney, who was assisting the prosecution, ridiculed the defendants' assertion that the expeditionists were "peaceful agriculturists." "There would be about as many furrows turned up by the plow, as many hillocks made with the hoe, and as many fields leveled by the harrow by them here." This was a "new breed of farmers," he asserted, who lived in hotels and frequented public houses to the tune of $1,000 a day! Concluding the hearing, the judge reduced bond for the two defendants to $1,000, released them on their own recognizance, and reset the trial for June 5.[25]

---

21 Blackwood's, March, 1856.

22 New York Times, April 30, 1855.

23 Scroggs, Filibusters, 102.

24 New York Times, May 8, 1855.

25 Ibid.

Marcoleta was not satisfied with the government's efforts, and he asked Marcy to prevent the departure from American ports of every vessel which may have been chartered by Kinney and company. "Mad enthusiasm" and "excitement," he remonstrated, had been created by a map of Nicaragua "embelished with likenesses of Kenny [sic] and Fabens, and in which the points are marked where the new cities of Montezuma, Cortes, Fabensville and Kennyville, are to be built."[26] Marcy replied that "the prosecuting attorney had availed himself of all the proof which Mr. Marcoleta could indicate or which could be otherwise obtained. . . . The government and its officers have done their whole duty in this matter."[27]

Marcoleta's importunities seem to have borne fruit in the surveillance of the United States, but the Nicaraguan agent did not rest. Shortly afterwards, he advised Marcy that Kinney now planned to hire a small vessel, the Grape Shot, and perhaps sail from another port. In that event, the United States should send a warship to intercept him at San Juan del Norte. Should Kinney land there, he "would at once place the de facto Government of that town at his disposal." Among other calamities this would cause, the peaceful settlement of diplomatic problems there would be seriously impaired.[28]

On June 5, Kinney secured a one-day continuance of his arraignment. When he failed to appear the following day, his trial was postponed until June 7, but by the latter date Kinney was safely at sea. By employing a ruse involving a mass meeting at dockside—where the United States was moored—to protest the government's treatment, Kinney distracted the federal marshals and quietly slipped the lines of a small schooner in another part of the port. The Times description of the coup was that in order to "cure a congestion in one part he claps a blister on a distant part."[29] Nevertheless, the White-Marcoleta plan had been reasonably successful, and when the schooner Emma sailed on the evening of June 6, Kinney's army of colonists had been reduced to a mere platoon. After an eventful voyage, including a shipwreck in the Turks Islands, Kinney and his argonauts arrived in July at San Juan del

---

[26] Marcoleta to Marcy, May 9, 1855, in William R. Manning, Diplomatic Correspondence of the United States: Inter-American Affairs, 1831-1860, IV, Central America, 1851-1860 (Washington: Carnegie Endowment for International Peace, 1934), 457-60.

[27] Marcy to Marcoleta, May 15, 1855, ibid., 68.

[28] Marcoleta to Marcy, June 1, 1855, ibid., 463.

[29] New York Times, June 18, 1855.

Norte, where one report asserted that their "arrival was hailed with enthusiasm."[30]

But if Colonel Kinney thought his major difficulties were behind him, he had misjudged the situation. In reality, he had walked into a rabbit warren of international and local intrigue. Mosquitia was a focus of the diplomatic battle between the U.S. and Great Britain over whether the Clayton-Bulwer Treaty was retroactive or prospective; that is, should Britain withdraw from its existing colonies and protectorates in Central America—particularly around the proposed canal route—or simply refrain from establishing new ones. Smouldering also was a conflict between the citizens of Greytown and the residents of the Accessory Transit Company's settlement across San Juan Bay on a sandspit called Punta Arenas. Generally speaking the Greytowners resented the company personnel's conducting their business independently and virtually ignoring the town. More specifically, it meant loss of a substantial financial windfall. The British government—this time in accord with the Clayton-Bulwer provision for free ports at each terminus of the transit route—had directed the town council not to collect duties. The transit company had ignored the council's decree that transit steamers using the bay should pay port fees instead. Finally, the town fumed because transit passengers were transferred directly from the ocean steamers to the river steamers, without setting foot in Greytown and thereby having the opportunity to spend some money in the local economy.[31]

The antagonism was exacerbated in February, 1853, when the council ordered the company to dismantle its settlement and move across the bay to Greytown. To aid in inducing the Americans, a band of men rowed over from Greytown and demolished some of the company structures. When a company official protested, he was summarily incarcerated for using "threatening and seditious language," and released only after posting a $7,500 bond. The physical damage could not have been much, as it was later revealed that the company property consisted of "three miserable shanties and one shed," but the affront as well as the menace was real. The company appealed to the United States government for protection, and the Navy responded by dispatching Commander George N. Hollins in the sloop-of-war *Cyane*. Upon entering the harbor on March 10, Hollins inquired as to which banner he should salute. When told he could choose among the American, British, Mosquitan, or Nicaraguan, he professed amazement at "persons who did not know the flag under which they were enjoying protection." On the

---

[30] Stout, *Nicaragua*, 176.

[31] David I. Folkman, Jr., *The Nicaragua Route* (Salt Lake City, the University of Utah Press, 1972), 60.

following day, the commander landed a small contingent of marines to prevent further destruction.[32]

A year later, on March 10, 1854, another crisis arose. Greytown deputies attempted to arrest Captain T. T. Smith aboard his river steamer Routh for having shot and killed a native in a canoe up river. Minister Solon Borland, who happened to be on board, intervened; but when Borland went to Commercial Agent Fabens' house in Greytown, a town mob held him in virtual house arrest for the entire night.[33] Finally, on May 15 some Greytowners stole a boatload of merchandise from the transit company.[34] For all these "outrages," the Navy Department again ordered Commander Hollins and the Cyane to San Juan harbor with these instructions:

> Now, it is very desirable that these people should be taught that the United States will not tolerate these outrages, and that they have the power and determination to check them. It is, however, very much to be hoped that you can effect the purposes of your visit without a resort to violence and destruction of property and loss of life. The presence of your vessel will, no doubt, work much good. The department reposes much in your prudence and good sense.

Unfortunately, "a resort to violence and destruction of property" seemed unavoidable to the sloop commander. When the citizens of Greytown were unable to make a hasty monetary restitution, the town was shelled (after proper warning to allow the inhabitants to escape with some baggage) for most of the day of July 13. Marines were sent ashore to fire those buildings still standing to ensure that the destruction was complete. The only British ship in the harbor, the outgunned H.M.S. Bermuda, stood helplessly by.[35]

Even though the facts make it appear that the catastrophe was the result of local indignation and precipitous action on the part of a

---

[32] New York Times, April 2, April 5, April 27, May 5, 1853.

[33] Ibid., May 26, 1854.

[34] Ibid., August 2, August 5, 1854.

[35] British and Foreign State Papers, XLVI, 859-88. When advised of Hollins' intentions, the Bermuda's Lieutenant Jolly expressed regret that "the force under my command is so totally inadequate against the Cyane, that I can only enter this my protest."

naval commander, ample evidence exists to indicate that it was a transit company-State Department affair. Colonel Kinney subsequently made public a letter (apparently provided him by Fabens) from Joseph L. White to Fabens:

> Captain Hollins, commanding the corvette "Cyane," leaves on Monday. You will see by his instructions, which I have written on the margin, that it is intended his authority would not be so exercised as to show any mercy to the town or people.
>
> If the scoundrels are soundly punished, we can take possession, and build it up as a business place, put in our own officers, transfer the jurisdiction, and you know the rest.
>
> It is of the last importance that the people of the town should be taught to fear us. Punishment will teach them. After which you must agree with them as to the organization of a new government, and the officers of it. Everything now depends on you and Hollins. The latter is all right. He fully understands the outrage, and will not hesitate in enforcing reparation.[36]

Further State Department involvement can be perceived by its negative response to British, Nicaraguan, and Costa Rican protests.[37] Apparently Washington felt the British should be convinced that the United States meant business in Central America, and Greytown happened to be a pawn in the big power conflict. But aside from the implications of Clayton-Bulwer interpretations, Kinney, at least, was convinced that the State Department was squarely under the influence of the transit company.

Kinney claimed that he had a copy of a letter (again probably given him by Fabens) from White to Secretary Marcy explaining the event. It said in part, that "the transit company had been plundered to the amount of thousands of dollars by a camp of savages pretending to exercise authority over Greytown, and that the lives of citizens of the

---

[36] Henry L. Kinney, "Pronunciamento," New York Weekly Post, September 6, 1855.

[37] London Times, August 14, 1854; Marcy to Marcoleta, August 2, 1854, National Archives, M99, 10/62; Marcy to Molina, October 4, 1854, Manning, Diplomatic Correspondence, IV, 61.

United States were imperilled by their cruelties." Marcy, in turn, used virtually the same language in his letter of vindication to British Foreign Secretary Lord Clarendon. Kinney also charged that "the object in these falsehoods was the overthrow of the then existing government at Greytown, and the establishment of a new government more pliable to the hands of the company."[38]

But in Kinney's eyes the real villains were White and the transit company. Kinney felt, Thayer wrote the Post, that "the sources of all his persecutions and troubles were Joseph L. White, whom he characterizes with all the vigor of the Texas vernacular, and M. Marcoleta, 'who signs himself,' the colonel says, '(as in one sense he might justly claim to be) Envoy Extraordinary from Nicaragua'."[39] Kinney accused Marcoleta of serving White for financial reasons (Marcoleta received no salary from the government of Nicaragua), and charged that White and Marcoleta had used the courts "to delay his departure, to dispirit his companions, and thus break up the enterprise."[40]

Apparently the transit company preferred to deal with Nicaraguans and Mosquitos rather than Anglo-Saxons; at least that is what Kinney thought was the true motivation for the company's actions. He maintained that the company knew it could not run roughshod over Americans as it had over Nicaraguans, avoiding or denying its contractual obligations. (The company had pledged a percentage of the transisthmian transit profits to the Nicaraguan government, and had committed itself to build a canal across Nicaraguan territory.) The company perhaps recognized that—with a large permanent contingent—the Americans would gain influence in the government, and would "discharge the obligations of that government to others, then would exact the obligations owed it."[41] Conversely, perhaps that was why the Greytowners, thinking they had found a champion against the arrogance and inconsiderateness of the company, "hailed their arrival with enthusiasm."

Though ostensibly a part of the Mosquito king's dominion, Greytown was largely inhabited by British, Nicaraguans, Americans, and Costa Ricans, plus a handful of Indians. Because of the town's battle with the transit company, Kinney felt he had natural allies in the place and—despite opposition to the expedition from Nicaragua, Britain,

---

38   Kinney, "Pronunciamento," ibid.

39   New York Weekly Post, September 6, 1855.

40   Kinney, "Pronunciamento," ibid.

41   Ibid.

Mosquitia, and the transit company—he issued an optimistic proclamation:

> I have . . . the fullest confidence in the opinion that not many months will elapse before Central America will throng with industrious Anglo-Saxon farmers and artizans, who need only the enterprise and business habits of their native land to insure an ample reward for their labors in developing its resources. . . . The native races . . . are ready, almost without exception, to give us a healthy welcome.[42]

Kinney forthwith moved to fill the vacuum in government which existed in Greytown and, on September 6, was "unanimously chosen Civil and Military Governor of the City and Territory of San Juan del Norte" by an assembly of Greytown citizens.[43] According to Marcoleta, it was a rump convention consisting of members of Kinney's party along with renegades who were responsible for the problems with the transit company. The Nicaraguan minister contended that "the native born citizens, and other foreigners . . . energetically protested. . . . Even the British authorities who were invited, and also the Captain of the vessel of War 'Eurydice' anchored in San Juan Bay, refused to acknowledge those proceedings."[44]

Nonetheless, Kinney's government issued a decree which provided that property owners—those with a "stake in the community"—would elect a governor and council. The governor, in turn, would choose subordinate officials and, with the advice and consent of council, establish laws and regulations. There would be no taxes without the consent of property owners, but ships must continue to pay existing tariffs.[45] With what appeared to be responsible government finally established, a flurry of activity began and the New York Evening Post reported that

> the expeditionists, before they had marked out their farms, set to work at once in San Juan, in the line of their respective vocations. One

---

[42] Kinney, "Pronunciamento," New York Weekly Post, September 6, 1855.

[43] Stout, Nicaragua, 177.

[44] Marcoleta to Marcy, October 8, 1855, Manning, Diplomatic Correspondence, IV, 480-1.

[45] Stout, Nicaragua, 179.

of them, for example, is a doctor, and has quite a run of practice. Another . . . has opened a school . . . whose benches are filled with urchins and little misses of various races and complexions. The Californians have taken to gold-seeking, and others have made arrangements for beginning trade on their own account.[46]

Diplomatic relations with the new officialdom of Greytown were a different story. Needless to say, the question of recognition of the independence of the new San Juan "colony" did not need to be referred to the purported sovereign, the King of the Mosquitos. But Kinney did "officially" notify the agents representing both the United States and Great Britain. Because Fabens had joined forces with Kinney, his designation as Consul and Commercial Agent had been revoked by the Department of State. Discharging these functions was E. F. Mason, the Vice-Commercial Agent.

On September 10, Mason acknowledged Kinney's announcement. The vice-commercial agent chose—in the absence of instructions from Washington—to employ the precedent established in 1852 by James Geddes, his British counterpart. Geddes, in turn, had based his decision for recognition on the judgment made by Daniel Webster on that occasion: "Meanwhile a temporary recognition of the existing authorities of the place, sufficient to countenance any well-intended endeavors on its part to preserve the public peace and punish wrongdoers, would not be inconsistent with the policy and honor of the United States." Mason also quoted former Secretary of State Edward Everett's belief that Nicaragua could give the citizens of San Juan del Norte "a government agreeable to them, and allow them to carry on their own affairs, according to the judgment of their own elective municipal officers." The American agent maintained that this was what Nicaraguan President Fruto Chamorro had meant in March, 1854, when he "recommended that the frontiers, being mostly occupied by foreigners, should be allowed their own local government." For his own part, Mason congratulated Kinney and said that he had "seen this movement in favor of a government, and am confident that it will be productive of great good to this place."[47]

But the Mason enthusiasm did not represent a chorus of diplomatic approval; the initial response of the British consul was one of stern rebuke. This attitude changed to grudging acquiescence when

---

[46] New York Evening Post, October 16, 1855.

[47] E. F. Mason to Kinney, September 10, 1855, New York Evening Post, October 16, 1855.

Kinney challenged the British agent to suggest an alternative. The consul's major liability in the maneuvering was his peculiar relationships with the various governments, i.e., Greytown, British, and Mosquito. In 1850, when the people of San Juan del Norte first organized a municipal government, their right to do so was expressly recognized by the British consul general for Central America, acting as the agent for the Mosquito king. When, in 1852, the Greytowners framed a constitution, the same consul general, on behalf of the British government, withheld his sanction from the constitution and the government organized under it. Nevertheless, the British did not object when Secretary of State Webster announced recognition of the government. Furthermore, the Greytowners simply ignored Britain's tacit disapproval and thereby effectively nullified its impact.[48] Eventually, with a British consul in Greytown, the British recognized the government, and that gentleman even served at one time as chief of the city council in one of the pre-bombardment governments.[49]

The British consul's position was rendered even more tenuous because the Foreign Office failed to back him up in his initiatives against the transit company with respect to collection of port fees and transfer of the company's operations to Greytown; in fact, the Foreign Office had specifically disavowed these acts. The British reaction to the bombardment of Greytown, presumably protected by the furls of the Union Jack, had been one of righteous indignation, but reparations had never been aggressively pressed despite the fact that British property (including the consulate) had been destroyed. Finally, with the twenty-six gun H. M. S. Eurydice in port and not an American naval vessel in sight, Kinney and his contingent were allowed to land unmolested.[50] In truth, the British consul may have begun to feel a bit abandoned by the Foreign Office.

Nevertheless, when Colonel Kinney notified Consul James Geddes of the new government on September 12, Geddes' reply was a formal protest. The consul claimed that Kinney's "assumption of authority was an infringement of the rights of the Mosquito sovereign, and in contravention of the Clayton-Bulwer Treaty."[51] He then appended a longer letter addressed to Geddes from Captain J. W. Tarleton of the Eurydice. Tarleton requested Geddes tell Kinney that the government established under the 1852 constitution, and recognized by both Great

---

48 New York Times, April 2, 1853; New York Herald, November 30, 1855.

49 Folkman, Nicaragua Route, 60.

50 New York Herald, November 30, 1855.

51 Ibid.

Britain and the United States, could only be dissolved by a majority vote of the citizens. Only about twenty persons—and those had "no legitimate qualifications to vote"—had attended Kinney's assembly which purported to erect a new government. Tarleton continued that even if he considered the Kinney election valid, he would still have to object to the title of "Civil and Military Governor" which would "confer powers inconsistent with the prerogatives of the King of Mosquito, and with the strictly provisional arrangements heretofore sanctioned by the governments of Great Britain and the United States."[52]

Again the question arises: under what authority were Geddes and Tarleton making the protest? The seal on the consul's letter displayed the British coat of arms with the word "Mosquito" underneath, and surrounded by the title, "H. B. M. agent and Consul General." With these impressive credentials, why then did Geddes feel it incumbent to refer the letter to a naval officer, and use that reply as the bulk of his response to Kinney? The latter gently alluded to this apparent discrepancy in procedure when he, in effect, presented the British with a rather awkward alternative to recognition of his government. He would assent "with equal cheerfulness" to the formation of a responsible government "by any duly empowered representative of Her Majesty's government." Judging from the correspondence, Kinney averred, it appeared that Tarleton was "clothed with special diplomatic powers." Therefore, "it would afford me pleasure to witness his effort" to achieve that goal.[53]

At this point, Tarleton retired from the debate, and Geddes seemed to have wished he could do the same. The consul responded weakly that he still could not grant his imprimatur to Kinney as long as he theoretically recognized the previous government; however, he fully conceded the right of the people of Greytown to elect their own officers, and would not interpose any obstacles to the popular will.[54]

For a brief moment things seemed to be going in Kinney's favor. Reports from the Nicaraguan capital were encouraging as John H. Wheeler, U. S. minister in Granada, observed that "the prospect of [Kinney's] undisturbed possession from the [Nicaraguan] Government seems fair."[55] An expeditionist wrote a friend in the United States that

---

[52] Tarleton to Geddes, September 13, 1855, Thayer Papers.

[53] New York Herald, November 30, 1855.

[54] Ibid.

[55] Wheeler to Marcy, September 21, 1855, Manning, Diplomatic Correspondence, IV, 478.

> Colonel Kinney yesterday [October 17] concluded a grant treaty with the various Mosquito tribes of Indians and indeed it was a grand sight to see the weather-beaten Indians smiling and rejoicing in spirit, to think that the great deliverer had at last come. . . . The contents of the treaty was that the Indians shall occupy their lands peaceable and that they will in no wise molest any person connected with the Kinney expeditions.[56]

Kinney's newspaper, The Central American, reported on September 29 that the Colonel had been invited to Granada to confer with the Nicaraguan chief executive, Jose Maria Estrada, and had even been sent a passport by the latter. Kinney did not immediately take advantage of this because "his multifarious business operations . . . prevented his leaving the immediate vicinity of his labors."[57]

Even assuming that this was a proper reading of the ambience in Granada, the situation on the Pacific side took a dramatic turnabout. William Walker, another American adventurer, had intervened with a band of filibusters on behalf of the Liberal Party in the Nicaraguan civil war. On October 12, Walker had entered the capital, formerly held by the Conservatives, with his small army and had assumed a control of its destiny that would endure for more than a year. Patricio Rivas, a former customs official, was Walker's handpicked man for president of Nicaragua, and Walker chose for himself the title "General-in-Chief of the Nicaraguan Army." His fellow American's success prompted Kinney to attempt to take advantage of the new situation. Despite the glowing reports dispatched to New York, the Mosquito Colony was not really prospering. Walker's domain—not Kinney's—was attracting the adventurers from the United States, and Kinney felt an alliance would be in his own interest. He therefore sent Fabens, J. R. Swift, and several others to Granada to make the proposal. Walker was unreceptive and replied that "Governor Kinney, or Colonel Kinney, or Mr. Kinney, or whatever he chooses to call himself"[58] "should be distinctly informed, that if he was caught in Nica. (and he considered San Juan del Norte as

---

[56] J. R. Swift to William Sidney Thayer, October 18, 1855, William Sidney Thayer Papers, Library of Congress.

[57] New York Evening Post, October 16, 1855.

[58] New York Herald, January 30, 1856.

part of her territory) that he would treat him as a Traitor and hang him in five minutes."⁵⁹

This blow to Kinney's aspirations was magnified when his entire delegation defected to Walker without returning to Greytown. On February 8, 1856, Walker's government issued a decree claiming and annexing the whole Mosquito territory as an integral portion of the state of Nicaragua, and thereby nullifying the Kinney purchase. The proclamation also stated that "the said Sheppard . . . and Kinney and all other persons claiming this unlawful acquisition, are declared guilty of an attempt against the integrity of Central America."⁶⁰ Strange talk from one filibuster to another! But the audacity of the approach encompassed even more. Walker's paper, El Nicaraguense, editorially observed:

> With a single decree the new government set at rest a matter about which the United States and England had quarrelled for years. Mosquito was annexed to Nicaragua, and there was no necessity for further protocols explanatory of the Clayton-Bulwer imbroglio. Truly, the cabinet of President Rivas deserves credit for so easy an adjustment of so important a matter.⁶¹

The decree did not specifically deal with what to do about Kinney. Walker's strength was unquestionably far superior to that of the Texas colonel, but a foray down river to dislodge Kinney might have seriously weakened Walker's forces in Granada. While Walker and his aides were still mulling over the question, Colonel Kinney, much to the amazement of the Granadinos, alighted from a lake steamer seeking an interview. According to El Nicaraguense:

> He almost forfeited his reputation for sanity, and today a great many point knowingly, and with a peculiar expression, to the head, when he is spoken of. He did not improve this impression by his conduct after his arrival. The Colonel entered the city on foot, and

---

⁵⁹ Wheeler to Marcy, November 12, 1855, Manning, Diplomatic Correspondence, IV, 487-88.

⁶⁰ New York Evening Post, February 28, 1856; Wheeler to Marcy, February 26, 1856, Manning Diplomatic Correspondence, IV, 508.

⁶¹ El Nicaraguense, February 16, 1856, quoted in New York Evening Post, February 28, 1856.

after composing his toilet, prepared for a formal visit to Gen. Wm. Walker, or "Uncle Billy," as he is known in this vicinity.[62]

The interview was short but probably enlightening for the self-styled governor. Kinney observed that "the difficulties under which we labor in forming a peaceable government for Nicaragua, may be consummated by dividing the country and creating two states, one of which shall be called Mosquitia." Walker icily replied that "if Nicaragua chooses to divide her territory, she will do so without advising with any one, and last of all with Mr. Kinney." The General also advised the Colonel that "he should be particular in his speech, or he might be guilty of uttering treasonable language."[63] Apparently Kinney did not heed Walker's admonition. On the following day he was placed under arrest "for some indiscreet remarks on the conduct of government," and was "banished from all the Nicaraguas." Kinney was escorted under guard back to Greytown, with the mayor of Granada acting as custodian.[64]

Upon his return home, Kinney launched a journalistic counterattack on Walker, declaring that Nicaragua's claim to Mosquitia was a simple assertion, unsupported by "a single proof or argument." He further pointed out that the grant to Shepherd had been in existence since 1839, and had not been publicly questioned by Nicaragua until after a lapse of seventeen years. Then it was done "only when the ruling Government has been overturned and another substituted under the dictation and control of an invading military power."[65]

Kinney's spirits were then temporarily buoyed by a Walker setback. An augmented battalion of Walker's army had been routed by the Costa Ricans at Santa Rosa, a plantation near the Nicaraguan-Costa Rican border. Then Walker himself was defeated in an assault on Costa Rican defenses at Rivas. In addition to the consequent scattering of his forces, Walker dismissed his French and German mercenaries, and all who could not speak English.[66] The New York Times chronicled the event:

---

62 Ibid.

63 Ibid.

64 New York Evening Post, February 28, 1856.

65 The Central American, March 3, 1856, quoted in New York Times, March 15, 1856.

66 William Walker, The War in Nicaragua (Detroit: Blaine Ethridge, 1971 (1860), 195-203.

> Deserters from Walker's army are hourly coming down the river, in a state of destitution. Most of them carry their arms and ammunition. They all say they were starved out, and for want of means to carry them to the states they are living on charity. Col. Kinney has given relief to about 22, all his house will hold; the rest are sleeping in sheds or on wharves, and make out a mouthful anywhere they can.[67]

Kinney jubilantly wrote to Thayer:

> Walker has been badly whipped by the Costa Ricans. He richly deserved his fate. Now. . . our day is coming and that soon. We will have a new Republic in a short time, and that American . . . . I have had a hard time of it . . . . but I think the day is dawning when we will have our labors reimbursed.[68]

But despite Kinney's momentary ebullience, the situation was inexorably deteriorating. The colony simply was not getting the recruits or the support from the United States that the founders expected. The New York Times reported in April that Kinney had been in Greytown over nine months, and notwithstanding all the inducements he had offered, and the several attempts made by different parties to cultivate the soil, there were not yet ten acres under cultivation. Worse still, with the rainy season aproaching, nothing more could be done for the next six months. The Times attributed the failure to the type of soil around San Juan, the precarious nature of the title to the land, and the unsettled conditions on the Isthmus in general:

> Everything connected with the Central American continent seems to be in a complicated dispute that will require centuries of time or the intervention of some strong Government to settle. Hundreds of Americans who have come out here during the past six months under false hopes and misrepresentations, have all gone back to Uncle Sam's dominions, poorer but much wiser than they left.

---

67 New York Times, April 28, 1856.

68 Kinney to Thayer, April 5, 1856, Thayer Papers.

Finally, the expectations of Kinney himelf may have been unwarranted all along. The Times correspondent described him as a "good-hearted, honest man" but "an enthusiast in this land speculation, and his anticipations never can be realized." It was noted that the Colonel himself was discouraged when trying to clear an area near the city; after one month's labor he gave up in disgust. In the eyes of the Times reporter, the situation was virtually hopeless:

> The inhabitants of San Juan del Norte present the most wretched appearance that animated nature is capable of being reduced to; and to acquire this phantom form every new comer must serve an apprenticeship of at least two years of chills and fever.
>
> The city can boast of about ten frame houses and a lot of bamboo native huts. There is one hotel, kept by a German, but the best and, indeed, all the other houses of accommodation are kept by gentlemen of color. The British Consul owns his own frame house, but the American Consul hires his rooms and dwells in the house with colored men. . . .
>
> The commerce of the place is entirely in liquor and plantains. These two articles make the eating and drinking of the inhabitants, but they always savor their food with a large dish of hope that San Juan is soon to become the greatest commercial city of the world.[69]

The last sanguine observation was but a pious trust which might or might not precede the millenium. For his part, Kinney remained in Greytown for more than a year thereafter, trying to knit up the frayed remnants of his forlorn colony. He finally capitulated to the inevitable in July, 1857, and set sail for Corpus Christi. Except for one bold but farcical attempt in 1858 to plant his flag once more in Mosquitia, the Colonel was never again to set foot in Nicaragua. Involvement in a local feud in Matamoros resulted in his being shot and killed in 1861.[70]

Kinney's expedition did not entice American colonists or enterprise into Mosquitia, but it did alarm the British sufficiently to cause them to station a warship of "considerable force" in San Juan Bay

---

[69] New York Times, April 28, 1856.

[70] Scroggs, Fillibusters, 132.

to deter similar efforts.[71] And it did—along with Walker's escapades on the Pacific side—serve to heighten the sensitivity of Nicaraguans to American ambitions on the Isthmus. It thus aggravated the difficulties of other Americans trying to establish and maintain a transit route through Nicaragua. As a result, the transit was abandoned and the canal was never dug. Between the Civil War and the Spanish-American War, Americans were distracted by internal development. By the turn of the century when American interest was again turned toward Isthmian transit, the precedent for a canal in Panama had been established, and Nicaragua had ceased to be the focus of international concern.

---

[71] E. H. Hammond to Admiralty, June 8, 1858, FO 53/42, f. 323.

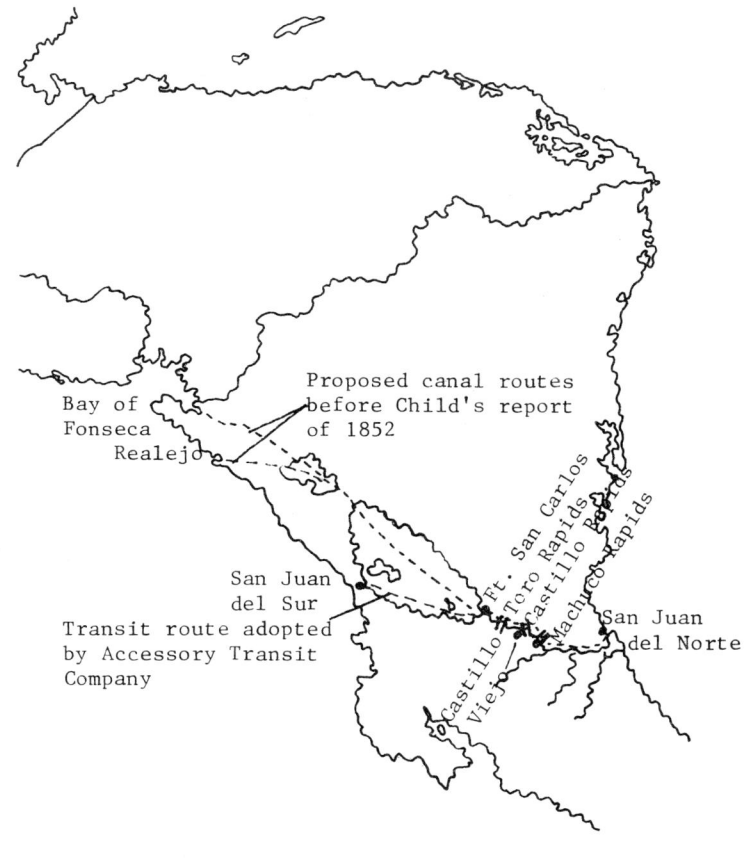

Figure 6. Nicaraguan Transit Routes

CHAPTER V

BRIDGING THE ISTHMUS

> [Regarding] the completion of that enterprize which has heretofore engaged the attention of philanthropists and statesmen for three hundred years without effect . . . tell the members of the Company who have with the aid of the United States obtained the power to construct this work that if there be any mean spirit of speculation indulged in by them, or any of them, to blight or disgrace so glorious an undertaking, they will merit and receive the execrations of good men, while on the other hand, if they be true to their own honor, their own interests and the best interests of their own country, and of the human race, their names will be handed down to posterity among those of the noblest benefactors of man.[1]

The grandeur of these instructions given by Secretary of State John M. Clayton to his consul in Central America, Ephraim George Squier, indicates the hopes and expectations that were attached to the project of building a canal through Nicaragua in 1850. More than three centuries had passed since Philip II of Spain had entertained the same dream, but in neither the colonial nor the national period did men or governments have the technology or the sense of purpose that activated Americans and some Europeans in the mid-nineteenth century. In global terms, the man who would become Napoleon III, Emperor of France, wrote in 1846:

> The State of Nicaragua can become, better than Constantinople, the necessary route of the great commerce of the world, and is destined to attain an extraordinary degree of prosperity and grandeur. France, England, and Holland have a great commercial interest in the establishment of a communication between the two oceans, but England

---

[1] Clayton to Squier, May 7, 1850, National Archives, M77, 27/104.

has, more than the other powers, a political
interest in the execution of this project.²

Americans had a sense of urgency about canal construction for a more mundane reason. Before the ink was dry on the Treaty of Guadalupe-Hidalgo whose terms ceded California to the United States, gold was discovered at Sutter's Mill on California's American River. This discovery, along with the long-range necessity of settling California and Oregon to assure their continued adherence to the Union, caused an almost overwhelming demand for some route—other than across the vast expanse of the American continent or the long and perilous voyage around Cape Horn—from the east coast to the west coast.

Central America was the logical place in which to undertake the establishment of some sort of transisthmian passage and, by 1850, a number of routes were already in some stage of operation. Two were in Mexico, one utilizing a Veracruz-Mexico City-San Blas route, and the other making a water and land crossing of the Tehuantepec Isthmus. Another, and by far the most popular, was the crossing in Panama (then still a part of Colombia) from Chagres on the Caribbean to Panama City on the Pacific. This route was served by a line of steamships with irregular schedules: calling at Chagres was the United States Mail Steamship Company; operating between Panama City and San Francisco was the Pacific Mail Steamship Company. Unfortunately for this route, the passage between the two coasts in Panama was both difficult and debilitating. Passing the night in the disease-ridden squalor of Chagres was so hazardous to the traveler's health that his insurance policy carried a cancellation clause in such an event.³ From Chagres, only canoes and mules were available for transportation to the embarkation port for San Francisco. In addition, by 1850, this route was vastly overburdened by the tide of humanity bound for California's gold fields. A railroad across the Isthmus at Panama, which a trio of American entrepreneurs had contracted to build in that year, would not offer relief until its completion five years later.

A more salubrious route, and one that promised to be more feasible, was through the state of Nicaragua. A few tentative efforts had been made by American companies to incorporate this route into a through service from New York or New Orleans to San Francisco. Initially, the passage across the Isthmus at Nicaragua was not much more inviting than that of Panama except for the beauty of the scenery, the attraction of the colonial city of Granada, and the tropical fruits

---

2   Napoleon Louis Bonaparte, <u>Canal of Nicaragua, or a Project to Connect the Atlantic and Pacific Oceans by Means of a Canal</u> (London, 1846), quoted in Folkman, <u>The Nicaragua Route</u>, 14.

3   Folkman, <u>Nicaragua Route</u>, 2.

that grew in abundance. The passengers debarked at the nondescript port town of San Juan del Norte and traveled by hollowed-out log canoes called bungos up the 122-mile San Juan River to Lake Nicaragua. En route, the passengers were forced to debark at least three times for passage of rapids while the bungos were either poled through or portaged around these cataracts. Upon reaching Fort San Carlos, where the San Juan flows out of Lake Nicaragua, larger craft were boarded for the crossing to Granada at the far corner of the lake. The trip across the lake could also become eventful, as an early traveler suggests: "The rapacious shark fins his way along, and the timid mariner witnesses waterspouts, and experiences the most sudden, dangerous squalls met with in any water on the globe."[4]

The last leg, from Granada to the Pacific port of Realejo, was accomplished primarily by cart pulled by either oxen or mules. The 134-mile journey was particularly difficult during the rainy season when the trail was turned into a quagmire. One other problem was that—as the Nicaraguan passage was not an established route—connections at both San Juan del Norte (for those traveling east) and Realejo were far from dependable.

One solution to the arduousness of this passage (which would later be implemented) was the employment of river and lake steamers for the water portions of the journey, and a shorter and more dependable route from Lake Nicaragua to the Pacific for the land leg. Another intriguing and more challenging solution was the construction of a transisthmian canal connecting the Caribbean and the Pacific, which would permit passengers to travel from the east coast of the United States to the west coast without debarking. Planners anticipated that the canal would employ the San Juan River or its corridor, Lake Nicaragua, and a channel which would be cut at some point between the lake and the Pacific Ocean. Original expectations were that the canal's western terminus would be Realejo, perhaps because Lake Managua, north of Lake Nicaragua, could be used to shorten the distance, and because this was the traditional access for Nicaragua to the Pacific. One major impediment was the necessity of constructing a number of locks in order to utilize Lake Nicaragua. The lake level was 128 feet above sea level, while Lake Managua was 156 feet,[5] thus entailing the construction of at least one lock between the two lakes. By comparison, it should be observed that Lake Gatun, created in the early part of the twentieth century by the impoundment of the Chagres River to provide a channel

---

[4] Peter F. Stout, Nicaragua: Past, Present and Future (Philadelphia: J. E. Potter, 1859), 19.

[5] Folkman, Nicaragua Route, frontispiece map drawn by E. G. Squier.

for the Panama Canal, rises only eighty-five feet above sea level[6] and requires three locks for ascension from either sea.

Selection of a route and contracting with the state of Nicaragua to build a canal, along with the necessary financing and technology, were not the only problems faced by prospective transportation magnates. A diplomatic impasse, long brewing in that region of the Isthmus, made Louis Napoleon's allusion to the special British interest quite prophetic. A major portion of this problem could be attributed to one man, the British consul-general in Central America, Frederick Chatfield, who had arrived in Central America in 1834 like a human hurricane, determined to ensure that British interest in trade—and perhaps territory—would predominate in that area. For the next seventeen years, Chatfield was the dominant foreigner in Central America, and so highhanded and overbearing were his tactics that a Salvadoran newspaper was moved to complain:

> The ravages of smallpox, cholera, civil war, tyranny, barbarism . . . all these pass away. . . . But there is an evil, horrible and interminable, there is a living curse which corrodes the vitals of Central America—and that is Chatfield, the eternal Agent of England.[7]

Although Chatfield was unpopular in some quarters of Central America—and in Britain—he was nonetheless effective. Lord Palmerston, who was British Foreign Secretary for thirteen of Chatfield's seventeen years in Central America, appeared on many occasions to allow his consul sufficient rein to virtually set British foreign policy for that area. The two men were similar in their thinking with respect to the leverage British imperialism should assume in newly-developing areas. The Royal Navy was directed to make shows of force at Caribbean or Pacific ports at Chatfield's behest, in order "to protect British nationals from interference in their commercial exploits."[8]

Chatfield's grand design, initially encouraged and endorsed by Palmerston, was British control of the Isthmus of Central America by supervision of the Mosquito Territory of the Caribbean coasts of

---

[6] *The Panama Canal, 50th Anniversary 1914-64* (Panama: The Panama Canal Company, 1964), 69.

[7] Cyril Hamshere, *The British in the Caribbean* (London: Weidenfeld and Nicolson, 1972), 177.

[8] Ibid.

Nicaragua, Costa Rica, and Honduras, and by occupation of islands and ports in the Gulf of Fonseca, shared by El Salvador, Honduras, and Nicaragua. This scheme implied British control of at least one of the anticipated termini of the "inevitable" canal, San Juan del Norte, and perhaps the others.[9]

Chatfield's opposition to Yankee expansion, particularly after the amicable settlement of the Oregon question and the Mexican War, finally affected Whitehall. The British occupied the Mosquito Coast early in 1848 and quickly extended the "boundary of Mosquito" down to the Colorado River, effectively controlling the three mouths of the San Juan River. They thus shut off any Caribbean outlet for a Nicaraguan canal not under British control. The British consul in New York, trying to interest American capital in a British-built canal, asserted, "From Machuca Rapids, about 30 miles below Lake Nicaragua, to the mouth of the St. John [San Juan], the navigation of that river belongs to Mosquito.[10]

Understandably, a degree of concern about British encroachment in the Isthmus was mounting in Washington. During the Mexican War, President Polk had appointed Elijah Hise as charge' d'affaires in Guatemala, instructing him to try to bring about a union of Central American states in order to resist the further incorporation of the area as a British sphere of influence. He was also to report on British activity, and to negotiate treaties of friendship and commerce with the

---

9   There seems to be some confusion over the location of Realejo. One author states, "[Chatfield] pointed out to Lord Palmerston that the ports of Realejo and La Union, both in the Gulf of Fonseca, were the most valuable ones between Peru and California. The former was the logical terminus of any interoceanic passageway through Nicaragua. . . ." Mario Rodriquez, A Palmerstonian Diplomat in Central America (Tucson: The University of Arizona Press, 1964), 282. Another identifies Realejo, the terminus of the early land transit route and of the projected canal as the present-day Corinto, which is about fifty miles south of the Bay of Fonseca on the Nicaraguan coast. Folkman, Nicaragua Route, 5. Squier's map also puts Realejo there. Robriguez's map calls the place Cortino (perhaps a misprint) and does not have Realejo. William Walker also places Realejo at the site of the present port of Corinto, when he refers to the proximity of the island of Cardon. William Walker, The War in Nicaragua (Detroit: Blaine Ethridge, 1971 [1860]), 36.

10   Miles P. DuVal, Jr., Cadiz to Cathay (Palo Alto: Stanford University Press, 1940), 51.

independent states.[11] When Palmerston and Chatfield learned of Hise's mission, they were determined to undermine and thwart it. Chatfield observed, "It will I think be necessary to take a high hand with the North Americans, if we are to hold our ground in Central America."[12] Palmerston's instructions to his consul were to defeat U.S. policy "as far as its object is hostile to the interests of Great Britain."[13] Upon Hise's arrival in October, 1848, he found considerable political confusion due to the efforts of British agents to foment disruption.[14]

Probably the major reason the United States did not take more vigorous action and confront the British occupation of Mosquito with the Monroe Doctrine was that Washington hesitated since the Central American states were doing so little for themselves. They seemed intent upon allowing their patrimony to be nibbled away by the British lion while being preoccupied with internal dissension and civil war. Nevertheless, Hise felt that it was necessary to quickly negotiate a treaty with Nicaragua to block the British efforts to control the canal route, and he forthwith asked permission of the Department of State to execute the agreement. Despite the lack of formal approval, he negotiated the Hise-Selva Treaty in accordance with Polk administration policies, signing it on May 31, 1849.[15]

Providing for a right-of-way for a canal, road, or railroad in perpetuity, the treaty permitted fortifications and guaranteed the integrity of Nicaragua. Both Hise and his treaty were repudiated by the less expansionist-minded administration of Polk's successor, Zachary Taylor, and Hise was replaced by Ephraim George Squier. With the arrival of Squier on June 6, 1849, the battle for hegemony in Central America between America and Britain was under way. The main problems for Squier to solve were which of the major powers would supervise the area as a sphere of influence, along with the capitalists and filibusters from the competing nations, and how much the respective governments could and should back the claims of their citizens.[16]

Secretary Clayton's instructions included an account of the history of the British claim to Mosquito, as well as the recent events and

---

11   Ibid.

12   Rodriquez, *Palmerstonian Diplomat*, 295.

13   Ibid.

14   DuVal, *Cadiz to Cathay*, 52.

15   Ibid., 53

16   Clayton to Squier, May 1, 1849, National Archives, M77, 27/98.

-77-

current situation, pointing out that Lake Nicaragua was the key to the passage to the Pacific. In treaty negotiations, Squier could assure the Nicaraguans that the U.S. government would use all moral means to dislodge the British from Mosquito. Squier was further directed to help acquire a canal contract for American entrepreneurs approved by the Nicaraguan government. He was not, however, to guarantee the independence of the territory of Nicaragua. The major thrust of the canal negotiations should be equality of transit for all:

"Our object is as honest as it is clearly avowed, to claim no peculiar privilege, no exclusive right, no monopoly of commercial intercourse, but to see that the work is dedicated to the benefit of mankind.[17]

The problem of securing a treaty favorable to and supporting a canal contract was not Nicaraguan intransigence. If anything, the Nicaraguans were even more anxious than the Americans to see the great dream brought to fruition. Their major concern was that the transit should benefit Nicaragua and not redound exclusively to the benefit of a foreign power or company. Early in 1849, Nicaragua had rushed into a contract with Gordon's Passenger Line of New York for the navigation of the San Juan River and for making a road across the Isthmus from Lake Nicaragua to Realejo. The peculiar situation in which the Secretary of State found himself in trying to remain disinterested was demonstrated by the fact that he himself had to caution the company through his consul. British interests had complained to Washington that the contract called for the company to have the privilege of maintaining four customs houses, a provision which would have conflicted with a contract for a loan made in 1826 by a British banking firm, the House of Barclay, Henning & Co., to the late government of Central America, by which the customs house revenues of that republic were pledged for the securing of the loan. Clayton suggested that a stipulation in the contract should provide for the assumption of a part of the payment of the loan. However, it seems that the customs question faded during the subsequent wrangling over transit contracts.[18]

The customs house issue became moot when the Gordon contract was abandoned or lost by default. The river steamer sent by the company proved defective, and passengers and crew were compelled to navigate upstream and through the rapids on the San Juan River by poling and paddling any serviceable craft they could obtain.[19] The Gordon fiasco provided an opening for Cornelius Vanderbilt, a giant

---

[17] Ibid., M77, 27/64.

[18] Ibid., June 19, 1849, National Archives, M77, 27/97.

[19] Folkman, Nicaragua Route, 5.

among transportation magnates, to obtain a charter from the Nicaraguan government for the transisthmian transit. Along with associates Joseph L. White and Nathaniel H. Wolfe, Vanderbilt organized the American Atlantic and Pacific Ship Canal Company, on whose behalf the contract was signed on August 26, 1849. The agreement granted to the company the exclusive privilege of constructing a ship canal across Nicaragua. The company agreed that the canal would be open to the transit of vessels of all nations, subject to fixed and uniform tolls.

The immediate benefits to Nicaragua would be an initial payment of $10,000 by the company, and a similar amount yearly thereafter until completion of the canal. In addition, Nicaragua was to receive $200,000 worth of stock in the enterprise, and ten percent of the net profits of any route which the company might establish. In the meantime, in order to begin competing immediately in a realistic fashion with the Panama route, the company could install river and lake steamers, plus a carriage route for the Lake Nicaragua-Pacific portion. Finally, in the event the construction of the canal proved to be unfeasible or impossible for engineering or other reasons, the company was committed to building a railroad across the Isthmus, or a rail and carriage route which would incorporate the utilitarian aspects of the existing water transit.[20]

While these negotiations were in progress, Squier was engaged in trying to negotiate a binational treaty that would provide official protection for the American entrepreneurs. He continually found himself frustrated by British intrigue and diplomatic maneuvering, and felt that these problems were not fully understood and appreciated in Washington. For this reason, Squier proceeded to negotiate a pact which provided for the neutrality of the canal, as the Department of State had directed, but also conceded a guarantee of Nicaraguan independence, which Clayton had specifically forbidden him to do. This latter infraction was one of the reasons for Washington's rejection of the agreement. The other was that the treaty had only a twenty-year duration, whereas the construction contract called for eighty-five years, and Squier's agreement was subject to annulment by either party on twelve months notice. In his message of rejection, Clayton advised Squier that more instructions would be forthcoming after the settlement of a treaty with the British to dislodge them from the Mosquito Territory.[21]

But Squier was still on the move. He negotiated another treaty, this time with Honduras, in which that state agreed to cede Tigre Island in the Bay of Fonseca to the United States for eighteen months and to

---

20   Ibid., 18.

21   Clayton to Squier, November 20, 1850, National Archives, M77, 27/101.

-79-

permit a naval station on the Gulf of Fonseca for the protection of the Pacific end of the canal. When the British received news of the Honduran treaty, Captain T.A. Paynter, on the advice of Chatfield, appeared at Tigre Island with a squadron on October 16, 1849. He seized the island and raised the British flag, thereby establishing British power on both sides of the Isthmus and presumably at the terminal points of the proposed canal. After Squier's protest that they were occupying U.S. territory was ignored by the British, the American diplomat issued an ultimatum threatening to use American force if the island were not evacuated within six days. The British backed down and withdrew.[22] Although the United States never subsequently implemented the terms of the Squier treaty, this was probably the closest that the two nations came to armed hostilities during the protracted conflict over transit and hegemony on the Isthmus.

A welcome note of harmony was introduced when the American Minister to Great Britain, Abbott Lawrence, addressed on December 14, 1849, an eloquent appeal to Lord Palmerston.[23] A canal built by "the two greatest commercial nations on earth," Lawrence said, would "perpetuate peace between Great Britain and the United States."

> It is our mission to extend commerce, the pioneer of civilization and child of peace, to all parts of the world, to cultivate friendly relations with all, to bring the distant near; and to illustrate by our example the elevating effects of Christianity.

The canal would be "given up to the use of the world, dedicated to peace, and [would bring] incalculable benefits to mankind." The two countries should invite all nations to join in guaranteeing the canal's neutrality to avoid the possibility of future friction.

To a large degree, this message prompted Palmerston to instruct Sir Henry Lytton Bulwer, British Minister in Washington, to work out a satisfactory agreement with Secretary Clayton. Clayton, who was taking time out from a distinguished senatorial career to serve as Secretary of State in the truncated administration of Zachary Taylor, was a commercial expansionist, but not an imperialist. In the Senate, he had opposed the annexation of Texas and the Mexican War, and he did not intend to see American sovereignty extended any further while he was the nation's chief diplomatic officer. As a result, he ran counter to the tides of Manifest Destiny that were sweeping the nation. Although he regarded the treaty he signed with Bulwer on April 19, 1850, as the

---

22   DuVal, Cadiz to Cathay, 55.

23   Ibid., 59.

crowning achievement of his political career, it was probably "the most persistently unpopular treaty" in American history because of the constraints it imposed upon American activity in Central America.[24] Clayton was almost euphoric in his description to Squier of what the treaty was designed to do.[25]

> The object is to secure the protection of the British Government of the Nicaragua Canal and to liberate Central America from the dominion of any foreign power. . . . [It will] secure the passage across the Isthmus and any and every other practicable passage whether by Canal or Railway at Tehuantepec, Panama or elsewhere. . . . All other nations that shall navigate the Canal will have to become guarantors of Central America and the Mosquito Coast. . . . The agreement is not to erect or maintain any fortification commanding the canal or in the vicinity thereof not to occupy, fortify, colonize or assume, or exercise any dominion whatever over any part of Nicaragua, Costa Rica, the Mosquito Coast, or Central America, nor to make use of any protection or alliance for any of those purposes.

Clayton then addressed the effect the treaty should have on Britain's Mosquito Protectorate. Warming to his subject, the Secretary betrayed a startling ingenuousness and an interesting insight into the attitude of the American government towards its own indigenous population.

> I trust that means will speedily be adopted by Great Britain to extinguish the Indian title. . . . We have never acknowledged . . . the existence of any claim of sovereignty in the Mosquito King or any other Indian in America. To do so would be to deny the title of the United States to our own territory. Having always regarded an Indian title as a mere right of occupancy, we can never agree that such a title should be treated otherwise

---

[24] Alexander de Conde, "John M. Clayton, 1796-1856," *Encyclopaedia Britannica*, V (Chicago: Encyclopaedia Britannica, Inc., 1970), 893.

[25] Clayton to Squier, May 7, 1850, National Archives, M77, 27/104.

than as a thing to be extinguished at the will of the discoverer of the country.

Following the Clayton-Bulwer Treaty, the American Atlantic and Pacific Ship Canal Company made preliminary plans for carrying out the requirements of their contract with Nicaragua. The company sent retired Colonel Orville W. Childs to make the canal survey across the Isthmus in Nicaragua. Starting work in August, 1850, he completed his report in March, 1852, after a thorough investigation and systematic elimination of undesirable routes. Childs' recommendation adopted the familiar route via the San Juan River and Lake Nicaragua, but deviated from the traditional version on the Pacific side by selecting Brito as the best terminus. The Caribbean side would have twelve locks, with thirteen on the Pacific slope. The cost was estimated at $31,538,319 and the time for completion at six years. The Childs report, which was presented to President Millard Fillmore, was checked by two U.S. Army engineers and found to be feasible.[26]

The report showed that a canal was technically and financially practicable, but the size was an unresolved question. It was to be seventeen feet deep, fifty feet wide at the bottom, and 118 feet wide at the top.[27] The fact that it would not meet the specifications in the charter to accommodate vessels of all sizes was brushed aside by Vanderbilt. Unfortunately, convincing British financiers of the feasibility of a limited-use canal proved to be more difficult. In the early summer of 1852, Vanderbilt commissioned Childs to present his report to British engineers and London capitalists. The engineers appointed by the British government approved the report, but those retained by the British banking firm of Baring Brothers were less sanguine. The latter examination prompted the London firms to demur from financing the project. They pointed out that while great advantage would accrue to the United States from such a project, the limited size of the proposed canal would prevent nearly two-thirds of the East Indian and western American trade—the only trade in which the canal would prove serviceable to Europe—from passing through the canal. Also, the Orient trade would probably opt to continue using the route around Africa as the distance was 1,500 miles shorter. In addition, the original plan for the Suez Canal had been drawn up in 1846, and the possibility of this route would be far more attractive to British shippers. Finally, the heavy toll of three dollars a ton proposed for passage would probably discourage even ships of the proper size from using the Nicaraguan canal. On a vessel of 1,000 tons, the toll would be $3,000—more than

---

[26] DuVal, Cadiz to Cathay, 67.

[27] The original locks of the Panama Canal could accommodate ships 110 feet wide and drawing forty feet in salt water.

the average earnings of such vessels on their voyages. Increasing the size of the proposed canal to accommodate all vessels would swell the cost to about $100,000,000, a sum beyond the private capabilities of any one country. As Vanderbilt and his associates felt they could not finance the construction alone, they were forced to abandon the project.[28]

In the meantime, however, Vanderbilt had proceeded with establishing an interim water and land route which ultimately became the only route. The traditional route on the Pacific side had been from Granada to Realejo, employing the only serviceable road between the lake and the ocean. Some Americans, early arrivals who hoped to get in on the ground floor of what they expected to be a bonanza, had already begun establishing businesses along this route. Several had married natives and had settled in to await inevitable prosperity. These men were subsequently disappointed when the lake-ocean route was changed, and buildings and businesses were abandoned at a great loss.

The British vice-consul at Realejo reported in December, 1850, that the Nicaraguans treated the passengers going through quite well, probably because those from California, particularly, spent liberally. The Nicaraguans especially needed forbearance because the Americans were a "turbulent set of people interspersed, here and there, with some of the most violent characters on earth." The commentator noted that the least respectable probably used the route as it was much cheaper than the Panamanian alternative. He then described the rest of the journey, across the lake by schooners because the transit company had been unable to get lake steamers up the rapids, and by *bungos* down the river. Viewing the difficulties and hardships of this trek, he was less than complimentary in his remarks about the transit company leadership.[29]

> The New York Company must have been much misled and ill-informed by their agents in this country; American enterprize and their great experience in River Steam Navigation are so prominent, that one is astonished at their want of foresight in almost everything relating to this

---

28   Folkman, *Nicaragua Route*, 35, 36.

29   John Foster to Chatfield, December 31, 1850. Foster made his report available to U.S. Navy Commander William L. Hudson, who forwarded it on June 14, 1851, to Navy Secretary William A. Graham. National Archives, T152, 1/19-26. Foster's report was outdated by the time it reached Chatfield's hands, and certainly so by the time Graham received it.

undertaking, as well in competent persons to direct, as in materials and money.

The vice-consul was equally indignant in his assessment of the Nicaraguan government:

> Amidst all the excitement, the government appears the only party who does not enter into the American spirit of go-aheadism. It gives not the least attention to matters of the most vital importance to its welfare and improvement, but squanders its time and money in idle disruptions and intrigues; whilst its Finances are in the most serious condition; and in its blind compliance to certain parties at the commencement of the California traffic, omitted to obtain the slightest privilege to improve its revenues.[30]

The situation pictured in the latter observation would continue to exist throughout the life of this transisthmian service. American financiers put together a serviceable and imaginative route, engaged in internecine strife over the control of the enterprise, and then watched the route deteriorate in struggles with American filibusters, and all without reference to the native Nicaraguan government.

With respect to the vice-consul's views on the route itself, problem-solving had already begun when he submitted his report. A lake steamer was winched past the worst of the San Juan River rapids in November, 1850, and immediately went into service. A series of small river steamers were introduced to ply between the rapids, though passengers continued to disembark to make the journey on foot around these cataracts. Later, a small railroad was built to carry the passengers and their baggage around Castillo Viejo, the largest of the river rapids. Vanderbilt himself went down to oversee the progress in January, 1851. Under his direction, a new lake-ocean route was laid out which would utilize the shortest distance between the two points. From Virgin Bay on the lake, to San Juan del Sur on the Pacific, the distance was only twelve miles, but forest and undergrowth had to be cleared to provide for passage of oxen- and mule-driven carts.[31]

San Juan del Sur, the site selected by the canal engineers for the Pacific terminus, was just a few miles south of Brito. It had been an

---

30 Ibid.

31 Folkman, Nicaragua Route, 26.

overlooked jewel on Nicaragua's Pacific coast. The entrance to the bay was guarded by towering cliffs, and though the tides were sometimes tricky, all the port needed were wharves and service areas. The port, probably because of its isolation, had previously been rarely used. American ships calling there had amounted to no more than four small brigs or schooners a year.[32] The service point on the Caribbean side was located at Punta Arenas, the sandspit which formed the bay of San Juan del Norte, and across from the town of San Juan del Norte, or Greytown, as the British called it. The selection of these sites completed the initial transit route design. The first east-to-west transit over the new route was made on August 30, 1851.[33]

In that same month, Vanderbilt turned his attention to a reorganization scheme for his company. A new corporate personality, the Accessory Transit Company, was grafted onto the existing organization, the American Atlantic and Pacific Ship Canal Company. The A.T.C. would have the responsibility for carrying passengers across the Isthmus, while the Canal Company would concern itself solely with the construction of the canal (the plan had not yet been abandoned). Finally, the Vanderbilt Line, a company operating ocean steamers, would carry passengers between ports in the United States and ports on the Isthmus.[34]

Before Vanderbilt could turn his entire attention to the transit project, he had to face the problem of the prior British presence. Although there would later be disagreements between Washington and London over whether or not the Clayton-Bulwer Treaty was retrospective in application, particularly with respect to British occupation of the Mosquito Coast, Lord Palmerston seemed initially to be conscientiously trying to live up to the spirit of the accord. The two countries had agreed jointly to support Vanderbilt's company in its efforts to construct a transit route through Nicaragua. In keeping with this commitment, the Foreign Secretary had encouraged British bankers to welcome Vanderbilt's request for financial support, and had promised the company that the authorities at Greytown would not interfere with transit construction.

One of the provisions of the agreement was the establishment of free ports at the termini of the passageway across the Isthmus. For this reason, Palmerston vetoed Chatfield's tariff schedule and made

---

32 Francis V. Clark (commercial agent at San Juan del Sur) to James Buchanan (Secretary of State), September 8, 1847, T152, 1/1.

33 Folkman, Nicaragua Route, 32.

34 Ibid., 33.

-85-

Greytown a free port. Unfortunately, this left Greytown without revenue for its garrison, so the citizens organized a municipality and began charging modest port fees. As fate would intervene, on November 21, 1851, the first ocean steamer to confront the new levies, the Prometheus, had carried Cornelius Vanderbilt on board. Vanderbilt objected, saying that these fees violated the Clayton-Bulwer Treaty and Lord Palmerston's assurances. But when the British warship Express, designated to enforce the municipal regulations, fired across the bow of the Prometheus, Vanderbilt paid under protest. Subsequently, he complained to the State Department and it referred the protest to the Foreign Office. On January 11, 1852, the British government disavowed the action and apologized. Repercussions were far-reaching, however, as Palmerston had resigned a month earlier, and Chatfield was recalled a few weeks later.[35] The only other major problem that Vanderbilt's company incurred with Greytown was the one which had resulted in the bombardment of the town by the American sloop-of-war Cyane on July 13, 1854. Joseph L. White, a director of the Accessory Transit Company, was implicated in that incident.[36]

One other diplomatic issue remained with respect to the transit route between Lake Nicaragua and the Caribbean: the long-standing claim of Costa Rica to the south bank of the San Juan River. Apparently, at one time or another the transit company had entertained the idea of damming the Colorado River, the southern-most distributary of the San Juan, at its juncture with the San Juan. Originally, this plan would have formed part of the canal-and-locks project. Later, it was probably anticipated that this diversion would insure that the major flow of the San Juan would exit by the northern-most mouth, at San Juan del Norte. This control of water flow would not only facilitate navigation over the San Juan River rapids, but would serve to alleviate silting conditions in the Bay of San Juan.

Felipe Molina, the Costa Rican minister to Washington, wrote a letter to the transit company president and other officers objecting to the plan, and forwarded a copy to the State Department. In addition, Molina alleged abuses of Costa Rican sovereignty at Punta Arenas (across the bay from San Juan del Norte) and at Castillo Viejo. He contended that these points were entirely within Costa Rican territory, and that Costa Rica had granted the canal concession to a competing American firm, the Costa Rican Transit Company. Molina called on the U.S. government to guarantee Costa Rican interests. The State Department advised him that adherence to his request was impossible.

---

[35] Mario Rodriguez, Central America (Englewood Cliffs, N.J.: Prentice-Hall, 1965), 87, 88.

[36] Henry L. Kinney, "Pronunciamento," New York Weekly Post, September 6, 1855.

The United States, it replied, protected American companies and citizens equally, but had no warrant to protect the territorial integrity of another state, that being the state's own responsibility. If Costa Rica could show that the transit company was clearly in the wrong, and could "legally claim and maintain" its title against the transit company, the United States would not interfere.[37] Under the circumstances, Molina was faced with a fait accompli, at least for the time being.

Except for the problems associated with the juridical status of the British protectorate of the Mosquito littoral and the Costa Rican claim, the transition to a major transisthmian route at San Juan del Norte was made with relatively few impediments. The story was different on the Pacific side at San Juan del Sur. There the transformation from a sleepy fishing village to a major terminal caused serious dislocations, many of them the results of interference by local Nicaraguan officials who had no instructions or conflicting ones from their government. The American consul at San Juan del Sur seemed most distressed at the workload the confusion gave him, and complained to the Department of State in January, 1852.

> I am now too old to endure all that I have gone thru here—and God knows—I have gone thru more since I have been here than all the rest of my life put together. For I do not much admire the idea of dying here like a dog—and I am now rather too poor to leave without something else in view, while I do stay I will endeavor to do my duty if Providence spares my life.[38]

---

[37] Molina To Marcy, November 14, 1854, National Archives, M99, 10/69.

[38] W. F. Boone to Daniel Webster (Secretary of State), January 13, 1852, National Archives, T152, 1/17, 18. Boone seemed to experience difficulties in finding his proper geographical niche. He was originally named to Realejo, but when the transit company selected San Juan del Sur as the terminal site, he requested that the State Department station him there, and give him the responsibilities of commercial agent for all of Nicaragua's Pacific coast. If this could not be arranged, he suggested to the Department that it find him another suitable port, perhaps Antwerp. Boone to Webster, August 31, 1851, National Archives, T152, 1/29. After his complaint about San Juan del Sur, he requested transfer to San Juan del Norte. Subsequently, he changed his mind when he heard that both climate and emoluments were worse at the latter place, but
(Continued)

The major early problem at San Juan del Sur, and on the entire East Coast-San Francisco transit, was one of numbers. The avarice of Vanderbilt combined with the pressure of masses wanting to make the journey placed an overload on the system. One of the passengers angrily inquired of the State Department if

> it is not time that the government should pass an act of Congress restricting the proprietors of California steamers from crowding their vessels with human souls without comfort or proper accommodations. . . . . A commercial agent should be appointed forthwith at San Juan del Sur to compel Vanderbilt to show mercy and justice to emigrants.[39]

Meanwhile, according to one authority, Vanderbilt was pocketing a sizable fortune through manipulation of rates; after two years of transit company operations, nearly two million dollars—virtually the entire earnings of the steamships—had found their way into the Commodore's coffers.[40]

On February 14, 1853, Vanderbilt sold his interest in the transisthmian passage to the Accessory Transit Company directors in preparation for a long-awaited European cruise. Unfortunately for Vanderbilt, his legacy of business acumen and ruthlessness was inherited by two former colleagues: Charles Morgan, company manager in New York, and Cornelius K. Garrison, Morgan's counterpart in San Francisco. Morgan and Garrison manipulated the company stock on the New York exchange to gain complete control of the Board of Directors. After Morgan was elected president of the Accessory Transit Company on July 18, the company charged Vanderbilt with indebtedness to the company and suspended further payments on the purchase contract.[41]

---

unfortunately, the Department had already issued the directive for his transfer and for the appointment of Loomis L. White as consul at San Juan del Sur. Boone to Webster, April 16, 1852, ibid., 1/67. White was not particularly popular among American transients at the Pacific port. One passenger complained to the State Department that White was buying tickets of dead passengers and selling them at double the price to live ones. Bernard O. Kane to Edward Everett (Secretary of State), January 26, 1853, ibid., 1/84.

39   Ibid.

40   Folkman, Nicaragua Route, 54, 55.

41   Ibid., 48.

When Vanderbilt returned from Europe in September and learned what had transpired, he promised to "ruin" the Morgan and Garrison faction for "cheating" him. His first move was to establish a competing line using the Panama route, and in a short time, both the Mail Steamship Company and Morgan and Garrison were compelled to buy him out. Part of the agreement was that Vanderbilt pledged himself not to open any more competing lines. The contract, however, did not provide for the cessation of his efforts to regain control of the Accessory Transit Company, which he continued attempting to do.[42]

Despite preoccupation with the Vanderbilt challenge, the company under Morgan and Garrison proceeded apace with improvements to the transit route across the Isthmus. Wharves were built at Virgin Bay, the lake port, and at San Juan del Sur, along with a macadamized carriage road between the two points. New carriages arrived in February, 1854, and the caravan of twenty-five carriages painted in the Nicaraguan colors of blue and white was an impressive sight as well as a luxury to the transients. In addition, by the spring of 1855, new lake steamers with sleeping quarters and dining facilities had been introduced. By then, the passage from New York to San Francisco had been reduced to twenty-one days, with only twenty-one and one-half hours of that time required for transit across the Isthmus. In 1854 alone, over 13,000 passengers made the trip, and by early 1855, the number was still rising.[43]

The government of Nicaragua was also aware of the success of the enterprise, and began to wonder officially what had happened to its share of the profits. The transit company had unfailingly submitted the $10,000 annual payment, but had just as unfailingly reneged on the ten percent of the profits that the contract anticipated. The company claimed that there were no profits, that all income from the transisthmian route had been reinvested in improvements on the line. The Nicaraguan government maintained that either there were profits, or the company had charged low rates through Nicaragua and high rates on the ocean to keep the profits down.[44] At any rate, the government sent two inexperienced agents to New York in June, 1855, to negotiate with the company regarding the amount that the company allegedly owed Nicaragua. In a tacit admission that the percentage had, in fact, been illegally withheld, the company bickered over the amount, not the question itself. Eventually, the matter was referred to specially selected commissioners to arbitrate, a move which was in accord with the provisions of the contract. It was at this point that the filibuster

---

[42] Ibid., 56.

[43] Ibid., 57-59.

[44] New York Herald, March 31, 1856.

William Walker arrived on the scene in Nicaragua, and both the negotiations and the arbitration were subverted.[45]

Walker and a number of men he recruited in the San Francisco area had been hired in June, 1856, as auxiliaries by the liberal faction in Nicaragua's civil war. His ambitions, however, were far more grandiose than those of merely helping weight the conflict toward one of the competing sides. Though historians are not in complete agreement about Walker's initial intentions, it appears that he planned from the very beginning to parlay his role into mastery of Nicaragua and, subsequently, to establish a superstate in Central America and the Caribbean. The transit route would necessarily play a major role in these plans, and it would be largely responsible for his early success, as well as ultimately the cause of the demise of his project.

Walker arranged with the liberal faction to have his American filibusters, along with a contingent of native auxiliaries, formed into a separate military unit, the American Phalanx. Rather than continue the liberal army strategy of frontal assaults on the conservative capital of Granada, Walker made his initial thrusts at the transit route, some seventy-five miles south of Granada. The primary reason for this strategy was that Walker realized it would be necessary for him to control the route and provide for continuing reinforcements from the United States if his overall plan of conquest was to be successful. The move produced an unexpected and significant benefit: the conservative army moved south out of Granada to intercept the anticipated filibuster march toward the capital. This maneuver left Granada virtually undefended, and Walker commandeered a transit company lake steamer to transport his troops north for an attack on the city. By October 13, Walker and his Phalanx were in control of the capital, and thereafter used the families of the conservative leaders as hostages to bring his opponents to terms. The result was that, for the next year and a half, William Walker was the de facto chief of Nicaragua.

In the meantime, although Morgan and Garrison were repeating the Vanderbilt story of manipulating the company for personal gain, their control appeared to be slipping. Vanderbilt had obtained an injunction against the issuance of more stock and against further contracts between the company and Morgan and Garrison. This injunction, plus reports of renewed hostilities in Nicaragua, caused the company's stock to decline severely. Vanderbilt and his friends were quietly picking up a large amount of the floating stock, and Morgan and Garrison realized that it was just a matter of time until the old Commodore used this leverage to regain control. They felt that some

---

[45] Scroggs, Filibusters, 136.

dramatic move had to be taken in order to put the company and its Nicaraguan contract beyond Vanderbilt's reach.[46] This move, they determined, could best be implemented in conjunction with the new Nicaraguan chief, William Walker.

Soon after Walker's coup in Granada, Morgan and Garrison dispatched agents to Nicaragua to discuss terms with him. The first of the agents, Charles J. McDonald, advanced him $20,000 in gold bullion on the spot. McDonald took the bullion from a shipment in transit from California, and gave the owners drafts on Morgan in New York, drafts that were subsequently honored. Walker secured the "loan" with he understanding that it would be deducted from the annual payments made by the company to the Nicaraguan government according to the franchise contract.[47] In San Francisco, Garrison showed his good faith by ensuring that every company steamer that left that port carried a number of filibuster recruits.[48]

To capitalize on this largesse, Garrison sent his son, along with Edmund Randolph, to explain to Walker how the benefactors were to be benefited. Randolph, grandson of the Virginia statesman of the same name, was an old friend of Walker from their days as struggling young lawyers in New Orleans before 1850. The acquaintance had been renewed in San Francisco, and Randolph helped Walker plan his expedition and later secured recruits in California to be sent to Nicaragua.[49] Randolph urged Walker to nullify Vanderbilt's contract on the basis of non-compliance with its provisions and to confiscate the transit company property. Walker would then negotiate a new contract with Morgan and Garrison in exchange for their continued support of his operations.[50]

While these negotiations were going on, a Walker agent, Parker H. French, was in New York enlisting Morgan's support for an arrangement whereby recruits would be transported to Nicaragua by the company at twenty dollars a head. The transportation fees would then be deducted from the amount the company allegedly owed because of its recalcitrance on profit percentage remittance which its contract with

---

46 Folkman, Nicaragua Route, 75.

47 Scroggs, Filibusters, 125.

48 Ibid., 133.

49 Charles Morgan to John P. Heiss, June 20, 1856, Heiss Papers, Tennessee State Historical Society, Nashville.

50 William O. Scroggs, "William Walker's Designs on Cuba," Mississippi Valley Historical Review, I (September, 1914), 202.

the Nicaraguan government called for. Not suspecting the preemptive arrangements being prepared in Nicaragua, Vanderbilt not only acquiesced in the scheme, but actively supported it, apparently feeling that stabilization along the route could be achieved by Walker and would eventually redound to the Commodore's benefit.[51] Randolph's terms were even more persuasive, however. Not only would the Morgan-Garrison faction provide passage at company expense for filibusters, but it would actively engage in recruiting efforts for Walker which would include advertising for "colonists" (the euphemism employed to circumvent U.S. neutrality laws) in New York and New Orleans newspapers.[52]

With all factions of the transit company at least temporarily supporting Walker in his efforts to introduce legions of Americans into Central America, hundreds of recruits began pouring into both terminals of the Nicaraguan transit route. This movement aroused the concern of Central Americans outside of Nicaragua. Antonio Jose de Irissarri, Minister for Guatemala and El Salvador at Washington, complained to Secretary Marcy that state authorities and the U.S. government were doing nothing about preventing the departure of the filibusters. Marcy advised Irisarri that the neutrality laws of the United States were quite adequate, and that they were being enforced in good faith. Unfortunately, it was not always possible to identify either the destination or purposes of passengers embarking for the transisthmian route, and Marcy disavowed any responsibility of the United States to go beyond routine enforcement. The Secretary conceded that some of the miners returning from San Franciso to their homes in the Atlantic states might have been converted to filibusterism en route. Obviously, these passengers could not be distinguished from any others at the port of embarkation. He deplored the civil war in Nicaragua and opined that peaceful changes in government were much to be preferred. Nevertheless, the United States did not feel constrained to interfere as long as the rights of its citizens were not affected.[53]

Apparently not fully aware of the extent of Vanderbilt's cooperation and that Vanderbilt had recently regained the presidency of the company, Walker went ahead with the charter cancellation decree. The steamer carrying word of the confiscation passed en route a steamer carrying two hundred and fifty Vanderbilt-sponsored recruits. Many of these men were foreigners, particularly Cuban revolutionists, among

---

[51] Scroggs, "William Walker and the Steamship Corporation in Nicaragua," American Historical Review, X (1905), 792-811.

[52] Scroggs, Filibusters, 139.

[53] Marcy to Irisarri, December 6, 1855, National Archives, M99, 10/96.

them Domingo de Goicouria. Upon his arrival in Granada on March 9, 1856, Goicouria was amazed at Walker's audacity in his challenge to Vanderbilt. Nevertheless, the Cuban subsequently served Walker in both military and diplomatic capacities.[54]

As soon as Vanderbilt received word of Walker's decree, he went into action. His first move—that of requesting Marcy to intervene—was desultory. The irony was that Joseph L. White, Vanderbilt's associate, had, only a few weeks earlier when his faction was supporting Walker, arrogantly disdained to recognize any U.S. jurisdiction in the entire issue. More appropriate and more effective was Vanderbilt's move to withdraw his ocean steamers and thereby isolate the transit route entirely. Unfortunately for Walker, Morgan and Garrison were not yet ready to take up the slack. When this news reached the stock exchange, company shares plummetted precipitously, and Wall Street thought Walker a fool.[55] The New York Herald lamented:

> The great mass of the American people sympathize deeply with the present government of Nicaragua and will regret to find that its gallant head has perilled its hitherto bright prospects. It will be seen that it is in Mr. Vanderbilt's power to kill off the new government by opening another route and thus cutting off Walker's communication with San Francisco and New York.[56]

Not only did Walker need recruits, but also a massive infusion of capital in order to stabilize his embryonic regime. He dispatched Goicouria to Great Britain to attempt to obtain a loan. The agent went by way of New York, and there initially monitored the activities of Randolph who was undertaking the same project with Morgan. Goicouria wrote to Walker that he didn't think the Morgan-Garrison clique could handle the loan, and offered a counter-proposal. The San Juan River and Lake Nicaragua should become international waterways, Morgan-Garrison should have the franchise over only the land portion of the route and would pay the Nicaraguan government according to tonnage and passengers, and the anticipated government income should be used to secure the loan in the open market.

In the meantime, the peripatetic Cuban determined on his own to approach Vanderbilt, who agreed to reopen service. Still hoping to gain

---

54 Scroggs, "Walker and Cuba," 203.

55 Scroggs, Filibusters, 152-53.

56 New York Herald, March 15, 1856.

exclusive control, the Commodore promised to advance the Nicaraguan government $100,000 on the day his first ship sailed for Nicaragua, and $150,000 more during the following year. Walker's response, probably because he found Vanderbilt's opportunism highly suspect, was an outright rejection of the offer. Upon the strength of rumors, Walker also accused Goicouria of being Vanderbilt's agent. The Cuban vehemently denied it, excoriated Walker's imperious attitude, and resigned. "The filibuster leader thus threw away his last chance to make friends with Vanderbilt and redeem the greatest blunder of his career."[57]

On another front, Vanderbilt took the issue to the courts. In New York, the company steamers were placed in his hands as trustee, but a number of stockholders sued in order to get a receiver to conclude the business of the company and distribute its assets. Vanderbilt asserted that the Walker revocation decrees had no validity as they were not issued by any lawful authority. The New York Supreme Court found otherwise on November 3, observing that the decrees were issued by a de facto government, and that the annulment of the charter was an historic fact, regardless of any considerations of justice.[58] The steamers were therefore placed in the hands of a receiver and sold. In December, Vanderbilt brought suit in the U.S. Circuit Court in New York in the name of the transit company against Morgan, Garrison, and Walker for the sum of $1,000,000, alleging trespass, conversion, and disposal of the company's goods, and fraudulent conspiracy to interrupt and molest the corporation in the discharge of its lawful business.[59]

The revocation decree that caused the legal skirmishing was issued by the Nicaraguan provisional government, which was under Walker's control, on February 18, 1856, and published in the New York Times on March 15. It pointed out that the original concession of September 22, 1849, and subsequent modifications called for the transit company to build either a canal, a railroad, or a railroad-carriage road across the Isthmus, none of which had been done. In addition, the company had failed to comply with the stipulated payments of $10,000 per year and ten per cent of the profits. Finally, the company had failed to respond to a request by Nicaragua on November 12, 1855, to appoint commissioners to arbitrate the differences as provided by the contract. Therefore, the privileges granted the company were dissolved and abolished. Cleto Mayorga, Edward J. Kewan, and George F. Alden were

---

57   Scroggs, "Walker and Cuba," 205-6.

58   New York Herald, November 4, 1856.

59   Ibid., December 22, 1856.

appointed a Board of Commissioners, with full powers to examine, liquidate, and ascertain the amount due by the American Atlantic and Pacific Ship Canal Company and Accessory Transit Company to the State, with full powers to send for persons and papers, and to enforce respect and obedience to all their orders and decrees.[60]

The commissioners were to notify the company's agents in Nicaragua to appear before the board to give evidence and to defend the interests of the company. The company property in Nicaragua was to be seized and held pending the determination of its value by board-appointed appraisers.

In a lengthy dispatch, replete with depositions and letters, the American minister to Nicaragua, John H. Wheeler, provided the Department of State with the history of the confiscation and the findings of the board.[61] Wheeler's report is largely the Nicaraguan government's version of the affair, as Wheeler had long since become identified with the fortunes of the Walker regime.

Previously, in June, 1855, Gabriel Lacayo and Raphael Garcia Tejada had been appointed by the conservative regime in Granada, at that time nominally the government of Nicaragua, as commissioners to arrange the matter in dispute with the transit company. The commissioners had gone to New York but had been unable to reach an agreement with the officers of the company. Nonetheless, a proposal (rejected by the commissioners) by Joseph L. White in July indicated that the company was aware that it had not fulfilled the terms of the contract with respect to both construction and payments. The news of Walker's occupation of Granada reached New York on October 28, and the company informed the commissioners "that a change of Government had made void [their] authority and that [their] powers to act were revoked unless renewed by the new government." Nevertheless, on November 14 the company sent the commissioners the names of the proposed arbitrators, among whom was Nathanial H. Wolfe, one of the original grantees of the charter! The commissioners replied that, under the circumstances, they could have no further relations with the company unless expressly directed by the new government.[62] On December 14, Parker H. French, an agent for the Walker regime, arrived

---

[60] New York Times, March 15, 1856.

[61] Wheeler to Marcy, August 2, 1856, National Archives, M219, 11/63.

[62] Deposition of Gabriel Lacayo, July 23, 1856, ibid.

in New York with instructions to arrange with the company for new arbitration commissioners to be sent to Granada. On advice of counsel, the company declined, on the basis that the matter was now out of the hands of both the company and the government as arbitration commissioners had already been appointed, and "a change of parties [did not] invalidate any previous act of Government."[63] There the matter stood until the decree of February 18.

Immediately after the publication of the decree annulling the charter, the board advised the president of the company in New York of the proceedings they had instituted, and forwarded a copy of the instrument of authorization. The same documents were sent to all the agents of the company in Nicaragua, and time was given to present any statement or evidence in defense of the company's interests.[64] Although the government could make the case that it was adhering to legal procedures, the lack of response on the part of the company could undoubtedly be attributed to its recognition that the outcome was a foregone conclusion, and its position that the act of annulment and confiscation itself was illegal.

Vanderbilt's response, far from sending representatives as supplicants before the Walker government, was to dispatch an agent, Hosea Birdsall, to San Juan del Norte to take charge of company property in that port. Birdsall's further instructions read: "If the Walker filibusters attempt to employ force to rescue the boat from your possession, you are authorized to ask for the assistance of the Commander of any Man of War of her Brittanic [sic] Majesty's Navy in the Port of San Juan to prevent such rescue." The ostensible pretext for the action was to protect Costa Rica, but it was apparent to all sides that the real reason was to prevent recruits from reaching Walker: "Unless our Boats are seized by the Filibusters on the Orizaba and the Charles Morgan [ocean steamers from New York and New Orleans], they cannot get into the Interior, and without large accessions, Walker must fail, and Costa Rica be saved.[65]

---

[63] Joseph L. White (counsel to the Accessory Transit Company) to Thomas Lord (company president), December 1, 1855, ibid.

[64] Report of the board of commissioners, ibid.

[65] Lord to Birdsall, April 8, 1856, ibid. This was not a precedent, as Vanderbilt had resorted to the employment of force during the previous year. On July 5, 1855, sixty men and six officers, dressed as American soldiers, had been dispatched to guard the strategic points along the San Juan River. The force was ineffectual, and many ended up in the Legitimist army. Marcy to Wheeler, September 1, 1855, M77, 27/242.

Although the company agent refused to surrender the property, Birdsall applied to Captain Tarleton, the officer in command of the British frigate Eurydice, to prevent alleged filibusters aboard the Orizaba and the Charles Morgan from going up river. After conferring with Captain Tinklepaugh of the Orizaba, Tarleton boarded that ship to examine the manifest and talk with the passengers. He came away unconvinced of Birdsall's charges, and refused to interfere in what appeared to be company internecine strife.[66]

In the meantime, the wheels of the confiscatory proceedings ground on. The appointed appraisers, Joseph N. Scott, Dolores Bermudas, and Byron Cole, obtained from the various agencies on the Isthmus a schedule or inventory of the real and personal property on and connected with the line and business of the company. Omitting the value of the roads and piers, the appraisers submitted a report to the board fixing the value at $141,129.05. The job of the board of commissioners in trying to determine company profits was a much more frustrating and difficult one. The commissioners observed that "the want of . . . necessary data has been the fruitful source of afflicting perplexity and embarrassment." The original grant had obligated the company to make and present an annual report and account to the government, setting forth its receipts and expenditures. It also conceded to the state "the right through any commissioners it may appoint for that purpose to inspect and examine at any time the books of the company, to satisfy itself of the correctness of said receipts and expenditures."[67] Not only did the company not submit returns of the company receipts and expenses to the government, but no records were kept by the company on the Isthmus. The company agent at San Juan del Norte testified:

> The supplies were chiefly furnished from New York by Agents of the company at that point—no invoices or account of purchases were ever furnished by the New York Agent, consequently [I] could not, nor could any other person ever be able to estimate the net profits of the company on the Isthmus without said invoices.[68]

---

[66] Wheeler to Marcy, August 2, 1856, National Archives, M219, 11/63.

[67] Report of the board of commissioners, ibid.

[68] Deposition of Joseph N. Scott, Agent and Receiver for the Accessory Transit Company at San Juan del Norte, July 24, 1856, ibid.

For whatever reason the company neglected to maintain or deliberately did not maintain records in Nicaragua, the omission did not long deter the commissioners. Information was obtained by interviewing recent agents of the company, poring over private notes and memoranda of the employees, and examining a few official records accidentally preserved. One source was the agency at San Juan del Sur. There the commissioners found memoranda of freight and passengers preserved in the office, not by authority of the employers, but as a private record. The statistics were obtained from waybills, and from accounts of the contractor who landed and embarked passengers and freight on the steamers in the port of San Juan del Sur.

Another fount was the documentary evidence preserved by a Mr. Gottel, the transportation contractor for the Isthmus. Gottel testified that since 1852, the average number of passengers per month traversing the Isthmus would not fall below two thousand. As the charge per person had never varied much from thirty five dollars, the monthly receipts for passengers alone would have amounted to $70,000. The estimate of receipts from the transportation of specie and freight was fixed at $8,000 per month. There was also the accumulation of receipts from internal travel and transportation of local freight. J. A. Ruggles, the company agent at Castillo from August, 1851, until December, 1853, revealed that the expenses of that agency were more than defrayed by the sums received from this branch of the business of the company. The agent at Virgin Bay testified that no drafts had ever been drawn on New York for expenses. The receipts were sufficient to cover expenses and pay for the improvements that were made there.[69]

After collecting this information, the commissioners had to determine the cost of the operation in order to ascertain the net profit. Concluding that the complete establishment of the route by the grantees out of their own capital was contemplated in the charter, disbursements relating to the construction of wharfs and piers, or construction and repair of roads could not be legitimately charged against the net profit from which the government would draw its percentage.[70] One of the considerations attendant upon this last item was that it appeared that the company had written off enormous losses for construction and repair due to "ruinous contracts with favorites."[71] The company had also paid "high salaries to employees and supernumerary officials, and diminished the ostensible receipts, and [this] was to the extent of the percentage, a

---

69 Report of the board of commissioners, ibid.

70 Ibid.

71 El Nicaraguense (Granada), March 12, 1856.

robbery of the government."⁷² With respect to the salaries, the commissioners observed:

> Considering the number of secretaries, clerks, and employees to whom also has been paid large salaries that have been retained in the employ or service of the company, it cannot but be admitted that the recompense to the principal agents has been not only liberal but characterized by an exhibition of even munificent prodigality.⁷³

At any rate, the final determination with respect to valid monthly expenditures for the operation of the route was $21,000. This figure would leave a profit of $57,000 per month or $696,000 per year. The government's share of ten percent would then have been $5,700 per month or an annual sum of $69,000 from August, 1851, until March, 1856. Added to this was a yearly interest of six percent, the receipts from specie shipments, and the annual payment of $10,000 provided in the charter. The final sum of company indebtedness to the government of Nicaragua was determined by the commissioners to be $412,589.96.⁷⁴

The amount due the government according to the commissioners was probably inordinately high. This could have been deliberate, in order to leave a buffer area between that figure and the estimate of the value of the company property which was confiscated, or it could have been a matter of misjudgment engendered by the paucity of information with which the commissioners had to work. Vanderbilt himself estimated the actual value of the company's property in Nicaragua to be between $700,000 and $1,000,000 (though this also could have been inflated), so it is unlikely that an investment of even this amount would have amortized itself yearly, as the commissioner's report would seem to have indicated.⁷⁵

For the next few months, events seemed to bode well for the Walker regime. The filibusters turned back an invasion by the forces of Costa Rican President Juan Rafael Mora, and service was resumed on

---

72   Ibid.

73   Wheeler to Marcy, August 2, 1856, National Archives, M219, 11/63.

74   Ibid.

75   Scroggs, *Filibusters*, 156. The commissioners set the profits at $696,000, close to the lower figure of $700,000 investment Vanderbilt claimed.

the transit route under the auspices of the Morgan-Garrison faction. A sham election was held in which only a portion of the Nicaraguan provinces participated, and Walker became the nominal president of the country. On July 18, 1856, Randolph met with Morgan and Garrison at Saratoga Springs, New York, and formally transferred the franchise to them for a consideration of $10,000. The confiscated Accessory Transit Company property in Nicaragua was later sold to the usurpers for $400,000, with the understanding that every Morgan-Garrison dollar would be counted as five dollars. Added to the $10,000 already assigned were the $20,000 in gold bullion which McDonald had given Walker in October, 1855, and $70,000 from steamer fares of recruits which the company had transported to Nicaragua. With this total of $100,000, the credit assigned to Morgan and Garrison was $500,000. Deducting the $400,000 cost of the company property, this left a balance of $100,000 which Walker covered by issuing government bonds bearing an interest rate of ten percent. Clearly, Walker's major interests were to tie the fortunes of the Morgan-Garrison company to those of Nicaragua, and to ensure that the company would continue bringing fresh reinforcements for the filibuster army.[76]

Faced with this *fait accompli*, and realizing that neither the courts nor the State Department were inclined to salvage his interests, Vanderbilt elected to pursue a more direct course. His correspondence with the presidents of other Central American states urged them to unite against Walker, but in view of the hapless efforts of Costa Rica, he determined that they would need more than moral support. By the fall of 1856, the Commodore had begun sending both soldiers and agents to President Mora, and by December, Vanderbilt was so sanguine about his chances of overthrowing Walker that he posted this advertisement in the New York Herald:

> Present appearances indicate a realization of my hopes that the company will be speedily restored to their rights, franchises, and property upon the Isthmus of Nicaragua, which has been so unjustly invaded.[77]

On November 28, under Vanderbilt's sponsorship, Englishman William Robert C. Webster and American Sylvanus H. Spencer arrived in San Juan, Costa Rica, to engage in secret talks with President Mora and to outline for the president a method of bringing about the capitulation of Walker. The key, they said, was to control the San Juan River; after that, everything else would fall into place. Spencer had formerly been an engineer on the transit boats, and knew both the river and the crews,

---

[76] Folkman, Nicaragua Route, 83, 4.

[77] New York Herald, December 25, 1856.

so the details of the planning were left to him. Mora called for Costa Rican volunteers for an expedition down the Serapiqui River, an obvious objective and one the filibusters would have anticipated since that river was Costa Rica's major outlet to the San Juan. Cunningly, Spencer's force clandestinely utilized the San Carlos River, twenty-seven miles north of the Serapiqui, floating on rafts and canoes into the San Juan on December 16. Stealthily descending the San Juan, the Costa Ricans quickly overpowered the surprised filibusters guarding the mouth of the Serapiqui.

Spencer then took his force down river to San Juan del Norte and seized four river steamers there. The boats' crews joined the Costa Ricans on the promise that their wages would continue to be paid, and with Costa Rican flags flying at their masts, the boats began chugging upstream. The U.S. commercial agent at San Juan del Norte, a Walker partisan, appealed to the commander of the large British squadron in the harbor, but the Briton refused to interfere in what he termed a business dispute.

Spencer's boats picked up a Costa Rican force of about 800 men armed with Vanderbilt-supplied Minie rifles brought down the San Carlos by General Jose Joaquin Mora, Commander-in-Chief of the Costa Rican army and brother to the President. Mora's army continued upstream and systematically captured the stategic forts along the San Juan River all the way to Lake Nicaragua, employing force and ruse. Utilizing a lake steamer commandeered at Fort San Carlos, the fortress guarding the outlet of the San Juan River from Lake Nicaragua, General Mora crossed the Lake and captured Virgin Bay. Along with another Costa Rican force that had occupied San Juan del Sur, Mora had now completely isolated the filibuster president. With no hopes for supplies or reinforcements, Walker capitulated on May 1, 1857, and his force was evacuated by U.S. Navy ships at San Juan del Sur.[78]

The rest of the story of the route during the period is denouement as the transit across the Isthmus, for various reasons, was never reopened. Nevertheless, without the benefit of prescience, the traditional competitors, joined by others, continued feverishly contending for the franchise. The three major rival groups were the American Atlantic and Pacific Ship Canal Company under Joseph L. White and company president H. G. Stebbins; the Accessory Transit Company of Cornelius Vanderbilt; and the Morgan-Garrison combine. The latter duo passed virtually out of contention as they were discredited by having been so closely identified with the defeated fillibuster. Vanderbilt's initial efforts were at least imaginative: working through Costa Rican General Jose Maria Canas, his proposal was to establish a new state out of both Costa Rican and Nicaraguan

---

[78] Scroggs, Filibusters, 270-85.

territory that would encompass the entire area of the transit route and which would do business exclusively with the Commodore. White appealed to Antonio Jose de Irisarri, who was now the Nicaraguan minister in Washington as well as that of Costa Rica. On June 27, 1857, Irisarri signed a contract with Stebbins and White which was subsequently confirmed by the new Nicaraguan government under President Tomas Martinez.

One of the major problems preventing the reopening of the route was the revival of the territorial dispute between Nicaragua and Costa Rica. The latter had traditionally claimed the south bank of the San Juan River, and now bolstered its argument with the assertion that it was necessary for defensive purposes. The Nicaraguans, their neighbors charged, could not defend that portion of the Isthmus if the reopening of the transit under Nicaraguan auspices engendered another invasion. Just such an invasion seemed imminent when Walker reappeared at Greytown in November, 1857, with a new band of filibusters. Although the U.S. Navy subsequently intervened and shipped Walker and his contingent back to the United States, both of the Central American countries were infused with a sense of urgency. As a result, Nicaragua largely capitulated to the Costa Rican demands, and a new bilateral treaty was signed on April 15, 1858.

In the meantime, Irisarri was negotiating a bilateral treaty with U.S. Secretary of State Lewis Cass, a treaty which would provide security for American investment in Nicaragua and particularly for any company which might obtain the transit franchise. In the U.S. Senate, the treaty became suspect when the exclusive contract Irisarri had previously signed with Stebbins and White was revealed. An almost insurmountable impasse for the treaty developed in Nicaragua when it became clear that President Martinez did not want the route reopened. Although the president sent the document to the Nicaraguan assembly for ratification, he had assumed that it would be rejected. When the assembly, much to the president's chagrin, approved the treaty on March 26, 1858, Martinez at first refused to sign and then resorted to subterfuge in an effort to prevent the accord from becoming law.[79]

Some evidence indicates that Martinez was more afraid of American sponsorship of the route than the reopening of the route itself. Despite his efforts to defeat the bilateral treaty with the United States, the president seemed at least reluctantly prepared to go ahead with a commercial contract. The Englishman Webster had entered into a contract, in the name of Vanderbilt, with the Nicaraguan foreign ministry for the reopening of the route. Martinez was hesitant about confirming the agreement for fear of retaliation by Stebbins and White, so the concession was made that the latter would be allowed until June,

---

[79] Ibid., 354-58.

1856, to "have their boats actually on the route, or forfeit their contract; in which event Webster's contract [would] be considered as valid." President Martinez felt the Vanderbilt contract would be more favorable to Nicaragua, and besides, "Webster [had] boasted that the old commodore is determined to have the line either by fair or foul means." Regardless of the commercial imbroglio, "The [Nicaraguan] authorities seem resolved that [the American] government should have no voice in the matter."[80]

The feuding among the American entrepreneurs was temporarily superceded with the arrival on the scene of an extraordinary Frenchman, Felix Belly. Belly landed at San Juan del Norte on March 3, 1858, and although subsequently revealed to have been merely the agent of a few obscure Parisian speculators, the mysterious aura surrounding the man convinced local newspapers that he was in fact the clandestine representative of Emperor Napoleon III. When Belly was received by President Mora in San Jose, his denials of official capacity sounded as if they were made for diplomatic reasons, and Mora was as convinced as the press of the legitimacy of Belly's mission. Mora signed a Costa Rican-Nicaraguan canal treaty which Belly conveniently had in hand, and then accompanied the Frenchman to Nicaragua to obtain the signature of President Martinez. After Mora and Belly arrived in Rivas on April 24, Mora and Martinez affixed their signatures to an international convention which gave exclusive canal privileges to a company to be formed by Belly. In addition, Martinez and Mora signed a treaty of limits making major concessions to Costa Rica, but committing Costa Rica to aid Nicaragua in any controversy between that nation and the United States.[81]

Finally, at the instigation of Belly, Martinez and Mora signed a joint Declaration placing their countries under the protection of France, England, and Sardinia, without the knowledge of the European governments concerned.[82] Included in the manifesto was an elaborate complaint against the U.S. government which was intended for European consumption. It charged the United States with sponsoring the preparation of a new invasion of Central America with the intention of annexing the Isthmus to the United States by force. To underscore the irony of the occasion, all the documents were signed on May 1, the

---

[80] Mirabeau B. Lamar (Minister to Central America) to Lewis Cass (Secretary of State), March 27, 1858, National Archives, M219, 11/6.

[81] Cyril Allen, France in Central America, Felix Belly and the Nicaraguan Canal (New York: Pageant Press, 1966), 21-141, passim.

[82] British Foreign and State Papers, XLVIII, 695-6.

anniversary of Walker's capitulation. Secretary of State Cass was justifiably annoyed with the manifesto, and through his representative, Mirabeau B. Lamar, compelled the two presidents to disavow the document.[83]

After the signing of the accords, Belly journeyed to Aspinwall in Panama, and then to New York, but upon his arrival at the latter port he was confronted with newspaper headlines that the French government had denied any association with him. He went back to France thoroughly discredited and leaving some very embarrassed Central American politicians in his wake. His chief accomplishment, if such it can be termed, was to protect the efforts of American financiers to reopen the transit route.[84]

Meanwhile, despite the grace period initially extended to Stebbins and White, their contract was revoked on January 28, 1858, and transferred to Vanderbilt on March 8. Unfortunately for Nicaragua, it turned out that the Commodore did not intend to reopen the route but, on the contrary, to block its reopening. This action was in consideration of a sum of $56,000 a month that the Pacific Mail Steamship Company was paying him to prevent the renewal of competition with the Panama route. In the fall of 1859, however, Vanderbilt broke with Pacific Mail, and declared his determination to reopen the Nicaragua route. Wall Street was startled by this news, and rumors were rife that the Commodore might even employ filibusters if necessary. But when one of his steamers with a cargo of arms was prevented by the authorities from leaving the port of New Orleans for Nicaragua, Vanderbilt finally and definitively withdrew from the field.[85]

Stebbins and White were no more successful. Their accomplice Irisarri was replaced in Washington in October, 1858, by Maximo Jerez, the most powerful of the leaders of the liberal faction in Nicaragua. Jerez had previously been in correspondence with Vanderbilt, and appeared to be a Vanderbilt partisan, so the degree of influence that the old financier had in both Nicaragua and the Department of State can be inferred by Jerez' appointment and reception in Washington. His first move was to thwart the continuing efforts of Stebbins and White. When a Stebbins-White steamer advertised a scheduled sailing to Nicaragua, Jerez published a warning that the company had no river or lake steamers and that the journey across the waterways of the Isthmus would have to be made in bungos. Although Secretary Cass rebuked the minister for this untoward affront to diplomatic behavior, the damage

---

[83] J. L. Cole to John P. Heiss, June 20, 1858, Heiss Papers.

[84] Allen, Felix Belly, 21-141, passim.

[85] Scroggs, Filibusters, 365-67.

was already done. Nevertheless, the steamer Washington set sail on November 7, 1858, with three hundred and twenty passengers. When it arrived at San Juan del Norte, the Nicaraguan government refused the transients permission to cross the Isthmus, and the company was forced to transfer them to Aspinwall. Even though Stebbins-White were successful in procuring another franchise from the Nicaraguan government on April 12, 1860, they never succeeded in reopening the route.[86] America's attention was by this time turning toward a far more serious internal conflict. Nicaraguan turbulence, on the other hand, substantially declined for the next thirty years, a situation remarkably uncharacteristic for that unhappy nation.

---

[86] Gordon Ireland, Boundaries, Possessions, and Conflicts in Central and North America and the Caribbean (Cambridge: Harvard University Press, 1941), 191.

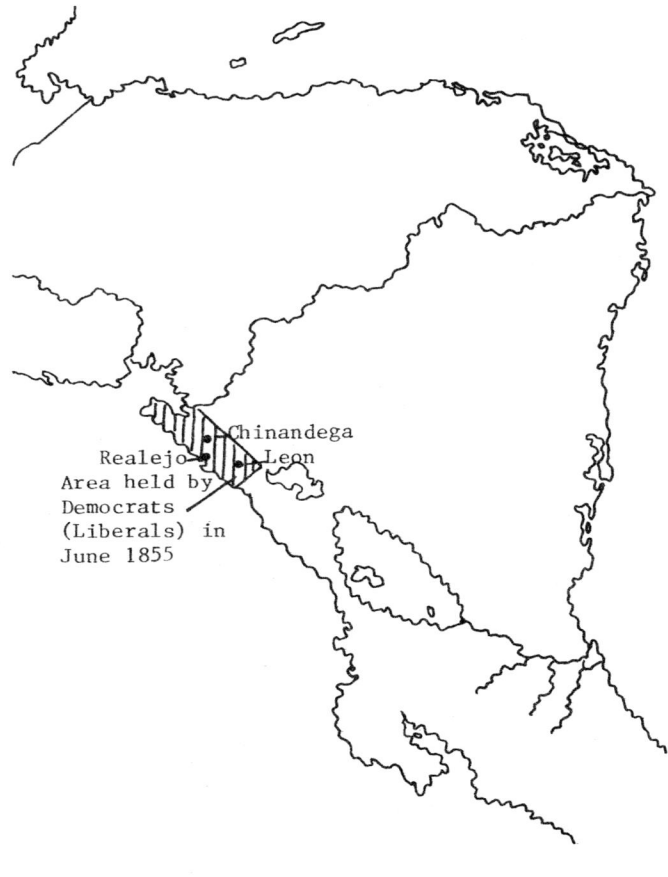

Figure 7. Liberal-held Territory in June, 1855.

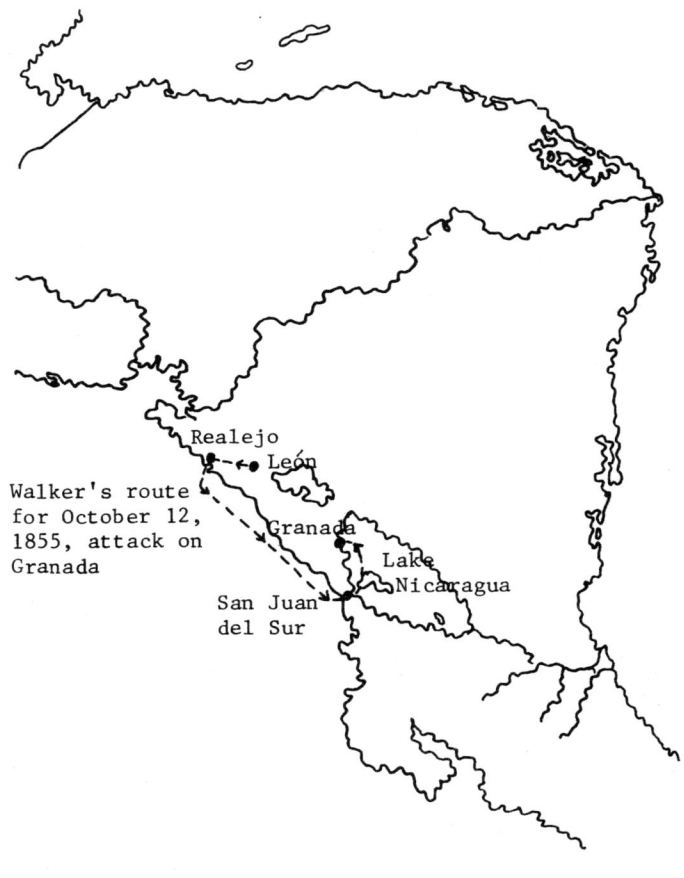

Figure 8. Walker's Granada Attack Route

CHAPTER VI

THE COMMANDER OF ARMS

"From such facts I reach the conclusion: If [Walker] doesn't drink, smoke, or have any devotion to Bacchus or Venus, it is clear that the only thing he desires is the sensuality of power; and for that reason a man without other passions, has turned into a filibuster. Lieutenant Lewis, forgive my frankness, but I have always distrusted men who do not render some homage to vice."

Upon returning to Granada, I told General Walker what the crazy Zavala—for that's what his own friends call him—had said, and saw a certain ironic smile sketched on his sphinx-like face.[1]

William Walker, the ubiquitous soldier-of-fortune who figured prominently in so many events, was the person to whom "the crazy Zavala" referred. Before Walker quit Nicaragua, he had managed to disrupt, confound, and quite destroy most of the carefully-conceived schemes of other Americans who had designs on that country. And in the process, he also had baffled and frustrated the Department of State.

Walker was born in Nashville, on May 8, 1824. He attended the University of Nashville, obtaining a degree in 1838 and subsequently securing a medical degree from the University of Pennsylvania in 1843. After living abroad, Walker returned to the United States and went to New Orleans, where he studied law and was admitted to the bar. While in New Orleans, he experienced his first exposure to the journalistic trade. After going to California in 1850, he continued working in that field, editing a newspaper in San Francisco and later in Marysville, Yuba County. It was there that he organized an expedition to seize and colonize Sonora and Lower California.

By January, 1854, Walker had proclaimed Lower California and Sonora an independent republic with himself as president. American authorities, concerned about apparent neutrality infractions, prevented food and supplies from reaching Walker's band, forcing him and the

---

[1] Gustavo Aleman-Bolanos, Centenario de la Guerra Nacional de Nicaragua Contra Walker (Guatemala: Imprenta Litografia, 1956), 57. Frederick Lewis was sent as a Walker emissary to Felix Zavala, Democratic Army General.

-108-

remaining members of his expedition to return to the border and surrender to officers of the San Diego army garrison. Walker was acquitted in a Federal court in May, 1854, of violating the neutrality laws.

Meanwhile, back in Nicaragua, Conservative President Fruto Chamorro had died from a liver infection during the 1854 Liberal siege of Granada. The emotional and physical stress he had undergone in an effort to maintain his position and his party in power had finally sapped his resistance. The Conservatives, fearing that news of the death of the strong leader might dishearten their supporters, made an effort to conceal this occurrence, and quietly named Jose Estrada as president. Subsequently, efforts to effect a reconciliation by Salvadoran and Guatemalan mediators in August and by the Presbyterian Remigio Salazar in September were rejected by Estrada, who refused to negotiate with the Democrats on the grounds that it would compromise "legitimacy."

The increasingly untenable position of the Democrats, and the inability of Honduran President Cabanas to continue supplying effective Honduran support for their cause, created a situation conducive to a search for other outside help. At this juncture, on August 15, William V. Wells and Byron Cole of the San Francisco Mining Company arrived at San Juan del Sur with the intention of exploring the possibility of developing mining resources in Honduras.[2] Cole, formerly a Boston editor, had left his Sacramento paper under the editorial management of Walker, recently reknowned for his filibustering expedition in Mexico. He suggested to Democratic leader Castellon that they should invite Walker to recruit and bring to Nicaragua a number of expeditionists to aid the Democratic cause. Because of his earlier impressions of American soldiery at the siege of Granada, Castellon was amenable to the idea of securing a number of American auxiliaries for his army. In addition, Walker's exploits in the ill-fated filibustering expedition to Lower California early in the year were known to Castellon.

There was ample precedent for the employment of foreign auxiliaries or legionnaires in the continual civil strife which Nicaragua had undergone since the initial Central American declaration of independence in 1821. Both the Liberal and Conservative causes had been augmented on occasion by, among others, American, French, and German soldiers-of-fortune. In fact, the Legitimists had recently sent Guadelupe Saenz to San Francisco on an unsuccessful mission to obtain foreign soldiers.[3]

---

[2] Scroggs, "William Walker and the Steamship Corporation in Nicaragua,"American Historical Review, X (June 1905), 792.

[3] Sofonias Salvatierra, Maximo Jerez, 80.

The terms of the first contract which Castellon offered, and which Cole took to California to present to Walker, called for three hundred Americans at a stated monthly pay and the distribution of 21,000 acres of land at the end of the campaign. This contract was rejected in November by Walker as he, according to his own account, regarded it as contrary to the U.S. Neutrality Law of 1818.[4] Walker outlined provisions for a new contract, and Cole returned with these to Nicaragua to renegotiate with Castellon. Castellon agreed to the terms and Cole once more voyaged to California, reaching Sacramento in February, 1855. The land grant was increased to 52,000 acres, the monthly pay was increased, the expeditionists were guaranteed the privilege of bearing arms even after the war, and—of major importance—they were to be regarded as colonists.

Walker took the contract to S. W. Inge, U.S. District Attorney for the Northern District of California in San Francisco, for a ruling on the validity vis-a-vis the neutrality laws. Inge agreed that no law would be violated by the implementation of the terms of the document. Next, Walker took the contract to General John E. Wool, U.S. Army Commander for the Department of the Pacific, who Walker believed had authority from secretary of War Jefferson Davis and from President Pierce to suppress expeditions conflicting with the 1818 law. Wool not only approved the contract and the aims of the expedition, but also wished Walker all success in the venture.[5] It is quite likely that Wool was influenced by the private views of the Secretary of State, William L. Marcy, who perhaps felt that a successful expedition would materially contribute to his presidential aspirations in the eventual annexation of pro-slavery territories.[6]

The stage was now set, as Walker believed, for the legal recruitment and transferral of the expeditionists/colonists to Nicaragua. He immediately proceeded to San Francisco and set about recruiting men and seeking financial support for his expedition. He received financial assistance from Joseph Palmer and Colonel John C. Fremont.[7] Walker rented the brig Vesta, loaded it with men, supplies,

---

4 William Walker, The War in Nicaragua (New York and Mobile: S.H. Goetzel and Company, 1860), 25.

5 Ibid., 27.

6 Albert H. Carr, The World and William Walker (New York: Harper and Row, 1963), 111.

7 Walker, War in Nicaragua, 29. Walker himself significantly—in view of his later repeal of abolition in Nicaragua—remarked that Palmer and Fremont were not fully aware of all the views he held on slavery.

and ammunition, and was ready to sail on April 20, 1855. However, the county sheriff seized the ship on behalf of a creditor of the owner, posted a guard, and took the brig's sails into custody. While Walker was attempting to resolve this problem, a U.S marshal served a writ for the same reason, and posted a cutter to prevent the sailing of the Vesta. With the help of a friend, Henry A. Crabb, Walker persuaded the creditor to grant easy terms and to let the brig sail.[8]

With the dismissal of the state and federal suits, the obstacle remained of the sheriff's costs for maintaining the guard over the brig, which the sheriff insisted Walker must pay. The sheriff, unaware of the dismissal of the suit, generously agreed to release the sails when Walker indicated he might take this portion of the matter to court. Walker persuaded the crew of the cutter to re-rig the Vesta and invited the sheriff's deputy, who was still posted as guard, below to his cabin. The deputy was advised by Walker, "There, sir, are champagne and cigars." From his pocket he drew a pair of handcuffs which he placed alongside the bottle. "And there are handcuffs and irons. Pray take your choice."[9] The deputy remained below partaking of Walker's hospitality, and after midnight early on May 4, the steam tug Resolute came alongside to tow the Vesta out into the harbor. The deputy returned ashore aboard the tug. A voyage followed which was laden with enthusiasm but otherwise uneventful. A pilot was taken aboard at Tigre Island and the Vesta reached shore in the Bay of Fonseca near Realejo on June 17.

When the Vesta arrived, the Leon provisional government (Democrats) was confined to the Occidental Department. The Legitimists held all of the Oriental and Meridional departments, and the departments of Matagalpa and Segovia, though not occupied by Granadan troops, were under Legitimist sway. In addition, the position of Cabanas, the Democratic ally, was weakening in Honduras. A force under General Lopez, aided by Guatemala, had invaded the Department of Gracias in the northern part of Honduras.

Rounding the circle of regional intervention, Honduran General Santos Guardiola (known to Central Americans as "The Butcher") had sailed from Iztapa, Guatemala, for San Juan del Sur aboard the Costa Rican schooner, San Jose, to help the Nicaraguan Legitimists. He had

---

[8] Ibid., 29-31. Walker observed in his narrative that he had pointed out to the creditor that he might find himself in an uncomfortable position should the troops aboard be forced to debark and abandon the mission, knowing that the creditor was responsible for its failure.

[9] New York Times, June 2, 1855.

arrived with his forces in Granada a few days before Walker landed in Fonseca. General Munoz, the old Nicaraguan warhorse, had come out of retirement in Honduras and had replaced Jerez as Commander-in-Chief of the Democratic forces. It was rumored that Munoz wanted to compromise with the Legitimists in order to secure for himself a position in a national government.

Castellon received the news of the arrival of the Americans in Chinandega with relief and optimism. He sent a personal emissary to escort Walker to the capital at Leon and, in a burst of exuberance, named the contingent of fifty-eight bearded, barefoot, robust Yankees, "the American Phalanx" (Falange Americana). His enthusiasm appeared to be unmixed with concern or suspicion over possible ulterior motives that Walker might entertain concerning the mission. With apparent justification he was imperceptive to the possibility that Walker's forces might develop into something more than mere auxiliaries serving in the ranks of the Democratic army.

Subsequent chroniclers have severely criticized Castellon for the Walker invitation. One observed:

> It is somewhat difficult to understand, on the supposition that Castellon was a man of intelligence, why he should have consented to take such a step. He ought to have known that it was the most fatal policy he could pursue. He ought to have known that by calling in these men, who could not possibly come to fight his battles merely for the purpose of helping him or his cause and who could not possibly be satisfied with playing any mere subordinate part in the public affairs of the state, he was introducing an enemy incalculably more dangerous than any native antagonist.[10]

However, the lessons to be learned from Walker's previous efforts in the filibustering field were not lost on General Munoz. With ambitions of achieving national power himself, he readily recognized the threat that this "Grey-Eyed Man of Destiny" represented.

The initial meeting of Walker with Munoz resulted in mutually penetrating and chilly appraisal. At the first opportunity afterward, Walker made it clear to Castellon that neither he nor his troops would serve under Munoz' command, to which Castellon agreed. Walker probably determined this course both from his initial personal dislike of Munoz and because of his immediate recognition that the general might

---

10 Theodore H. Hittell, "History of the Filibuster, William Walker," unpublished ms., 1915, Sutro Library, San Francisco.

thwart him in his ambition. There seems little doubt, in view of Walker's subsequent actions and testimony, that his intended service on behalf of the Democratic forces was to be but a stepping stone to greater political rewards. He was little concerned about the relative merits of the Liberal and Conservative causes, nor did he feel that the financial and territorial rewards agreed upon under the contract were sufficient inducement for such a bold and dangerous undertaking. It is unlikely that Walker had a concise and predetermined plan for the political reorganization of Nicaragua; however, his flexibility on this question did accomodate the possibility that he would eventually become Chief of State.

> Walker had seen enough of his new friends to convince himself that his ambition had nothing to fear from such rivals. Castellon was an amiable and irresolute gentleman; Munoz was ambitious and vain, but incapable. The native soldiery were ill-trained and feeble-minded. Faction had stifled any faint sparks of patriotism in their breasts.[11]

Some writers have obliquely alluded to the possibility that Munoz' real quarrel was his jealousy of and his antagonism toward Castellon. Though this remains conjecture, certain it is that Munoz had always been opposed to American aid on the grounds that it would lead to foreign domination. Walker, who aimed at such domination, instinctively knew that Munoz would try to block him.[12] Although Walker himself left no written record of his grand design for reorganization of Nicaragua and adjacent territories, there are indications that the design extended east to Cuba, and C. W. Doubleday, one of the Americans who participated in the siege at Granada, said that Walker planned to make himself emperor of a mighty slave-holding empire stretching from Texas to the Isthmus of Panama.[13]

Although Castellon was primarily concerned about the security of the Democratic position at Leon and warned Walker to keep his troops as a defensive force, this strategy did not coincide with Walker's plans. He convinced Castellon that the stalemate had to be broken and that the quickest, most assured way of achieving this end was to occupy Rivas and the transit road. This move would provide, he contended, revenue for the Democratic cause, lighten the tax burden of the citizens in the

---

[11] James Jeffrey Roche, <u>By-Ways of War, The Story of the Filibusters</u> (Boston: Small, Maynard and Company, 1901), 97.

[12] Meritt Parmalee Allen, <u>William Walker, Filibuster</u> (New York: Harper and Bros., 1932), 60.

[13] Ibid., 59.

Democratic area, and add new spark to the now feeble torch of assistance against Granadan domination. His private design, which he did not divulge to Castellon, was to occupy the transit route and thereby be in a position to recruit more American adventurers who would be traveling between the coastal areas of the United States.

The plan was authorized by Minister of War Buenaventura Selva, who also appointed Walker a colonel in the Democratic army on June 20, and offered commissions to other Americans whom the latter chose to recommend. Under the Constitution of 1838, a simple declaration by a person born in one of the American republics was sufficient to establish citizenship, and most of the Phalanx immediately became naturalized citizens of Nicaragua.[14]

For his part, Castellon provided for a civil governmental organization in the event the expedition was a success and gained a foothold in the Meridional Department. Maximo Espinosa, owner of a cacao plantation near Rivas and a Democratic sympathizer, was to be Minister of Government, while Francisco Vaco would be appointed Prefect of the Department and Commissioner of Revenue.

While General Munoz remained with the major part of his force to guard Leon, Walker's forces, along with 200 native troops under General Ramirez, embarked on the Vesta and sailed down the coast. Munoz now turned his open resistance to Walker into treachery, and sent word to general Guardiola, commanding the Legitimist garrison at Rivas, that Walker intended to attack. In addition, it is highly probable, judging from Ramirez' subsequent action, that he had been influenced by Munoz' determination to see the Walker forces destroyed.

On June 20, Walker landed at Agua Callito (above San Juan del Sur) and the next morning marched toward Rivas. His forces encountered General Boscha, commanding 480 men, on the plain outside of Rivas. The native troops, who had been continually lagging behind on the march, deserted en masse at the first sound of gunfire. Walker's band was forced to take refuge in and make a citadel of a nearby house. Though Boscha's troops could not carry the stronghold during the day, they succeeded in setting fire to the house under cover of darkness, and Walker's men were forced to fight their way out. Ten of the Walker band were killed in the battle, but the skilled American riflemen accounted for 180 Legitimist casualties.

The Walker contingent was not pursued and arrived at San Juan del Sur, hoping to find the Vesta waiting. When Walker found that the Vesta had not arrived, he decided to commandeer the San Jose, a sloop commanded by Captain Alvarado. When Alvarado pleaded neutrality,

---

[14] Walker, War in Nicaragua. 41.

Walker pointed out that the sloop had brought Guardiola from Guatemala to Nicaragua, and was thus already deeply involved in the conflict. A short way up the coast, the San Jose fortuitously rendezvoused with the Vesta, to which the filibusters transferred.

The Vesta arrived at the Bay of Fonseca on July 6, and the Walker contingent remained aboard. Walker sent a message to Castellon, charging that the desertion of Ramirez was ordered by Munoz, and threatened to leave Nicaragua if retribution were not directed. Castellon, desperately trying to hold his forces together, urged Walker to overlook this possible malfeasance. Walker rejected Castellon's entreaties and remained aboard the Vesta. Actually, Walker later confessed that his refusal to debark was partly strategy to gain more leverage in the use of his men, and partly to give his wounded an opportunity to recover. In the meantime, Mariano Salazar, a brother-in-law of Castellon, came aboard and urged Walker to return to Leon because of an imminent attack by Granadan General Ponciano Corral. Finally, Castellon came to Realejo with Salazar and persuaded Walker to return to Leon.

The next meeting among Walker, Castellon, and Munoz saw no discussion of Walker's charges; however, future utilization of the American Phalanx was the subject of heated disagreement between Walker and Munoz. The latter wanted the Phalanx divided into squads and scattered among the various units of the army. Walker insisted on keeping his command intact and launching another attack against the transit road. Further to confuse the conference, Cabanas was now in deep trouble against his conservative foes in Honduras and was calling for help from his Democratic allies. The negotiations in relation to the disposition of Walker's troops spanned the period from July 6 to August 23. Munoz, trying to arrange an armistice, sent Dr. Roasalio Cortez to Granada, pleading that there was still time to derail Walker before he beat Guardiola and marched on Granada. General Corral made no reply to the communication.[15] On July 19, news of the battle of Saouci in Segovia transformed the situation. Though the forces led by General Munoz had routed those of Guardiola, Munoz had been killed in battle.[16]

Walker almost unilaterally commissioned himself for a second attempt at the transit road. An Indian named Jose Maria Valle, Subprefect of Chinandega and a warm friend of the Americans, agreed to help. Castellon wrote Valle, asking him and then ordering him, not to join the expedition, pointing out that the Democratic capital was still

---

[15] Sofonias Salvatierra, Maximo Jerez, 82.

[16] Wheeler to Marcy, September 21, 1855, National Archives, M219, 10/23.

threatened. Valle forced his faltering chief to withdraw the order when he indicated that he would alternatively ignore it.[17]

Walker's band, accompanied by 136 native soldiers, set sail on the Vesta and the schooner Esperanza. Arriving in San Juan del Sur on August 28, they made preparations until September, when they began marching for Virgin Bay. Shortly after arriving at the unoccupied hamlet, the Democratic forces heard firing about one mile from town. Over five hundred Legitimist troops under Guardiola swarmed across the plains. With the native contingent of the Democratic forces performing as brilliantly as the Americans, Guardiola's forces were routed. The Democrats, while suffering only fourteen wounded, inflicted about a hundred casualties on the Legitimists and captured arms, ammunition, baggage, and the papers of Guardiola himself. Walker's forces then returned to San Juan del Sur where many Legitimist deserters joined them, indicating that the opposition armies were either becoming demoralized or scattered. However, Corral and Guardiola, with six hundred troops, fell back on Rivas on September 12.

From September 13 until October 3, Walker remained in San Juan del Sur, receiving new recruits from San Francisco. During this time over six hundred Nicaraguans died of cholera. The epidemic had begun in Granada during the siege and had inexorably spread north. Among the victims was Castellon, who was replaced by Nazario Escoto. After hearing this news, Walker also learned that Corral and Guardiola had quarreled and that Guardiola had returned to Honduras. Adding to his American reinforcements, Walker recruited native troops and attended to further financing. He levied "contributions" of $100-$150 on resident Americans and other foreigners in San Juan del Sur. Consul John Priest was forced to pay when Walker's troops seized his house and took him prisoner. In reply to Priest, Walker said he neither recognized Priest, who was accredited to the Legitimist government, nor his protest.[18]

On September 10, Walker took his reorganized and reinforced troops again to Virgin Bay, presumably to consolidate control of the transit route. However, upon reaching there he intercepted dispatches and letters to Corral from Corral's adjutant general, Fernando Chamorro. The interceptions disclosed a rather destitute condition of the government at Granada and its inability to assist its commander-in-chief at Rivas with more men. In addition, they indicated that Granada was almost entirely undefended, that the spirit of the people was sagging, and that the chiefs of the party had begun to despair of

---

[17] Walker, War in Nicaragua. 80.

[18] Priest to Marcy, September 11, 1855, National Archives, T152, 1/6.

maintaining the war much longer if vigorously pressed by the Democratic forces.

Walker's first reaction to this intelligence was to advise Corral of the interception and to intimate that an armistice would be good for both. Corral merely acknowledged receipt of the message and rather mysteriously included some penned signs. According to Walker's advisors, the signs were Masonic and indicated that Corral was willing to negotiate with another Mason. At this point, the correspondence ceased.[19]

It is possible that Walker actually had no intention of negotiating with Corral then, because it would have been impossible to negotiate from a position of sufficient strength to have obtained his desired goals. It is likely that he merely wished to confirm the validity of the intercepted reports by determining whether or not Corral would be willing to negotiate an armistice. Although the transit road had been Walker's number one objective, its occupation was merely a means to an end, the end being the subjugation of the Legitimist forces. With the knowledge of the weakened condition of Granada, he probably perceived a shortcut to this goal. Therefore, when the Accessory Transit Company's steamer Virgin anchored close to the Virgin Bay pier on October 11, Walker took a party and boarded it. For three hours on the afternoon of October 12, he embarked his men for Granada.

Possibly Walker had earlier anticipated utilizing in some fashion the services of the transit company to supply his troops and conduct his campaign. Before leaving Leon on the second expedition to occupy the transit route, Walker had unrealistically been authorized by the government at Leon to settle the differences between the Nicaraguan government and the transit company. On October 3, while Walker was still at San Juan del Sur, the steamer Cortez arrived from San Francisco. Aboard the steamer was C. J. McDonald, a confidential agent of Cornelius K. Garrison, the San Francisco manager of the transit company. McDonald apparently proposed a scheme to Walker whereby control of the transit company could be wrested by Garrison from Vanderbilt. Garrison would see that men and supplies were shipped to Walker aboard the company's ships and that the lake steamers were made available for Walker's campaigns in Nicaragua. Walker, in turn, upon assuming authority in the republic, would revoke the company's present charter, presumably on grounds of failure to pay the contractual profit percentage, and then re-award the charter and the nationalized capital equipment to Garrison.[20] It is in this light that Walker's commandeering of the Virgin for an attack on Granada must be viewed.

---

[19] Walker, War in Nicaragua, 104.

[20] Scroggs, "Walker and the Steamship Corporation", 792-811.

Actually the transit company was already involved in transporting mercenaries, but not to fight for Walker. On July 5, 1855, about fifty men had left New York bound for Nicaragua aboard the company's steamship <u>Star of the West</u>. They had been hired as soldiers by White, company counsel in New York, and by Jose de Marcoleta, the Nicaraguan Minister to the United States, with the transit company paying the expenses. The band had been organized as a military company to protect the interests of the transit company. American Minister John H. Wheeler added that it was "for the further purpose of aiding the present Legitimist government of Nicaragua, as will appear by a letter from the commanding general of the Nicaraguan army (presumably Corral) to Colonel Gazynski." Shortly after their arrival, according to Wheeler, the group disbanded. Some (with Gazynski) returned to the United States, some joined a colonizing expedition on the Caribbean side, and others enlisted as soldiers in the Nicaraguan army.[21]

Despite the reference in Corral's letter to Gazynski concerning services in the Nicaraguan army, White, surprisingly enough, seemed to be unaware of the entire nature of the expedition. Writing to Colonel Gazynski on August 6, he reminded Gazynski that he had been sent to Nicaragua in the services of the transit company and for no other reason. "Your place is on the river," he pointed out, and threatened to replace Gazynski.[22]

Wheeler's reference to a letter from Corral to Gazynski is confusing. In a letter written August 28 by Corral to Gazynski, Corral turned down Gazynski's offer of services, protesting that Gazynski's price was too high.[23] It appears that Gazynski had an agreement with Marcoleta about which White was not aware. Either the terms under which Gazynski's troops would serve the Legitimist banner were not firm, or he raised the price upon arrival. It is also possible that Corral knew nothing of the deal before the <u>Star of the West</u> docked at San Juan del Norte. In any event, when Gazynski encountered the rebuff, he packed up and returned to the United States, leaving his erstwhile companions on their own. A significant result of this episode was that Walker later used Gazynski's offer as part of his pretext for fulfilling his part of the bargain with Garrison.

At midnight on October 12, Walker, with two hundred Americans and three hundred native troops under General Valle, disembarked two

---

[21] Wheeler to Marcy, September 21, 1855, National Archives, M219, 10/23.

[22] Joseph L. White to Colonel Titus Felix Gazynski, August 6, 1855. <u>ibid</u>.

[23] Corral to Gazynski, August 28, 1955, <u>ibid</u>.

miles northeast of Granada. After a short battle early the following day, the city fell and the President fled.[24] Walker calmed the citizens by issuing a proclamation providing for the protection of persons and property, and by keeping strict discipline, in contrast to traditional ravages by conquerors in the long civil war. According to the account of the battle in the first edition of El Nicaraguense, Walker's fledgling newspaper, the Walker forces released 80 prisoners—men, women, and children—chained in the San Francisco Church.[25] Walker, in turn, imprisoned the major leaders of the Legitimist party who had not escaped during the confusion and the initial occupation. The next day, October 14, was a Sunday, a traditional day in Granada for political activity. The day opened with a sermon in the main cathedral by Padre Augustin Vijil, who exhorted the citizens to peace, moderation, and the putting away of revolutionary passions. According to William V. Wells, an early chronicler of Walker's adventures, efforts were made by prominent Granadinos to persuade Walker to accept the presidency. A resolution to this effect was signed by Rosario Viva, Sebastian Maranco, Pedro Quadra, the Lacayos, and others. Wheeler reported, "A proposition of peace has been made by which Walker is appointed provisional president for one month and an election to be ordered by the people, and the President-elect to take office at the end of one month."[26] Walker declined the office in favor of Legitimist General Corral,[27] but it appears that Walker's rejection of the offer was not as magnanimous as it was pragmatic. Rather than become a temporary figurehead, Walker perceptively surmised that his best course was to obtain control of the armed forces and thus wield the ultimate weapon in the jockeying for power. At this point, Wheeler was persuaded by the Granadinos to offer Walker's peace terms to General Corral at Rivas.

Wheeler had been commissioned by the Department of State to secure the adherence of Nicaragua to the international neutrality laws then being sponsored by the United States[28] and to re-negotiate a bilateral treaty which in its initial form had been unacceptable to the U.S.

---

24 Wheeler's account listed the American troops as ninety-two and estimated battle time as fifteen minutes. Wheeler to Marcy, October 14, 1855, ibid., 10/25.

25 El Nicaraguense, October 20, 1855.

26 Wheeler to Marcy, October 14, 1855, National Archives, M219, 10/25.

27 Wells, Walker's Expedition, 66.

28 Marcy to Wheeler, October 18, 1854, National Archives, M77, 27/2.

Senate.[29] After arriving in Nicaragua on December 22, 1854, and after an interlude at San Juan del Sur, Wheeler left for Granada from Virgin Bay on January 26, 1855. Because of internal strife, he regarded the trip by steamer as too dangerous, and he arrived at Granada via horseback on January 29.

Upon his request, the besieging Democrats allowed him twenty-four hours to enter the city and retrieve the American Ministry's archives. While in the city, Wheeler promised Chamorro neutrality on the part of the United States and said that he would dissuade any Americans from taking part in the war. He indicated that he would retrieve the archives and return to Virgin Bay until the war had ended and new orders were received from the Department of State. Chamorro agreed that this was the proper course.[30]

When the Democratic siege was lifted and the Legitimists were advancing on Leon, it appeared to Wheeler that the war was drawing to a close. He therefore advised the State Department that he would go to Granada on March 26 and added, "If justified by circumstances, I shall present my credentials to the President (Estrado [sic])."[31] On March 31, Wheeler arrived in Granada and on April 7, he presented his credentials to the Legitimist government, congratulating the government that the war was about to end.[32]

Wheeler never seemed to take the Democratic threat seriously until the surprising fall of Granada, and he carried on normal, diplomatic intercourse with the Legitimist government up until that time. However, he was well aware of the devastation and anarchy resulting from the war, and the possibility of peace at last arrived like a millennium. In addition, though there is no documentary evidence of it, he was undoubtedly influenced in his later support of the filibuster government by the strong and determined will of Walker. Therefore, he accepted the commission to carry Walker's offer of peace negotiations to Corral at Rivas.

Wheeler, accompanied by his private secretary, Thomas F. Van Dyke, and by Juan Ruiz, Minister of War under Estrada (Ruiz had given his "parole of honor" that he would return), left at midnight on October 15 and found that Corral was not there. Wheeler waited a few hours, and when he announced that he intended to return to Granada, he was

---

[29] Ibid., October 23, 1854, M77, 27/3.

[30] Wheeler to Marcy, February 3, 1855, M219, 10/6.

[31] Ibid, March 20, 1855, M219, 10/9.

[32] Ibid, April 11, 1855, M219, 10/10.

placed under house arrest by the Legitimists. After two days, the steamer Virgin forced his release at cannon point and Wheeler returned to Virgin Bay to await Corral's response.

Corral's message of October 17 accused Wheeler of interference, advised him that he intended to inform the Secretary of State and the newspapers in New York, and disclaimed any responsibility for the American minister's future safety. Wheeler rejected the accusation in his October 18 reply and informed Corral that he would wait two more days for the Legitimist chief's response to Walker's offer. After the two days were up, Wheeler returned to Granada from his unsuccessful mission.

The reverberations from Wheeler's trip were felt in Washington, and he was reprimanded for interference by Secretary of State Marcy.[33] Wheeler attempted to explain the situation and the reason for his action: "No other course could be taken than that which was pursued by me. . . . I could feel assured, therefore, that the President and you, on a full knowledge of the facts and history of the case, will justify and approve of my course."[34] Later, Nicaraguan historians berated Wheeler's action, calling him "the filibuster minister."[35]

An event again involving the transit company assumed significant stature in the developments. On October 15, the steamer Cortez had arrived at San Juan del Sur from San Francisco with Colonel Birkett D. Fry's Nicaraguan battalion of sixty men, recruited and accompanied by Parker H. French. The band was under the misapprehension that a swift and unexpected blow might topple Legitimist resistance, and believed that consolidation of command of the transit route was still of major importance. On October 18, they boarded the Virgin at Virgin Bay, along with other passengers and cargo, and crossed Lake Nicaragua with the intention of forcing the surrender of Fort San Carlos at the eastern entrance to the lake. Their demand for surrender was rejected, the Virgin fired upon, and an attempted landing by riflemen repulsed. The other passengers now had to content themselves with returning to Virgin Bay.

An hour after the attack, the transit steamer San Carlos arrived at Fort San Carlos, having come up the San Juan River with passengers from New York. The fort fired on the steamer, damaging the engines and killing a woman and her child. After the misunderstanding was cleared up, the steamer was allowed to proceed to Virgin Bay. The next

---

[33] Marcy to Wheeler, November 8, 1855, M77, 27/13.

[34] Wheeler to Marcy, December 15, 1855, M219, 10/32.

[35] Sofonias Salvatierra, Maximo Jerez, 85.

day, Legitimist troops from Rivas entered Virgin Bay, attacking and killing some of the detained passengers. When no Walker troops were found, the remaining passengers were allowed to go to Granada to be put under the protection of Wheeler.[36] Mateo Mayorga, a Legitimist cabinet minister who had been in asylum in Wheeler's house, was delivered up by Wheeler to Walker, who arranged for his execution under the pretext of reprisal against the attacks on American citizens. Walker determined on this course because the Legitimists threatened to throttle the transit road, and Walker could not abandon Granada to prevent it. He felt he had to aid the transit company to assure its support, and he could not punish French and Fry without risking encouraging the enemy.[37]

The Legitimist threat to isolate Walker in Granada necessitated a dramatic move. This move was the execution of Mayorga and a message to Corral that the remaining prisoners would be executed if Corral continued to refuse to negotiate. The Legitimists then faced the possibility that Walker might effectivly devastate the ranks of the leaders of the Legitimist party and might even execute members of the families of the Legitimist leaders outside of Granada. In addition, Corral probably expected the peace terms to name him chief executive in a provisional government. He persuaded Estrada to authorize negotiations by pointing out that an agreement would mean that Walker would henceforth collaborate with the Legitimists.

Corral arrived to negotiate on October 23 and agreed on some general terms with Walker. Hostilities would be suspended and the two governments which had existed since the beginning of the revolution would disappear. Selected provisions of the Constitution of 1838 would be respected. The governmental seat would be in Granada, with Patricio Rivas, customs officer in San Carlos, who was nominally a Legitimist but actually almost apolitical, as provisional president for fourteen months. Four ministers of state would by appointed by the President, with Corral serving as Minister of War. A general amnesty was proclaimed and plans were made for the reduction and disarmament of both armies.

Walker actually allowed Corral to take the initiative in the negotiations and to virtually dictate the terms of the treaty; thus, "nearly all causes were of Corral's authorship." Walker then trapped Corral by quietly insisting on being named Commander-in-Chief of

---

[36] Affidavits of George B. Slocum, Captain of the steamer San Carlos, and others, given to Wheeler, October 23, 1855, Wheeler to Marcy, December 15, 1855, National Archives, M219, 10/32.

[37] Allen, William Walker, 84.

Arms.[38] From this point on, Walker—as he had anticipated—was virtual master of the situation. The treaty was formally signed by Walker and Corral on October 23 and consecrated in a solemn Te Deum in the cathedral in Granada a week later.

Walker represented himself as acting on behalf of the Democrats, and declared he would subdue them if they did not agree to the convenant. When the news of the settlement reached Leon, there was surprise and consternation. A meeting was called among the Democratic leaders to determine what attitude should be assumed in the face of these events. Many wanted to disavow Walker, but Norberto Ramirez, a former chief-of-state, declared that the choice was two abysses, one soon and the other later. Thereupon, the Democrats approved the provisional government and sent a delegation to Granada which arrived on October 31.

Corral, who had expected a unilateral cabinet, was anguished at the introduction by Rivas (at Walker's behest) of the Democrats into the ministries.[39] Jerez was named Minister of Public Credit. Minister General Fermin Ferrer was a wealthy Granadino who, like Rivas had taken no part in the revolution.

Even before the new government could be established, an unsettling event occurred. Corral, brooding over what he regarded as a betrayal by Walker, wrote letters to Legitimist General Pedro Xatruch and to General Guardiola, both at Tequcigalpa. The letters obliquely requested intervention by these generals with troops before Walker's control could be solidified. They were intercepted, and General Valle delivered them to Walker.

Walker immediately had Corral arrested and at his subsequent court-martial, Corral admitted authorship. The court sentenced Corral to execution, but recommended that the Commander of Arms (not the President) grant mercy. Even Corral's wife and daughters formally called on Walker and begged reprieve in tearful wails. "But upon the countenance of Walker, there was not visible a particle of emotion. His features were calm and placid, and his cold, passionless gray eyes relaxed nothing of its [sic] ordinary frigidity."[40] According to Walker's own testimony, he felt compelled to sustain the sentence to avoid

---

[38] Laurence Greene, The Filibuster (New York: Bobbs-Merrill, 1937), 123.

[39] Sofonias Salvatierra, Maximo Jerez, 91-94.

[40] J. C. Kewen in the San Francisco Herald, December 14, 1855.

further conspiracies by either Corral or other Legitimist leaders. Corral was executed at 2:00 P.M. on November 8, 1855, in the main plaza.

Walker's action was exceedingly unpopular, and cost him much of the support he had enjoyed from his initial moderation. "Whichever way he turned, immediately there arose a cry from the Legitimists or the Democrats, the transit company or its rivals, the northern states or the southern states, the Central American republics or England, that he should have turned some other way."[41] Subsequently, Buenaventura Selva was named to replace Corral as Minister of War.

With his apparent imperturbability and his single-mindedness of purpose, Walker rode out the storm of protest. He perhaps felt that respect for his new government was far more important than ephemeral popularity and the good will of the rank-and-file Granadinos. He now turned his attention to the two major tasks at hand: the organization of the government and recognition of its legitimacy.

---

[41] Allen, William Walker, 93.

Figure 9. Nicaraguan Political Divisions

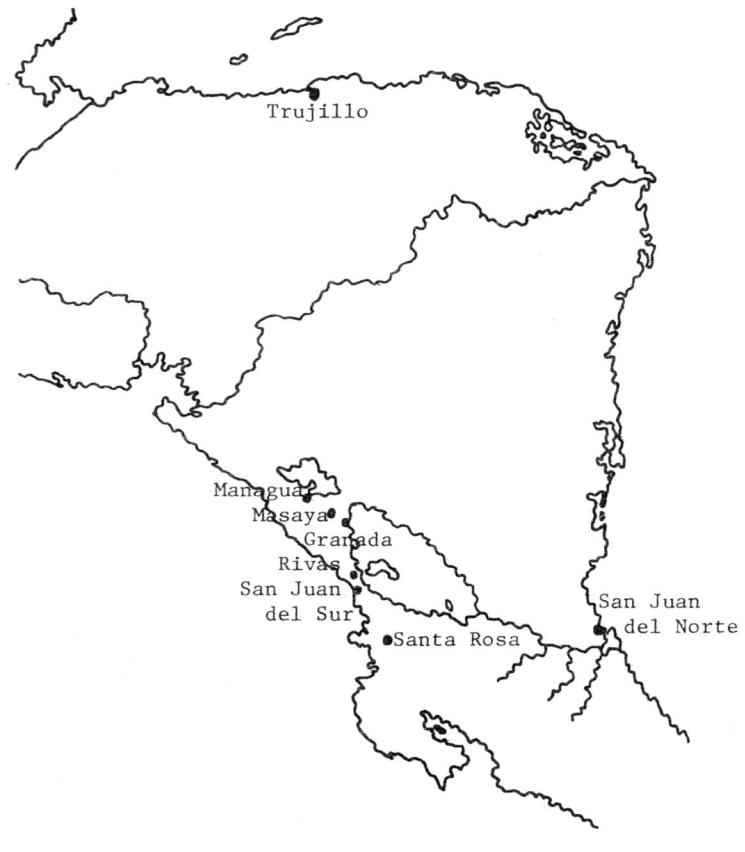

Figure 10. Major Battle Sites

CHAPTER VII

A FILIBUSTER GOVERNMENT

Perhaps American influence will tend to purify Nicaraguan businessmen's principles and elevate their conduct. With this idea it will prove a blessing if the whole of Central America becomes Americanized by the industrious and enterprizing from the North.[1]

On October 23, 1855, Wheeler informed Secretary Marcy of the peace treaty which had just been signed between Walker and Corral, and said that he would await instructions from the Department regarding recognition. The observation, however, that this was the first apparent peace in thirty years, and that El Salvador, Honduras, and Nicaragua would form a federal republic, indicated something of his feelings vis-a-vis the new government.[2] On November 6, Wheeler advised the Department of the constitution of the new government and the execution of Corral. Quoting from Wheaton's Elements of International Law concerning de facto recognition, he observed, "I shall feel authorized to present myself to the President of the provisional government, believing that this course will meet your entire approbation."[3] Two days later, he presented his credentials to the new government and, according to an account in Walker's newspaper, "acknowledged on the part of the government he so ably represents, the independence and sovereignty of the government established by the treaty of 23d ultimo."[4] Shortly afterward, Wheeler told the Department that the new government would be permanent, and that El Salvador and Honduras sent their congratulations.

> Costa Rica must fall in. Guatemala, the determined foe of Nicaragua, will seek and find ready cause of Quarrel and will attack her—in which aided by San Salvador and Honduras and the adventurous spirits from the United States and elsewhere, Guatemala will be badly whipped. Then will come a confederated union of the five republics and

---

[1] Wheeler to Marcy, June 15, 1856, National Archives, M219, 10/57.

[2] Ibid., October 23, 1855, ibid., 10/27.

[3] Ibid., November 8, 1855, ibid., 10/28.

[4] El Nicaraguense, November 10, 1855.

with it, I trust Peace, Science and Civilization.[5]

The Department's reply was delayed in arrival, and demonstrated a major difference in assessments of the situation:

> It has more the appearance of a successful marauding expedition than a change of government of rulers. Should the mass of people of Nicaragua be unwilling or unable to repel this inroad or shake off this usurpation, and ultimately submit to its rule, then it will become de facto a government and responsible for the outrages which have been committed upon the rights and persons of American citizens. Then this government will demand and exact, ample indemnity and satisfaction from it.[6]

This exchange brings dramatically into focus the cross-purpose between Wheeler and Marcy. Wheeler had experienced the trials of the savage civil war and had seen the devastation it was causing. He was caught up in the prevailing spirit of optimism that—it was fervently hoped—a final settlement had been found. To this end, he wanted to lend the prestige of his office to the consolidation of the armistice. Marcy was concerned about neutrality and about identifying a legal government on which damages could be assessed. Nonetheless, Wheeler acceded to the instructions from his superior: "Since the reception of this despatch . . . I have abstained from all official intercourse with the persons now exercising control over this republic and will not establish diplomatic intercourse until instructed."[7]

In addition to addressing the routine problems of organizing a revolutionary government, Walker turned his attention toward two other efforts: colonization and recognition. In order to stimulate colonization, he issued decrees guaranteeing life and property, and attempted to attract American scientific and industrial talent. J. W. Fabens was appointed Director of Colonization, and on November 28 he issued a homesteading decree which provided two hundred and fifty acres for a single person, with an additional one hundred for each person with a family. A non-transferable title would

---

[5] Wheeler to Marcy, November 12, 1855, National Archives, M219, 10/29.

[6] Marcy to Wheeler, November 8, 1855, ibid., M77, 27/13.

[7] Wheeler to Marcy, December 24, 1855, ibid., M219, 10/35.

be granted after six months' occupancy; the colonizers would be free from import duties, taxes, or public service except in emergencies.[8] As a result of this decree, American colonists began arriving in Nicaragua on both sides of the republic.

As important as recognition by the other Central American nations was recognition by the United States. French resigned as Minister of Hacienda (Finance) and was appointed minister to the United States. He left San Juan del Norte on December 3 for New York, carrying a letter of introduction from Wheeler and the treaty Wheeler had negotiated, for the purpose of exchanging ratifications.[9]

From New York French went directly to Washington and sent a note to Marcy on December 12. The note said French was the accredited Nicaraguan representative to Washington and requested an early interview before presenting his credentials. Marcy's note of December 21 said that the President "has not yet seen reasons for establishing diplomatic intercourse with the persons who now claim to exercise political power in the state of Nicaragua." Marcy also charged that those who overthrew the former government were not citizens and that citizens had not had an opportunity to express their will. Until such time, the President would not receive French or anyone else from that government.[10]

As a result of American non-recognition, Guatemala, Honduras, and Costa Rica refused even to correspond with the new government. Friendly efforts to establish commerce with the Central American states were rebuffed with unequivocal indications of hostility.[11]

In the meantime, Walker was still receiving support from the Garrison faction of the transit company. McDonald, the company representative, had taken $20,000 in gold bullion from a shipment crossing the Isthmus and had given the owner drafts on Charles Morgan, Garrison's accomplice and company manager in New York. The bullion found its way into the coffers of the new government, and the government in turn, agreed to deduct the amount from the transit company's annual payment.[12]

---

[8] Wells, Walker's Expedition, 98.

[9] Wheeler to Marcy, November 30, 1855, National Archives, M219, 10/31.

[10] Wells, Walker's Expedition, 99.

[11] Ibid., 147.

[12] Scroggs, "Walker and the Steamship Corporation," 795.

In addition, French, with Morgan's support, proposed in New York that the transit company transport immigrants to Nicaragua and deduct twenty dollars a person from the debt. Neither Vanderbilt nor White suspected the ulterior motives of the Garrison-Morgan faction, despite Wheeler's caution to Marcy concerning the situation: "The Government will early institute an inquiry by what warrant the transit company owns their charter, and the inquiry may result in it being declared forfeited so far as the transit over the isthmus is concerned."[13] It is likely that Vanderbilt suspected nothing concerning the conspiracy. At any rate, from December, 1855, to February, 1856, about one thousand immigrants were transported by the transit company.[14]

On December 3, General Cabanas arrived from Costa Rica where he had been in exile since being deposed in Honduras. He now requested a return on his investment in helping the Liberals mount the May, 1854, revolution. There still remained two months in Cabanas' presidential tenure in Honduras, and he wanted help in overthrowing Guardiola, now in power, in order to assure legitimate succession. Walker refused the aid because he regarded Cabanas as old and useless:

> The very obstinacy with which he asked to be restored before the expiration of his time was proof of the tendency of his mind to dwell on unimportant points. Incapable of looking at the affairs of Central America with general views, he seemed a Morazan Federalist, dwindled by age to a Honduras official.[15]

Walker also claimed that he did not help Cabanas because he wanted more time to prepare for the inevitable blow that the other states would strike. It was later alleged that Walker actually refused because he saw he could not manage the old warrior.[16] Both Jerez and Buenaventura resigned from the cabinet in disgust when Walker refused to cooperate with Cabanas.

Wheeler's view of Cabanas was more sympathetic than that of Walker. He referred to the old Honduran as being "esteemed as one of

---

[13] Wheeler to Marcy, December 15, 1855, National Archives, M219, 10/32.

[14] Scroggs, "Walker and the Steamship Corporation," 796.

[15] Walker, War in Nicaragua, 162.

[16] Ricardo Duenas Van Severen, La Invasion Filibustera (El Salvador: Director General of Publications, 1962), 84.

the most liberal and honorable men in Central America." Probably for that reason, and because it befitted his role as a "diplomat," he was more patient with Cabanas. The latter wanted to know whether the United States approved of its citizens coming to Central America, or whether it would prevent the attempt to "destroy the nationality of Central America." Wheeler replied that American policy since President Washington had been non-interference in domestic difficulties of other nations. He pointed out that the United States had stopped Colonel Kinney, and had indicted officials of the British government for recruiting for the Crimean War. But if American citizens left their country and enlisted in a foreign service, the United States was no longer responsible—either to restrain or protect them.

Wheeler assured Cabanas that the United States would not intervene to aid Walker if Guatemala—joined by other states—made war on him. Cabanas then observed that if Walker did not get reinforcements, Guatemala led by Carrera, and Honduras, with Graudiola at the helm ("both unscrupulous and unprincipled, desperate and bloody") would run the filibuster out or kill him. This was ominous—and eerily prescient —but Wheeler remained sanguine. He asserted that they would get whipped if they tried, for every steamer brought more people—farmers, merchants, miners—but mostly soldiers. The American government was not involved, he continued, but the spirit of enterprise and adventure was strong in the American character.

Then Cabanas changed the subject slightly, expressing admiration for the Monroe Doctrine and saying that he hoped the United States would force the British out of Central America, whom he styled as "oppressive, arrogant, and insulting." He observed that the British had just taken Roatan Island, which commands the Honduran coast, and were extending their control in other parts of Central America.[17]

Cabanas' feelings about Great Britain were agreeable to both Wheeler and Walker. Wheeler said that the United States was aware of British activities, and would either make Britain conform to the Clayton-Bulwer Treaty or unilaterally abrogate the agreement.[18] A recent article in El Nicaraguense had said:

> England, the ever grasping and never satisfied, has long looked with lustful eyes on our republic, and the collection of States which formed the Central American Confederation; and has more than once

---

[17] Wheeler to Marcy, December 24, 1855, National Archives, M219, 10/35.

[18] Ibid.

unblushingly asserted her desire to promote British interests at the expense of North America.[19]

Even if this were—as the Walker apologists seemed to contend—the official policy of the British government, there were still some thoughtful men in England. The Times of London proposed that Great Britain give up its claims to Belize, Mosquito, and Roatan, if the United States would force the filibusters out of Nicaragua. The article referred to Walker and his colleagues as "murderers, robbers, and pirates." It further contended that European—especially English—enmity and interference had prematurely forced the United States to action, for example in the cases of California and Texas. Europe, it said, should welcome a strong Central American Confederation as a counter-balance to United States expansion. Nonetheless, it mourned, all efforts by Nicaraguan leaders to establish relations had been rebuffed, and the consequences would surely be that "General Walker will build up a strong American auxiliary to the United States on the Isthmus."[20]

Unfortunately for Walker, the reality seemed otherwise, and with the rebuff of his minister to Washington, he was tentatively looking elsewhere for financial and perhaps moral support. El Nicaraguense, Walker's paper, editorialized that Nicaragua had two traditional courses, American and European, and as the United States had virtually shut the door on one of them, the only alternative was England and Europe. The problem had always been that English capital usually took over once invited in. The editorial cited as an example Mexico, "which is in debt slavery, [and] can't make a move without consulting England." Nicaragua, however, was now strong enough to have no fear, and it needed European capital. The state was too poor to build the things it needed: a ship canal, railroads, quartz machines, and saw mills. Why should Nicaragua not trade directly with the manufacturing source, Liverpool rather than Boston? Nicaragua's coffee, sugar, cotton, cocoa, indigo, and rice did not need transshipment. The merchants of Hamburg, Liverpool, Antwerp, and Bordeaux would buy as readily from Nicaragua as from the merchants of New York, and the costs and commissions to New York agents would be saved. Perhaps as a result, the tide of industrious European immigrants might be diverted from the United States to Nicaragua, as the latter would offer more promising inducements of resources to be developed and fortunes to be made. Finally, Nicaragua was not bound by the Clayton-Bulwer Treaty, and that should prove to be a major advantage.[21]

---

19 El Nicaraguense, November 17, 1855.

20 Quoted in ibid., March 15, 1856.

21 Ibid., March 22, 1856.

But there was still the Mosquito problem with the British government. On February 8, 1856, Walker's government had issued a proclamation affirming that the Mosquito Coast was an integral part of Nicaragua. This was presumably to nullify the formal renunciation forced upon Nicaragua by the British in 1848. The decree was largely ignored by the British, so Walker sought other measures to gain British acceptance. In June, General Domingo de Goicouria was dispatched to England as Nicaraguan minister with full powers to settle the Mosquito question, in addition to negotiating treaties and loans.[22] Unfortunately, his mission came to little. It was not until 1860—long after Walker ceased to play a role in Nicaraguan affairs—that a treaty was signed with Great Britian which provided for nominal incorporation of the eastern coast with the nation, under the form of an autonomous reservation. And it was not until the end of the century that full Nicaraguan jurisdiction over the Mosquitos was established.

Investment, however, was not the most immediate of Walker's foreign problems. His first priority was securing men, and the authorities in the United States were impeding his efforts in this respect. The New York Herald reported that on Christmas Eve, 1855, Captain Faunce of the revenue cutter Washington had received orders from the New York District Attorney to forestall the sailing of the Accessory Transit Company's Northern Light. At the Battery, Captain Faunce took off two hundred men from steerage who had no tickets; these were apparently bound for Nicaragua to help Walker, and were characterized as "stowaways." (It appears that the company initially disavowed them, despite the earlier agreement.) The men claimed to be colonists who had been promised two hundred fifty acres for cultivation upon their arrival in Nicaragua. About twenty-five in cabin class did not have tickets either, but Joseph N. Scott, the company agent at Greytown, explained that these men were being transported down to work on projects of the company, e.g., build fences, make stonewalls, work with stone quarries, build a coal depot, and build a wharf on the Pacific side. He opined that the natives would not work, and that all the "whites" were either with Walker or headed for California as soon as they got the money. As a result, the company constantly needed resupply. The men would be given tickets as soon as the ship cleared the bay.

But Joseph L. White, the attorney for and one of the directors of the company, was still fighting Walker's battles. In a letter to District Attorney John McKeon in New York, he declared that the company did not wittingly carry mercenaries to Central America, but ammunition and other supplies as paid freight to a duly-constituted government was another question. In response to McKeon's assertion that the Clayton-Bulwer Treaty forbade colonists, White denied it. The treaty said that

---

[22] Wheeler to Marcy, June 22, 1856, National Archives, M219, 10/58.

the United States and Great Britian as "corporate entities" could not colonize, but it did not refer to individuals. This, he continued, was up to the Nicaraguan government, under whose laws the company was incorporated. The company would continue to operate in this fashion no matter what the position of the United States might be with respect to recognition.

He did concede that the company had made a deal with the non-accredited Nicaraguan minister, Parker H. French, for delivering colonists at nominal rates. But McKeon's assertion that French's activities were illegal on the grounds that the United States did not recognize the Nicaraguan government was rebuffed.

> It will be new to them—it is to me—that the United States held any supervisory or other control over their political action. Whenever a government may be established in Nicaragua, and of whatever kind, and however the same may be changed or modified, are questions which affect only that state, and which are to be decided by them alone.[23]

Besides, White continued, the company had no choice. It was not a government it had helped establish, but no other was in prospect, and the company could not operate in a state with no government to recognize rights and protect concessions. Finally, he dissembled, the company did refuse transit to Colonel Kinney when he seemed to be mounting an invasion, and would do the same to prevent others going to Nicaragua for "soldiery," but not for colonization.[24]

About two weeks later on January 5, according to El Nicaraguense, French had a confrontation with McKeon. The District Attorney went to French's quarters at the St. Nicholas Hotel in New York. He accused French of violating American neutrality laws, asserting that he had proof of French's "criminality." The latter steadfastly maintained he was only the Minister from Nicaragua, his country had advertised for colonists, and the transit company had agreed to transport the prospects for twenty dollars a head. Beyond that, he had done nothing. He dared McKeon to arrest him, and then showed him the door.[25]

---

[23] New York Herald, December 26, 1855.

[24] Ibid.

[25] El Nicaraguense, January 12, 1856.

After the frantic exchanges of letters and words over the larger issue of American responsibility versus the prerogatives of its citizens, the actual trial of the Northern Light "stowaways" was somewhat anticlimactic. It was first heard on February 7, but was continued until the first Monday in April. El Nicaraguense claimed that nearly all those arrested had given up prominent positions to go to Nicaragua, and that most were heroes of the Mexican War. For example, "Colonel Hall was a captain in the New York Volunteers—who on his return was breveted Major by the Legislature for his bravery, and since then has served as Colonel of the Brooklyn Militia."[26] Having cut themselves off from their former occupations, and being lightly overseen, many simply proceeded to Nicaragua. The more prominent ones assured the American Minister in Nicaragua that they would request furlough to return for the trial, but the case was effectively closed, and the District Attorney's efforts to stop Walker reinforcements were even less effective than his moves against Kinney.

Nonetheless, the action—or inaction—of the U.S. government made itself felt in another fashion. It is unquestionable that in Central America, recognition of a government which claims de facto existence is of major significance. It was perhaps even more crucial to Walker's regime, given its precarious political balance and the predilection of other Central American states for intervention. In this respect, the new government was in immediate trouble, as evidenced by Marcy's response to Wheeler's announcement of its formation. The Secretary directed his minister to have no intercourse with the new government, as the Department did not regard it as legal.

> It appears to be no more than a violent usurpation of power, brought about by an irregular self-organized military force, as yet unsanctioned by the will or acquiescence of the people of Nicaragua.[27]

If those holding power should establish themselves as a de facto government, Marcy advised, the United States government could then hold them accountable for claims the American government might make on behalf of its citizens.[28]

Marcy wanted a government to berate, while Wheeler wanted one to support, believing—as did most Americans in Nicaragua—that the

---

[26] Ibid., March 15, 1856.

[27] Marcy to Wheeler, November 8, 1855, National Archives, M77, 27/13.

[28] Ibid.

Walker adventure was, in the long run, in the best interest of the United States. Marcy did later concede that Wheeler's role in maintaining some sort of informal contact with the government in Granada was of vital importance. The U.S. government needed "the most accurate information in regard to the actual political condition of the State of Nicaragua." Marcy acknowledged that the reports which had been received at the State Department were of a conflicting nature: "While some of them represent that the present political organization is satisfactory to the people . . . others [say] it has no foundation in the hearts of the people."[29]

The major popular support in the United States for Walker's efforts (among those Americans who were aware of the filibuster's activities) came primarily from the South and the West. Southerners continued to harbor interest in the extension of the slave-holding areas, and Westerners particularly were still caught up in the impetus from Manifest Destiny. An example of this latter feeling was an Oakland (California) Leader editorial:

> Walker is the Government of Nicaragua . . . his is not the vain ambition of lording it over the narrow territory and native population of Nicaragua. Central America may limit his aspirations—a federal government composed of independent, sovereign states, with a system of laws similar to our own, and a population invited from all quarters of the world, to give force, dignity, and character to his government, and infuse somewhat of enterprise into the present effeminate native population must be his ultimate hope.[30]

The British did not seem as reluctant to recognize the government at Granada as was the Department of State. Thomas Manning, the British vice-consul at Leon and a resident of Nicaragua for thirty years, discussed the situation with Wheeler in Granada. He assured Wheeler that "the present condition of political affairs in this Republic meets their hearty approval and acquiescence."[31] Manning subsequently conceded recognition in an official note to the Nicaraguan government.[32] He may, however, have been acting on his own judgment, as

---

29   Ibid., January 8, 1856.

30   Reprinted in El Nicaraguense, January 25, 1856.

31   Wheeler to Marcy, January 15, 1856, M219, 10/40.

32   Ibid., January 22, 1856.

Wheeler had done previously. Or it may have been that the British were accustomed to Central American governments with foreign advisors who were, in reality, the powers behind the throne. At any rate, it was at most a recognition of the government of President Rivas, and did not commit the British to recognition of the later government under Walker without the presence of a native chief executive.

Nevertheless, the main problem remained with Washington. El Nicaraguense, sarcastically commenting on the American refusal to accredit French, observed that the same standards would have left the United States a part of Great Britain, "after the filibusters Dekalb, Lafayette, Von Steuben, et al had come over." Instead, Great Britain immediately received John Adams as minister.[33]

In a note to the Department, Wheeler complained that self-respect would normally have made him demand his passport, but his explicit instructions from the President were to "stay and report." In the same communication, he subtly raised the specter of a Nicaraguan-British "understanding" (perhaps seeing Nicaragua in the role of another Mexico). Finally, he closed the dispatch by berating the British for their opportunistic diplomacy.[35]

One more problem was the continued recognition by Washington of Marcoleta as Nicaraguan Minister. Walker's newspaper again resorted to sarcasm: to whom did he send his dispatches, or from whom did he get his instructions? Marcoleta, the organ asserted, had "invented" a government, a cabinet, and an army at the ancient city of Segovia. It would be embarrassing for the U.S. government if the United States-Nicaraguan treaty pending before the Senate were sent to this imaginary government to exchange ratifications.[36]

The impasse was temporarily broken when the Walker-Rivas government replaced French with a native Nicaraguan. Wheeler broke the news by announcing that he had learned "incidentally" that the government was sending Padre Augustin Vijil as Envoy Extraordinary and Minister Plenipotentiary, and that the friar would leave in a few days. Wheeler called Vijil a "distinguished ornament of the Church," and assured the Department that he would faithfully represent Nicaragua

---

33 El Nicaraguense, January 12, 1856.

35 Wheeler to Marcy, January 22, 1856, National Archives, M219, 10/41.

36 El Nicaraguense, January 26, 1856.

and would be acceptable to the diplomatic corps.[37] The appointment was apparently enough to assuage the sensitivities of officials in Washington, and Marcy notified Wheeler that the President had decided to recognize the Nicaraguan government and to receive Vijil.[38] In addition, it appears that pressure may have been brought upon the government from other sources. Sympathy in the Senate had apparently been aroused by the letter Walker wrote Senator John B. Weller of California, apprising him of the situation.[39]

Finally, from Marcy's note it appeared that Commodore Vanderbilt had been urging President Pierce directly to recognize the government in order to have leverage with respect to the transit problems. Marcy advised Wheeler:

> The interest of the United States as well as that of many individuals has been injuriously affected by the interruption of the transit through Nicaragua across the Isthmus. It is alleged that the proceedings by which this result was brought about are in disregard of the rights granted by Nicaragua to the Accessory Transit Company in which the citizens of the United States had made large investments. This government has been called on by its citizens who have been injured by these proceedings to make reclamations for the losses they have sustained. . . . [Report on this.][40]

These happier circumstances were short-lived, however, as events in Nicaragua were outrunning the capacity of Washington to respond to them. By the time Wheeler acknowledged Marcy's communication on July 7, a political transformation had taken place. As Provisonal President, Rivas had ordered national elections to be held, but owing partly to the defection of feasible candidates, only Walker was a realistic choice. When Walker consequently won the post of chief executive, Rivas refused to acquiesce in the results. He, in turn,

---

[37] Wheeler to Marcy, April 17, 1856, National Archives, M219, 10/48.

[38] Marcy to Wheeler, June 3, 1856, ibid., M77, 27/18.

[39] El Nicaraguense, June 14, 1856.

[40] Marcy to Wheeler, June 3, 1856, National Archives, M77, 27/18.

defected to an invading coalition army on June 17.[41] In addition, on June 23, Padre Vijil—after only six weeks in Washington—notified Marcy that he would be absent from the country, and that John P. Heiss, another American, would be Charge d' Affaires.[42] These two events were more than the State Department could countenance, and recognition until the end of the Walker interlude became a moot issue.

Of more immediate concern to Walker was the prospect of a Central American coalition putting an army into the field against him. After Walker had refused to aid Cabanas in regaining power in Honduras, the latter went directly to El Salvador to incite the government of that country against the Americans. Cabanas was reported to have proclaimed a fierce war of extermination against the army of Walker, and to have expressed the belief that in its destruction lay the only safety for Central America.[43] In addition, it appeared that the other Central American states were preparing to join in an alliance to make general war against the Americans. Walker's paper, El Nicaraguense, feigned perplexity at these developments. It noted that a league had been formed among Guatemala, Honduras, Costa Rica, and El Salvador, and that—contrary to custom—Nicaragua had not been included. All the people of Nicaragua, the editorial intoned, were offended by this and felt "their government is required to have the incivility rectified or apologized for." Nicaragua had always tried to maintain a correct posture toward these states and could not but regard this as an unfriendly action.[44]

Then the newspaper went on to treat separately the adherence of each of the countries to the "ill-advised league." El Salvador, it asserted, had hitherto been considered the inveterate foe of the Conservative Party, and at the same time a staunch friend of democratic principles. Its position had been so well understood that contemporary writers called it the "Switzerland of America," because it was hemmed in with rocky mountains, "in whose fastnesses were firmly protected the liberal ideal of its people." Moreover, El Salvador had previously expressed a sympathy for the existing government in Nicaragua, and had made offers of peace and friendship. How strange that it would then lend its name and influence to an alliance against a

---

[41] Wheeler to Marcy, August 25, 1856, ibid., M219, 10/67.

[42] Viljil to Marcy, June 23, 1856, John P. Heiss Papers, Tennessee State Historical Society, Nashville.

[43] El Nicaraguense, February 16, 1856.

[44] Ibid.

government which was "founded on the theory her people have sustained with so much fidelity."[45]

Neither Honduras nor Guatemala had responded to the formal proposition submitted by Nicaragua to the other four powers for a convention of all the states to adopt measures to provide for the general good and to guarantee the independence of the contracting parties. It was perhaps hoped that this proposal (and the subsequent convention) might allay the fears of the other states of an expanding Americanization of the entire Isthmus. They were aware, of course, that Walker only negotiated from a position of strength, and contractual arrangements, therefore, always seemed to redound to his benefit. But it was Costa Rica—the most immediate and most formidable threat—for which El Nicaraguense reserved its most scathing invective. The loss of Costa Rica's friendship was "a doubtful injury." That state had allowed to congregate on its borders Nicaraguan political refugees who continually attempted to foment discord within their native country. The Costa Rican government had never made any effort toward establishing friendly relations with the current government in Nicaragua.

> All these faults, heretofore disregarded, will rise up to condemn her present suicidal policy; and when the long account is settled, if they force us to hostilities, all these defalcations must be answered for. We have stood to the faith of nations; we have acted honorably and with a most conciliatory spirit to all the republics of Central America, and will still pursue the same unequivocal policy; but yet we are prepared for the desperate alternative; and should discontented politicians inflame against us the ignorant people of adjoining states, we can only adjudge them, as it has been done since the beginning, "those who draw the sword, shall perish by the sword."[46]

Unfortunately, threats, cajolery, and appeals availed the Americans nothing. On March 1, Costa Rican President Juan Rafael Mora declared war, taking special pains to make it clear to native Nicaraguans that this action was aimed at the American contingent only. And it was to be a war to the death, as Mora decreed that "all

---

[45] Ibid.

[46] Ibid.

prisoners taken with arms in their hands were to be shot."[47] When the news reached Nicaragua on March 11, Walker announced plans for an immediate invasion of Costa Rica—perhaps an almost instinctive effort to avoid fighting a two-front war. He acknowledged that his coalition effort had failed, and that the "Servile" parties all over Central America were declaring their enmity. As the Legitimists in Nicaragua seemed to be joining the allied cause, Walker ordered that his troops should thenceforward wear the Red Ribbon, emblematic of the Democratic (or Liberal) Party in Nicaragua. An editorial in El Nicaraguense assured the Costa Rican people that the Nicaraguan army was coming "to regenerate rather than destroy" (perhaps hoping for a repetition of the Nicaragua story).[48]

With the arrival of 250 more men on March 9, Walker's army rose to 850, with about five hundred more Americans "capable of bearing arms engaged in civil business either at Granada or along the line of the Transit."[49] Wheeler fixed the total figure at 1,300.[50] In contrast, Mora had put out a call for nine thousand men,[51] though his active force was probably far below that. Mora's real strength came from other quarters according to Walker. He maintained that his rival's audacity was the result of encouragement by the policies of both the United States and Great Britain.[52] Wheeler partially confirmed this view in a report to Marcy that a Nicaraguan blockade of Costa Rica had resulted in the seizure of British mail. "I beg your patient attention to all these letters," he said, "they are genuine, and completely unmask the jesuitical policy of Great Britain."[53] The "mail" included Costa Rican diplomatic dispatches from their consul general in Great Britain, E. Wallerstein, to the Costa Rican foreign minister, Joaquin Beru de Calvo. A letter of February 16, 1856, from Wallerstein to British Foreign Secretary Lord Clarendon acknowledged a previous note from the British ministry telling Wallerstein (on Clarendon's direction) that the British Admiralty on the Pacific station would send cruisers to protect British interests.

---

[47] Walker, War in Nicaragua, 175.

[48] El Nicaraguense, March 5, 1856.

[49] Walker, War in Nicaragua, 175.

[50] Wheeler to Marcy, March 17, 1856, National Archives, M219, 10/44. Wheeler indicates that he is including "capitalists, merchants, farmers, mechanics, laborers, [and millers]."

[51] Folkman, Nicaragua Route, 81.

[52] Walker, War in Nicaragua, 165-76.

[53] Wheeler to Marcy, March 31, 1856, National Archives, M219, 10/46.

telling Wallerstein (on Clarendon's direction) that the British Admiralty on the Pacific station would send cruisers to protect British interests. Wallerstein's letter requested that the British navy also protect Costa Rica's interests as the filibusters were threatening that country. He pointed out that the United States had stationed a warship at Greytown, and therefore must be conspiring in the action with the intention of annexing Central America and introducing slavery.

A note from the Foreign Office to Wallerstein dated February 9 advised that the War Department had approved the sale of two thousand muskets to Costa Rica. A letter from the consul general to President Mora asked for instructions regarding this purchase. He indicated that he had already asked permission to examine some of the weapons. Wallerstein also said that when he mentioned to Clarendon that Costa Rica had eight hundred troops on the Nicaraguan frontier, Clarendon had replied that "that was the right step." Wallerstein judged that Clarendon had approved the small arms sale because Costa Rica was doing something about Walker. He also expressed the opinion that there would be no war between the United States and Great Britain because the United States recognized that Britain was "determined to punish the Yankees very severely for the least insult to the national honor." He added, however, that such a war would be in Costa Rica's best interests.

Also bolstering Costa Rican courage was a February 24 dispatch from their minister in Washington, Luis Molina, to Calvo. He said that news from Paris indicated that there was interest there in helping Central America maintain its independence, but no action would be taken until those countries affected did something to help themselves. Referring to the Clayton-Bulwer Treaty, Molina said that Britain had told the United States that it had given all the explanations and apologies it planned to with respect to the activities of its consuls in Central America. The British would be willing to submit the question of treaty interpretation to arbitration, but apparently the United States did not want this.[54]

The Costa Rican mobilization and declaration of war was only partly due to the support and encouragement of foreign governments. Mora and his government probably genuinely feared that Costa Rica, lying hard by the heartland of Nicaragua, would be the next target for the northern filibusters. Perhaps it would be more prudent to move now, before the Americans could become firmly entrenched and organized, than to wait to be plucked at a later date. Perhaps Mora wished to

---

[54] Molina to Calvo, February 24, 1856, ibid.

create confusion in Nicaragua, and under this veil, seize more territory along the San Juan River in an effort to control the transit route. At any rate, war had been declared, and Walker had to react.

CHAPTER VIII

DREAMS OF EMPIRE CRUMBLE

The course of General Walker in reference to Costa Rica and his honest, frank, and manly manifesto seems to have been generally received with favor throughout the state, and I understand it has drawn to his standard many wavering adherents of other and hostile factions. When will they begin to learn that he is the chosen instrument of a manifest destiny, and that though by their puny efforts they may for a moment stem the current, it will eventually but render the torrent more dreadful in its ravages and engulf them in its onward course?[1]

Walker wasted no time in ordering his army to march south in an invasion of Costa Rica. By the middle of March, a battalion of three hundred and fifty men under the command of a German Jew, Colonel Louis Schlessinger, marched out of Virgin Bay with banners streaming, intent upon the first objective, the capture of Guanacaste (Nicoya). The force included two companies of Americans and one each of French and German mercenaries. Some of the French were old Chasseurs de Vincennes, "bronzed with the sun of Africa, and familiar with the use of that most deadly of weapons, the Minnie Rifle; these bringing with them musicians . . . and the air was soon resounding with songs of home and fatherland."[2] El Nicaraguense reported that no problem was anticipated in the capture of Guanacaste. The spirited army, mounted on "fine, caparisoned horses," was moving so rapidly, "Costa Rica [wouldn't] even have time to muster the militia." The government organ confidently speculated on which direction the army would move after the conclusion of the initial stage of the campaign.[3]

Unfortunately, Colonel Schlessinger had been selected more for his linguistic ability than for his knowledge of military science. On March 20, he called a halt in the march at the plantation of Santa Rosa, about eighteen miles north of the capital of Guanacaste. Schlessinger failed to post sentries, and when an alarm announced a surprise Costa Rican attack, general confusion reigned. The Costa Ricans poured in a murderous volley of fire; one witness testified that they fought "like

---

[1] "Corporal Pipeclay," in El Nicaraguense, March 22, 1856.

[2] El Nicaraguense, March 15, 1856.

[3] Ibid., March 22, 1856.

tigers."[4] The German and French companies were told to fall back to better positions, but they apparently misinterpreted the command as an order to retreat. Colonel Schlessinger followed the withdrawal, as he later characterized it, "to rally the fugitives." The engagement was over in about fifteen minutes. The retreat became a general rout, and for days stragglers struggled back to Virgin Bay in ones and twos.[5] Schlessinger was subsequently court-martialed for his role in the fiasco, but the damage was already done and the myth of the invincibility of the Yankee long-rifles had been shattered.

One of the most untoward events of the war followed on the heels of the Costa Rican victory. Mora moved north and entered undefended Virgin Bay on April 7. His troops surrounded the office of the Accessory Transit Company and fired a volley of about one hundred rounds, killing nine Americans, most of them employees of the company. A witness reported that the Costa Ricans "systematically bayoneted and stabbed with swords the wounded on the ground, robbed the dead, and broke in and robbed the Transit Company office, then burned the wharf."[6]

Wheeler immediately sent a letter to President Mora protesting this "slaughter of unarmed and inoffensive" American citizens. Wheeler pointed out that this atrocity was an implementation of Mora's twin proclamations of death to filibusters and elimination of all Americans from Nicaragua and Costa Rica. He reminded Mora of Molina's December letter to Marcy giving assurance that Costa Rican laws would grant land and protection to American immigrants. He also pointed out that Article XII of the 1851 United States-Costa Rican treaty guaranteed protection of persons and property of American citizens in Costa Rica.[7] Satisfaction, however, was not forthcoming, and claims for indemnity and restoration—processed through the Department of State—dragged on for years.

---

[4] Philippe Egan Toohey, an Irishman who was pardoned by Mora after being captured in the battle when he got written confirmation from the New Orleans Delta that he was a correspondent and not a filibuster. Wheeler to Marcy, April 17, 1856, National Archives, M219, 10/48.

[5] Ibid., April 14, 1856, 10/47, and New York Times, April 21, 1856.

[6] Deposition of Charles Mahoney, engineer for the Transit Company, taken by Wheeler. His statement was corrobated by other survivors. Wheeler to Marcy, National Archives, April 17, 1856, M219, 10/48.

[7] Ibid.

Along with information from Leon that a coalition army from Honduras-El Salvador-Guatemala was poised on the northern border and that invasion was imminent, Walker's intelligence reported that Mora's army numbered eight thousand. This dire news made Walker decide to barricade himself in Granada. However, neither of the reports proved to be well-founded (Mora's army was probably somewhere between two and four thousand), so Walker decided to attack Rivas, which had been occupied by Mora upon the withdrawal of the filibusters. On April 11, Walker led this assault himself, and his troops—some five hundred strong—attacked with fervor, catching the enemy off guard. The plaza was taken in five minutes, but the Costa Ricans had to be rooted out of barricades and fortified houses. As the day-long battle raged, it became clear to Walker that he occupied an untenable position. As a result, he was compelled to order his troops to slip out under cover of darkness, conceding a somewhat pyrrhic victory to the Costa Ricans (considering their losses and the subsequent events).[8] The Costa Ricans retained the town, but they were also left with a severe epidemic of cholera. Within a few days, the remaining five hundred Costa Ricans were forced to withdraw, and the war temporarily went into a state of suspended animation.[9]

Taking advantage of the lull in the fighting—due as much to the rainy season setting in as to Costa Rican exhaustion and the dilatoriness of the other governments—Walker determined to put the government on a more permanent footing. Provisional President Rivas, along with his cabinet, had been in Leon since March 1, but before leaving he had entrusted the southern and eastern departments to the care of Walker under a kind of martial law. A decree had been issued over the President's cachet calling for national elections on May 1. Delegates would be elected from each of the departments, and they in turn would elect a president, senators, and representatives. The two candidates for president were Rivas himself, and Mariano Salazar, both from what was formerly the Liberal or Democratic Party.[10] The forty-one delegates assembled in Managua on May 25, and began their balloting. With the city located in one of the departments under Walker's jurisdiction, and the oral voting conducted in front of the assembled delegates and observers, there was some basis for concern about intimidation. At any rate, Walker was nominated from the floor for president, and it appeared that he might be "swept" into office.

To forestall any charges of coercion or collusion, the balloting was temporarily suspended, and Walker made a "courtesy call" on Rivas

---

8   El Nicaraguense, April 14, 1856.

9   Allen, William Walker, 114.

10   Wheeler to Marcy, May 3, 1856, National Archives, M219, 10/51.

in Leon. There Walker apparently advised Rivas that he would be willing to accept the presidency only on the basis of a direct popular election. On June 11, Rivas issued a proclamation cancelling the previous elections and calling for a new one on the basis of Walker's recommendation. Feeling that the situation was well in hand, Walker rode south, only to be startled the next day by news that Rivas and his cabinet had abandoned Leon for Chinandega. In addition, Secretary of War Maximo Jerez had ordered the fortifications at both Realejo and Leon dismantled, and the small American contingent at Leon to abandon the city. When word reached Walker of this turn of events, he ordered his troops in Leon to obey because he "was not disposed to have the coming struggle occur on any such issue [i.e., disobedience to lawful authority]." He determined to have the contest conducted on more formal grounds.[11] In addition, he was concerned about having his forces strung out—in increasingly hostile territory—from Leon to Fort Castillo, and felt it more prudent to congregate them in the vicinity of Granada and perhaps in the immediate area of the transit route.[12] Upon the American withdrawal, Rivas returned to Leon and apparently invited in the troops from the northern states which had been poised on the frontier.[13]

Although Walker's visit probably had caught Rivas by surprise, and merely precipitated a course which the president had already decided to pursue, El Nicaraguense explained it in a more exotic fashion. It had been traditional in Nicaragua, the paper averred, for defeated candidates either to flee or to be summarily executed. The impending election had undoubtedly aroused an atavistic dread in the former president.

> This circumstance convinces us that the approach of an election, and an invading army at the same time so frightened President Rivas that he hardly knew what he was doing; and in a moment of partial insanity and chronic deceitfulness, he left the Presidency and thus lost all hope for the future.[14]

Despite this turn of events, Walker proceeded with the elections on the following bases: (1) the elections had been legally called by the

---

[11] Walker, War in Nicaragua, 226.

[12] Ibid.

[13] Wheeler to Marcy, June 30, 1856, National Archives, M219, 10/59.

[14] El Nicaraguense, June 21, 1856.

provisional president, even though that gentleman had subsequently forfeited his right to govern; (2) the October 23 agreement between Walker and Cabanas, which Walker regarded as the foundation of all subsequent Nicaraguan government, ceded the right to the commander-in-chief (Walker) to organize a new government upon the dissolution of the existing one; (3) the departments which would be subject to the elections were also legally under Walker's authority through the martial law concession made by Rivas upon his departure for Leon on March 1. In the interim, Walker appointed as provisional president Fermin Ferrer, most recently the Minister of Hacienda and the only member of Rivas' cabinet who had remained loyal to the filibuster government.[15]

The candidates for the new election were still Rivas and Salazar, as well as Ferrer and Walker. Not surprisingly, Walker swept all five provinces which participated in the voting, getting three times the vote of Ferrer, his nearest rival.[16] Even in the event the results were arranged, probably no candidate could have been honestly elected. The Legitimists did not vote and the natives in the outlying districts did not even know about it or feared going to the polls.[17] Provisional President Ferrer issued a decree declaring Walker president, and the latter was duly inaugurated on July 12.[18] Ferrer was named Secretary of State in the new government.

As reported by El Nicaraguense, the toasts at the inaugural dinner presaged an auspicious future for the infant regime. A Mr. DeShields waxed eloquent with: "General William Walker, President of the Republic of Nicaragua—the scholar, gentleman, and soldier, responding to the call of down-trodden and oppressed humanity, entered Nicaragua at the head of his invincible fifty-six, and established the nucleus of a great Republic!" Not to be outdone, Ferrer responded after the band played "See the Conquering Hero Comes" with: "Our Brethren from the United States who come here to teach the art of self-government, in company with William Walker, our champion in war and protector in peace."[19]

Perhaps to reassure itself of the legality of the election, El Nicaraguense editorialized that there was no sovereign law in the country except the treaty of October, 1855. The ultra-liberal

---

15   Ibid.

16   Ibid., July 12, 1856.

17   Allen, William Walker, 118.

18   El Nicaraguense, July 12, 1856.

19   Ibid., July 19, 1856.

constitution of 1838 had been wiped out by the revolution of 1854, and the ultra-conservative constitution of 1854 was never implemented. In addition, the treaty specifically had lifted only certain articles from the 1838 constitution, thereby indicating that the whole constitution was not intended. In essence, the paper maintained, the law was William Walker, elected under the provisions of 1855. The editorial also emphasized the duty and responsibility—not to mention the necessity—of foreign nations recognizing de facto governments for legal and practical reasons.[20]

Perhaps unfortunately for Walker, his sense of urgency to achieve reforms and to put things in order impelled him toward acting like a monarch. He overhauled the constitution, revised the tariff laws, annulled inoperative statutes, and changed the flag design among other things, all by executive fiat. He seemed to sow confusion in the ranks of his supporters: he appeared to be for and against slavery, Nicaraguan independence, annexation to the North American union, and conquest of Central America. Perhaps there was method to his madness, and all the feverish activity was either a "fog or smokescreen . . . for his true purposes" which may never have really come to light. At any rate, he created suspicion and alienated his friends at an inopportune time.[21]

Walker's enemies were again massing. At occupied Leon, hundreds of troops from Guatemala and El Salvador joined a large continent of Nicaraguan Legitimists. The filibuster forces held a line from Managua to the transit route, and from San Juan del Sur to Fort Castillo down the San Juan River. Only sixty miles separated the poised, contending armies in the north. Of some concern to Walker was the arrival of a British naval squadron at San Juan del Norte. The fleet consisted of thirteen ships of war, all steamships except one; among

---

[20] Ibid.

[21] Allen, William Walker, 119, 120. One of Walker's projects that excited both approbation and resentment was the Confiscation Decree of July 16, 1856, which provided that all persons who had "assisted the known enemies of the state" since October 23, 1855, or who had been declared traitors since April 22, 1856, should have their property confiscated and inheritances forfeited. Within ten days of confiscation, an account of the confiscated property would be published; thirty days after that—save the possibility of a successful contest of the action—the property would be sold, with the proceeds going to the Ministry of Hacienda. El Nicaraguense, July 19, 1856.

them was the Orion of ninety-six guns, making the total force two hundred and sixty eight guns and two-thousand-five-hundred men.[22] Further, American fears of British intervention were exacerbated by a rather peculiar stroke of fortune.

Walker had issued a decree on August 4 declaring all Central American Atlantic and Pacific ports blockaded (except the Nicaraguan transit route).[23] This was a paper blockade, since the Nicaraguan navy consisted of one outfitted schooner. Good use was made of this craft, however, when it captured a Salvadoran launch carrying General Salazar, who was credited with having persuaded Rivas and his cabinet to defect. The general carried a letter from Thomas Manning, long-time British vice-consul in Leon, to a Salvadoran business acquaintance.[24] The letter left no question about the way Manning must have been advising his government about affairs in Nicaragua.

The vice-consul expressed the fear that Walker had a personal vendetta against him, and that all Leonese were apprehensive that the filibuster might attack the city. Walker would be very difficult to drive out of Nicaragua, Manning said, if he received money and reinforcements. Considering the way troops were dribbling in from the other Central American states, the allies might be delaying too long, "and the expenses and sacrifices are made in vain."

> I am much afflicted to think that, under these circumstances no more activity is used in so serious an affair. At the present there are 500 men from Salvador, 500 from Guatemala, and 800 belonging to this place, and according to my judgment double that number is required.[25]

Although there was initial consternation in Granada over the juxtaposition of these events, cooler heads pointed out the unlikelihood of Great Britain's risking war with the United States over an internal conflict in Nicaragua. El Nicaraguense observed that Great Britain could not be held responsible for the aberrations of one obscure representative whose actions were contrary to the laws of both nations. In addition, Lord Clarendon had assured Ferrer by letter that Great

---

22   Wheeler to Marcy, August 16, 1856, M219, 10/66.

23   El Nicaraguense, August 1, 1856.

24   Ibid.

25   Manning to Florintine Souci, San Miguel, El Salvador, July 28, 1856, ibid.

that if this were not done, every American settler would have to leave or be in great danger from the "natives." He assured the Department that "unless a force of our government is placed at San Juan del Sur, murder and rapine will ensue."[31] Unfortunately, Wheeler's bargaining position with the Department was eroded, as he had already been recalled, probably due to his second unilateral recognition of a <u>de facto</u> government.[32]

With as many as three thousand opponents now congregated in Masaya, Walker again had to address problems on his southern flank. A new Costa Rican force under General Canas had occupied San Juan del Sur on November 7, and Walker—needing to keep the transit route open at all costs in order to receive reinforcements—took the major portion of his army there to dislodge them.[33] The garrison of two hundred and fifty men he left in Granada then underwent the cruelest siege of the whole war. The defenders, forced back to the main plaza, were compelled to turn the cathedral into a citadel. When they had drunk and eaten all their provisions, they were reduced to consuming mule meat— four inches square for every twenty-four hours. They died at the rate of three per day, and were buried only three yards away. Many of those marooned in the edifice were American civilians, and they labored in the same jobs as the soldiers. Survivors were finally picked up by Walker in a lake steamer, but the seventeen-day siege had taken a dreadful toll: One hundred and twenty died of disease, forty deserted, and only one hundred thirty-five made it to the steamer, many of these succumbing later to disease or wounds.[34]

The city Walker was finally forced to abandon on December 14 was but a shell, having been virtually destroyed during the protracted battle. He proceeded to concentrate his forces at Rivas—a smaller, cleaner, more defensible town. At this point, the tide had definitely begun to ebb. The land had been wasted by war, and the few hundred remaining Americans were exposed to cholera, dysentery, typhoid, and yellow fever. They were attacked by troops from four nations, and most Americans in the United States had lost interest because of distraction by the fall presidential campaign.[35]

---

31   <u>Ibid.</u>

32   Marcy to Wheeler, September 23, 1856, <u>ibid.</u>, M77, 27/25.

33   Allen, <u>William Walker</u>, 124-126.

34   Scroggs, "Walker-Heiss Papers," 319.

35   Allen, <u>William Walker</u>, 126-127.

The succeeding theatre of war was the transit path on the Caribbean side. Vanderbilt, who was still determined to rid himself of his pretentious adversary and to regain control of the route and the company, resolved to cut off Walker by seizing this portion of the crossing. His instrument was Sylvanus H. Spencer, another bold American soldier of fortune,[36] who led a Costa Rican force (armed by Vanderbilt with the latest weaponry) against the filibuster garrisons along the San Juan River. By decisive strokes, Spencer not only captured the filibusters but the river and lake steamers as well. This campaign cut Walker off from the Caribbean and gave the allies communication between their northern forces at Granada and their southern troops at Virgin Bay and southward.

In Walker's subsequent account of the action, he alluded only to the Vanderbilt involvement, without mentioning the Commodore by name; however, he did fulminate against Marcy (and President Pierce, by implication) for not asserting the United States' prerogative and responsiblity for protecting American property (i.e., the transit steamers). Walker employed the somewhat specious argument that had the vessels been Nicaraguan, the state of war between the two countries would have conceded the legality of the Costa Rican action. As they were neutral ships operating in Nicaraguan territorial waters, where they were not masters of their own fates, rather than on the high seas, they should not have been subject to belligerent seizure.[37] This assertion was in the face of the compelling fact that this waterway was the only route by which the Walker force could be resupplied and reinforced from the Atlantic ports of the United States.

The beginning of the end for the filibuster effort came when the allies moved in and occupied San Jorge, a town virtually within sight of Rivas, on January 28. For more than three months, skirmishes and assaults occupied the opposing forces. Walker held on to his position, continually hoping that a contingent he had sent to try to reopen the route to San Juan del Norte would be successful. Eventually, as the forces of the enemy increased and their partial encirclement of Rivas became more effective, the rations of the filibuster forces became—if not reduced—at least less palatable, as mule meat replaced beef. But the major blow was the increasing desertion rate, now no longer confined to European mercenaries but including long-time American comrades-in-

---

36 Ibid., 143.

37 Walker, War in Nicaragua, 350-351.

arms. President Mora had reversed his psychological tactics (from his former proclamation of complete extermination of the Americans), and now made it clear that the war was against one man: William Walker. Mora's new proclamation assured amnesty to all deserters, and this promise was scrupulously observed.[38] Apparently the seeming hopelessness of the American position was sapping the men under Walker's command, and although replacements continued to trickle in form California, the morale factor of the desertions could not be ignored.

Meanwhile, in San Juan del Sur, an uneasy truce continued up until early April. The Costa Ricans had not penetrated the city, probably because it was under the guns of the Nicaraguan "navy"--the sloop <u>Granada</u> continued in port. In addition, U.S. Navy Commander Charles H. Davis had brought his sloop-of-war <u>St. Mary's</u> into the port in late January "with orders to do what he could for the Americans."[39] As a result, Walker was able to keep the wires and routes open to the port town, and to continue receiving news, men, and supplies. Davis himself undertook to enforce a truce while, under agreement with both sides, he evacuated the American women and children from the besieged Rivas. Eventually however, the allies erected fortifications along the transit route.[40]

On April 30, Walker emissaries met with Davis at Costa Rican headquarters in San Jorge at the commander's invitation in order to receive a proposition for evacuation. Davis pointed out that Walker's position had become entirely untenable: the contingent on the San Juan River had embarked for the United States, so no help could be expected from that quarter; the Garrison and Morgan faction of the transit company had decided to send no more steamers from California, so there would be no more recruits arriving; Davis did not intend to allow the <u>Granada</u> to leave port, and would be seizing it shortly, so it would be of no help to Walker; and finally, Walker's provisions were running out, so he could not hold on much longer under any circumstances.[41]

With this discouraging news, Walker was compelled to sign an agreement with Commander Davis. Walker and sixteen of his top staff would surrender themselves to Davis, and would be transported from San Juan del Sur to Panama. The remainder of the force, along with American civilians in the government, would be moved under the

---

[38] Allen, <u>William Walker</u>, 154.

[39] Ibid., 156.

[40] Walker, <u>War in Nicaragua</u>, 414-429 passim.

[41] Ibid., 421.

protection of Davis to San Juan del Norte to embark for Colon. Guarantees for the lives and property of Nicaraguans in Rivas and still loyal to the filibuster government would be the responsiblity of Davis. The accord was signed on May 1, 1857. Walker remained convinced that Davis was acting on direct orders from Secretary Marcy, not to remain neutral and merely safeguard lives and property of American non-combatants, but rather to be instrumental in the capitulation of Walker.[42]

Of the immediate impact of the filibuster foray, personnel figures tell part of the story: Of the 2,518 Americans who "enlisted"[43] under Walker, about one thousand were killed or died of disease, two-hundred fifty were discharged, eighty were captured, and the rest either survived at Rivas or were unaccounted for. The allied force—counting the entire war—numbered seventeen-thousand eight-hundred. Of these, 5,080 were battle casualties, while uncounted thousands died of disease. In other terms, the transit route was never effectively reopened, and the "breach of ill-feeling between Central America and the United States had been widened."[44]

The Legitimist General Tomas Martinez assumed the reins of the presidency upon Walker's departure, but the situation remained unstable. By July, the filibuster was already thinking in terms of another expedition and had written to friends in Washington to intercede with the Buchanan administration, assuring the government that he would scrupulously avoid violating the neutrality laws.[45] In September, he wrote the same correspondent again about reassuring the administration, and referred to the efforts of the Costa Rican, Guatemalan, and Salvadoran representatives to persuade Secretary of State Lewis Cass to use U.S. naval forces to prevent Walker's landing in Central America in the event his departure from the United States could not be forestalled.[46] In the meantime, former filibusters and new adherents were busily recruiting and raising money in eastern seaboard and Gulf Coast cities for a second assault on the little Central American country.

---

42   Ibid., 414-429 passim.

43   An Irishman captured at the Battle of Santa Rosa, before he was executed, wrote to his cousin to discourage any other immigrants: "You don't even get the 250 acres but are forced into the army." Costa Rican Army Bulletin, March 27, 1856.

44   Allen, William Walker, 158.

45   Walker to John P. Heiss, July 25, 1857, Heiss Papers.

46   Ibid., September 24, 1857.

Walker's second effort was a landing at Greytown on November 23, 1856, under the guns of the U.S. sloop-of-war Saratoga. Commander Chatard of the Saratoga was later criticized for allowing it, but the officer was somewhat confused with respect to his responsibilities in the matter. Chatard wrote his commanding officer, Commodore Hiram Paulding, whose vessel was standing off Aspinwall. Paulding immediately full-steamed north with his flagship Wabash, followed by the Fulton. The British Leopard and Brunswick also joined in. The American and British navies were now unwilling to risk letting the situation get out of hand again.

By the time Paulding arrived, Walker and his band of two-hundred seventy had already attacked. A contingent under the command of "the gallant Colonel Frank Anderson" had taken possession of Fort Castillo, which commanded a strategic spot on the San Juan River, along with the river and lake steamers that had previously fallen into the hands of the Costa Ricans.[48] As Walker prepared to move inland, Paulding's marines stormed ashore and interposed themselves between the filibusters and their destiny. Paulding took Walker into custody, and subsequently deposited him back at Mobile. For this action, which enraged some of the congressional expansionists, the Commodore had to justify himself before a congressional investigating committee.[49]

Walker's third try was even more ill-fated. On December 4, 1858, one hundred twenty men under Colonel Anderson, a soldier-of-fortune who had been with Walker since the earliest days, sailed from Mobile without a clearance in the schooner Susan. Walker was to meet them later, but the band never arrived. On December 16, the vessel struck a coral reef about sixty miles from Belize, and left the men stranded on a small island. They were subsequently rescued by the British sloop-of-war Basilisk, and transported back to Mobile.[50] The fourth effort was

---

[48] Scroggs, "Reminiscences of Ratterman," 326.

[49] James Rood Doolittle, Justification of Commodore Paulding's Arrest of Walker (Boston: Buell & Blanchard, 1858), passim. Paulding's attitude toward Walker's efforts had altered somewhat since the previous year. On January 4, 1856, he had written to Wheeler complimenting Walker's character and closing with: "Be pleased to express to the General, my profound acknowledgements, and my best wishes for his success in giving to Central America security and repose." Wheeler to Marcy, January 15, 1856, National Archives, M219, 10/40.

[50] Scroggs, "Remniscences of Ratterman," 329.

even more embarrassing, as the company Walker had organized in Mobile was stopped by the authorities before it left the harbor.[51]

Walker's fifth and final opportunity to reestablish himself in Central America came as a result of a dispute over the ownership of Roatan Island, off the Caribbean coast of Honduras, among Great Britain, the United States, and Honduras. It was resolved in favor of Honduras, but the citizens—being principally British—decided to seek extra-legal avenues for redress: early in the spring of 1860 they looked to Walker for deliverance. Walker was delighted, and on April 20 began sending down a few men at a time to rendezvous on Cozumel Island, east of Yucatan. After Walker joined them, they took the old Spanish fortress of Trujillo on Cape Honduras (the traditional northernmost point of the Mosquito Territory). After Walker had declared Trujillo a free port, the British ship *Icarus* arrived, and its captain, Newell Salmon, sent a message of protest to Walker, pointing out that the customs of the port had been mortgaged to Great Britain for a Honduran debt,[52] and that Walker had acted illegally in taking it, along with $3,000 from customs fees. Salmon further advised Walker that he should return the money, surrender his force, and accept the protection of the British flag.[53]

Walker was astounded by this turn of events. He apologized for taking the customs house, but protested ignorance with respect to the missing sum. (Later writers have speculated that the money may have been taken by native officials.) With his small band of seventy men, Walker tacitly declined the offer of protection and stole out of the town under cover of darkness, intent upon making his way south along the coast. His rear was beset by Honduran troops, and he was forced to carry on a running fight to the banks of the Rio Negro. At this point, Walker could not cross and could not retreat, and Salmon appeared on the river. The British captain took Walker and his men prisoners, and turned them over to Honduran officials. President Guardiola, a man who perhaps felt justified in his vindictiveness, was in charge. The curtain rang down on the Walker saga and the decade of intervention when the filibuster fell before a Honduran firing squad on September 12, 1860.[54]

---

51   Allen, William Walker, 171.

52   Chatfield had long held this over the Hondurans.

53   Ibid., 172.

54   Ibid., 173-174.

CHAPTER IX

DIPLOMATIC FRUSTRATION: REPRISE

After Walker had seized control of Granada in October, 1855, he had begun a flurry of diplomatic activity. One of the filibuster leader's first moves was the cancellation of Jose de Marcoleta's commission as Nicaraguan envoy to Washington. Complicating matters, the former conservative (Legitimista) president, Jose Maria Estrada, had escaped to the northeastern province of Segovia and there proclaimed his government still in existence. Walker's Granada regime, under the dissembling provisional presidency of Patricio Rivas, was, according to Estrada, illegitimate and invalid.

Having been appointed by Estrada, Marcoleta clung to his office and defied removal. When Walker's government named a replacement, the Department of State found itself in a dilemma. If the government withdrew its recognition of Marcoleta, it would seem to be indicating its approval of the filibuster government, which the Department considered at best as unrepresentative of the will of the Nicaraguan people. On the other hand, Marcoleta was an embarrassment to the Pierce administration since everyone recognized that the Nicaraguan represented a phantom government. The question was raised as to whom did he send his dispatches, and from whom did he get his instructions.[1] As it was believed that Marcoleta had never received a regular salary from the government of Nicaragua, the New York Herald sarcastically editorialized:

> The generosity of this gentleman in serving a government which could not pay is only equalled by his piety in continuing to serve it after it is dead. He continues with a constancy and disinterestedness unparalleled in the annals of diplomacy to represent its spirit long after the body is dead and buried.[2]

The wording of a State Department note to Marcoleta on December 10 is obscure, but Marcy seemed to assure the Nicaraguan diplomat that his recall by the Walker government did not constitute withdrawal of

---

[1] El Nicaraguense, January 26, 1856.

[2] New York Herald, January 12, 1856.

Marcoleta's credentials.[3] Nevertheless, such a withdrawal appears to have been conveyed to Marcoleta shortly thereafter.

Even before Marcoleta's dismissal, Walker began to send a succession of representatives to Washington. The leader of the parade was Parker H. French, an American who had been a short-lived member of "President" Rivas' cabinet.[4] The choice was not an inspired one, as it emphasized the foreign character of the Granadan regime. Nonetheless, the State Department was under heavy pressure from various sectors—both political and journalistic—to receive French. Some were in sympathy with the Walker cause, while others pointed out that he was the accredited representative of a de facto regime, and it was not within State Department prerogative to pass judgment on that regime. But the Department remained adamant in its position, refusing to recognize the government or its representative.

Domestic political considerations now entered upon the scene to alter the situation. Pierce's administration was beginning to be criticized for being soft on British imperialism and not devoted enough to the cause of Manifest Destiny. As the Democratic nominating convention was nearing, and Pierce was actively seeking re-nomination, an about-face on the issue of recognition of the Walker government was executed.[5] This time the Nicaraguan emissary was Padre Augustin Vijil, a respected cleric and former lawyer.[6] Marcy received Vijil on May 14, 1856, thereby implying recognition of the Granadan regime, and asked for the padre's legation personnel list on May 16.[7] The resumption of relations was a cause for celebration in the streets of Granada and among Walker's supporters in New York.

---

[3] Marcy to Marcoleta, December 10, 1855, National Archives. M99, 10/98.

[4] French had published a rival newspaper to Walker's in Sacramento before going to Nicaragua. In Granada, French offered his services to Walker and was appointed Minister of Hacienda and later Nicaraguan Minister to Washington. Marcy refused to accept him and, after American newspapers published a revelation of French's shady past, Walker dismissed and repudiated him. William O. Scroggs, Filibusters and Financiers (New York: Russell & Russell, 1969, orig. pub. 1916), 89, 168-71. Senate Report 455, 33 Cong., 2 Sess.

[5] Scrogg, Filibusters, 171.

[6] Wheeler to Marcy, April 17, 1856, National Archives, M219, 10.

[7] Marcy to Vijil, May 16, 1856, ibid., M99, 10/112.

The official recognition alleviated the pressure on John H. Wheeler, who had been appointed U.S. Minister to Nicaragua on August 2, 1854, and who had already engaged in premature diplomatic activity.[8] Wheeler had presented himself to the new government directly upon its formation,[9] and had been rebuked by Marcy for this show of initiative. The Department, Wheeler was informed, had embarked upon a course of watchful waiting and would therefore delay its judgment about the validity of the new regime. In the meantime, he was to assess the situation and keep the Department posted:

> It is very important that this government should have the most accurate information in regard to the actual political condition of the state of Nicaragua. The accounts which have been sent on here are conflicting. While some of them represent that the present political organization is satisfactory to the people of that state—others represent that it has no foundation in the hearts of the people, who would very generally shake off the power of Walker if it were possible for them

---

[8] John Hill Wheeler, lawyer, diplomat, and historical writer, was born in 1806 in Murfreesboro, North Carolina, the son of a merchant and shipper. He graduated from Columbian College (now George Washington University) in 1826, was licensed to practice law in 1827, and received an A.M. degree from the University of North Carolina in 1828. Wheeler served in the North Carolina House of Commons from 1827 to 1830, was superintendent of the Charlotte branch of the United States mint from 1837 to 1841, and was North Carolina state treasurer during 1842-1844. After serving again in the North Carolina legislature in 1852, Wheeler was appointed Minister to Nicaragua on August 2, 1854. He resigned under pressure from Secretary William L. Marcy on March 2, 1857. After living in Washington, Wheeler returned to his native North Carolina at the onset of the Civil War, then journeyed to Europe in 1863 to collect historical material. He then went back to Washington and historical writing until his death in 1882. His major publication, Historical Sketches of North Carolina, which came out in 1851, was undistinguished and error-riddled. The biographical portions were so partial to his own party that it was nicknamed "The Democratic Studbook." J.G. de Roulhac Hamilton, Dictionary of American Biography, XX,50.

[9] Wheeler to Marcy, November 8, 1855, National Archives, M219, 10/28.

to do so, and that terror is its sole foundation. Your situation is favorable to the acquisition of a correct knowledge of the internal affairs of that country.[10]

Unfortunately, the creaking wheels of packet-ship diplomacy could not keep pace with the events occurring in Nicaragua. Wheeler's acknowledgement of Marcy's dispatch granting recognition carried the news of a political change in the Isthmian state. The government in Nicaragua was no longer that of Rivas, who had defected to an opposition faction, but of President Walker, who had been chosen in an election of questionable validity.[11] At this intelligence, the perplexed State Department simply refused to act, and for the remainder of the Walker period did nothing with respect to official recognition. Walker himself sought to minimize the importance of his break with Rivas, and asked Vijil to reassure Washington that no substantial change had occurred.[12] By the time Walker's message reached Washington, however, Padre Vijil had already departed, leaving John P. Heiss as charge' d'affaires of the legation.[13]

Heiss had been sent to Nicaragua in February, 1856, as a bearer of dispatches from the State Department. When Heiss arrived in Granada, Walker won his fellow-Nashvillian's enthusiastic support. The latter then returned to the United States a "naturalized" Nicaraguan and devoted his energies to the filibuster cause. After first acting as charge for the legation, Heiss was designated by Walker as a special commissioner to the United States and Great Britain to adjust the continuing controversy over the British Mosquito protectorate. Inconveniently, neither government accepted Heiss' diplomatic overtures. This setback notwithstanding, he continued to serve Walker in other ways as when Walker needed publicity in the press, or a defense against the attacks of his critics, or a spokesman with an entree to the realms of power and influence in Washington. Warm letters were exchanged between the two men into 1857, but silence thereafter suggests a rupture in their relationship.[14]

---

[10] Marcy to Wheeler, January 8, 1856, M77, 27/253.

[11] Wheeler to Marcy, June 30, 1856, ibid., 219, 10/59.

[12] Walker to Vijil, June 29, 1856, John P. Heiss Papers, Tennessee Historical Society, Nashville.

[13] Vijil to Marcy, June 23, 1856, ibid.

[14] Elleanore Ratterman, "The Walker-Heiss Papers. Some Diplomatic Correspondence of the Walker Regime in Nicaragua," Tennessee Historical Magazine, I, No. 4 (December, 1915), 331.

Another American, Appleton Oaksmith, was the last of the Walker regime's nominations as representatives to the United States, and Oaksmith was also summarily rejected by the Department of State.[15] One of the victims of this diplomatic imbroglio was the bilateral treaty. Wheeler had negotiated a "Treaty of Friendship, Commerce, and Navigation" on June 20, 1855, even before the arrival of Walker. Nicaragua had ratified the accord on September 27, 1856, and in a September 30 dispatch, Wheeler urged action by the State Department. The American Minister pointed out that the treaty had met the approval of the Department when he first presented it, and that the President's annual message had indicated that it would be sent to the Senate. In order to comply with the time period designated for ratification, Wheeler counseled, the treaty would have to be approved during the current congressional session. His dispatch also enclosed a copy of the decree of the Nicaraguan government repealing the Act of the Federal Congress of Central America of 1824 which abolished slavery on the Isthmus. As if in explanation, the minister gratuitously observed:

> The short experience of any person who may reside for even a short space of time in Nicaragua will convince the most fanatical, that the rich soil so well adapted to the culture of cotton, sugar, rice, corn, cacoa [sic], indigo, etc., can never be developed without slave labour.[16]

In response, the Department not only ignored the treaty but recalled Minister Wheeler.[17]

Meanwhile, the problem of trying to determine just who should be the authentic representative from Nicaragua continued in Washington. In early October, 1856, Patricio Rivas, ensconced with a rival government at Leon, nominated a minister to the United States. But the anointed, Antonio Jose de Irisarri, already accredited as Minister from Guatemala and El Salvador, began an ill-starred year of efforts to secure reception by bungling his presentation of credentials. In acknowledging Irissari's note which referred to an accompanying introduction from the Nicaraguan Foreign Minister, Marcy quickly advised him of the faux pas: I have the honor to acquaint you, that the

---

[15] Marcy to Oaksmith, September 13, 1856, M99, 10/116.

[16] Wheeler to Marcy, August 6 and August 30, 1856, M219,10.

[17] Scroggs called Wheeler's support of the decree "the proverbial straw that broke the back of the camel" in sealing the Minister's fate. Scroggs, Filibusters, 216.

> accompaniment to your note is of a different
> character, being a letter to me from the
> same functionary upon the subject of Mr.
> Walker's alleged election as President of
> Nicaragua. It is presumed that this was
> accidentally substituted for the letter
> referred to in your note.[18]

On October 28, Marcy informed Irisarri that the President had declined to accredit him. The Secretary observed that there was too much confusion regarding who had the authority to speak for Nicaragua or to act as a <u>de facto</u> government, and some reason to believe that there may very well have been no one.[19]

After Walker was overthrown by a pan-Central American army on May 1, 1857, a new government was organized in Nicaragua. The chiefs of the political factions, Legitimist Tomas Martinez and Democrat Maximo Jerez, formed a coalition and ousted Rivas, who went into exile in England. Martinez was named president, with Jerez serving in various cabinet posts, and the new chief executive renamed Irisarri as the Nicaraguan delegate to Washington. In August, Lewis Cass, the new Secretary of State under President James Buchanan, advised Irisarri that the Nicaraguan's reception (and subsequent treaty negotiations) would be delayed until formal diplomatic relations were restored between the United States and Nicaragua.[20] While waiting for the State Department to make up its mind, Irisarri lived in New York until he received a summons from Cass in September: "Wishing to have a personal conference with you I will thank you to come hither so that I may see you on Tuesday morning of the 29th instant."[21] Whether from petulance, prior business commitments, or indisposition, Irisarri declined to make the trip immediately to Washington. Either Cass' suspicions or his ire was raised, as he revealed in his next communication:

> I have just received your letter of the 25th
> instant and much regret that your health is
> so impaired and especially, that it suffered in
> consequence of your late visit to this place.
> I am unwilling to subject you to a recurrence

---

[18] Marcy to Irisarri, October 20, 1856, M99, 10/118.

[19] Ibid., October 28, 1856, 10/119.

[20] Cass to Irisarri, August 28, 1857, M99, 10/131.

[21] Ibid., September 23, 1857, 126.

> here, of course the question of the recognition of the existing government of Nicaragua, which has been submitted to the President must be determined without the benefit of your presence. It was upon that subject I desired to converse with you, and I invited you to repair hither by the direction of the President. The President is now absent, but will return at the beginning of the ensuing week. . . . I think your presence here . . . would be useful in the consideration of this matter.[22]

In October, Cass again delayed a decision due to a report from the British Minister "and other sources" that Nicaragua and Costa Rica planned to form a confederation. Cass indicated that the United States would have to await the outcome of this new development, and requested that Irisarri send the Department a copy of the proposal if such existed.[23] In response, Irisarri reassured the State Department that Nicaragua intended to remain a sovereign state, and that the rumors of a confederation probably grew out of the amicable boundary negotiations currently underway between the two countries. Irisarri was then duly received, and negotiated a standard bilateral treaty with Cass on November 16, 1857.

After the recall of Wheeler, the State Department was severely circumscribed in its efforts to obtain independent intelligence on Nicaragua. Cass tried sending down a special agent, William Cary Jones, who ostensibly reported from July to September of 1857. Apparently, Jones also remained inebriated for that period of time and was singularly ineffective as a State Department correspondent.[24]

The advent of the new year saw a full-fledged professional named by the Department of State to carry out the difficult job of identifying

---

[22] Ibid., September 26, 1857, 127.

[23] Ibid., October 15, 1857, 128.

[24] New York Herald, January 1, 1858. Scroggs claims that Jones "was rarely sober and never diplomatic, and was called home without having furnished any information." Scroggs, Filibusters, 356. A dissenting voice in the case of Jones was that of Dr. J.L. Cole, who claimed that Jones' inebriation was a facade in order to take advantage of "in vino veritas," and that the ploy was quite successful. In addition, according to Cole, Jones was the only American agent who had not been "humbugged" by the local authorities. Cole to Heiss, June 20, 1858, Heiss Papers.

factions and political currents in Nicaragua, and of trying to secure ratification of the Cass-Irissari Treaty. The man selected was Mirabeau Buonaparte Lamar, a veteran of over twenty years of international diplomacy. Lamar had been President in 1838 of the new Republic of Texas, an office he won largely by default and whose duties he did not discharge with any conspicuous degree of success. One historian credits Lamar with having "destroyed whatever chance there might otherwise have been of Mexican acceptance of the loss of Texas."[25] Most recently Lamar had been the Minister-Resident to the Argentine Confederation.

Cass's instructions indicated just how complex was the task which the former Texan was about to undertake. First priority went to the treaty, for without it, Americans residing in Nicaragua could not be assured of adequate protection from their own government. Cass cited William Carey Jones' report that citizens were under surveillance, restricted in their movements, and threatened "with the penalty of instant death if they attempted to escape from the harsh and arbitrary measures which were imposed upon them." Cass noted that Lamar could not appeal to treaty provisions for protection, but pointed out that amity between nations required that unoffending aliens be properly treated. Jones had also reported that the mails were violated in order to guard against filibuster movements. Lamar was directed to enter a strong protest and to report to the Department immediately if the official mails were disturbed.[26]

The second item on Lamar's agenda was the boundary dispute between Nicaragua and Costa Rica. Cass suggested that in order to settle their differences, the two nations should retire within recognized territory and begin negotiations where they were left off when William Walker interfered. If that did not work, they could resort to the provisions of the Clayton-Bulwer Treaty (either to mediation by the United States or Great Britain under Article 6, or to the establishment of an international zone under Article 4), or, finally, to mediation by any friendly power. Cass observed that Costa Rica appeared to be trying to

---

[25] Henry Bamford Parkes, A History of Mexico (Boston: Houghton Mifflin Co., 1838), 205. Biographies of Lamar are: Herbert P. Gambrell, Mirabeau B. Lamar, Troubadour and Crusader (Dallas: Southwest Press, 1934), and Asa Kyrus Christian, Mirabeau Buonaparte Lamar (Austin: Von Boeckmann-Jones Co., 1922). Both of these deal primarily with Lamar's activities in Texas, and make only passing references to his diplomatic service. Also, see: Harriet Smithers, ed., The Papers of Mirabeau Buonaparte Lamar (Austin: A.C. Baldwin & Sons, 1921). These were edited from the original papers in the Texas State Library, and volumes V and VI deal with Lamar's diplomatic posts.

[26] Cass to Lamar, April 15, 1858, National Archives, M77, 27/309.

convert her success against Walker into territorial aggrandizement, and the Department did not approve. Lamar was directed to urge again that the Central American governments unite, since no "political or geographical considerations" separated them, but only divisions inherited from the Spanish colonial system. They could prosper and avoid conflict, Cass felt, by using the United States federation as a model.[27]

There was also the continuing problem of the differing interpretations of the Clayton-Bulwer accord, a topic not strictly within the province of Lamar. The Minister was advised, however, that British legate William Gore Ouseley was then in Washington to try to resolve the conflicting construction of the treaty. The United States would never agree to the British interpretation, Cass reflected, and had thought at one time that the British would give in, but recent events had made that possibility seem unlikely.[28]

The final issue was that of the reopening of the transit route and the confusion engendered by the companies competing for the franchise, not to mention the apparent Nicaraguan intransigence toward reopening it at all. Lamar was aware before leaving the United States of the aggressive attitude of Vanderbilt, and perhaps of the conspiratorial nature of the association between Irisarri and the Stebbins-White company.[29] Cass was unequivocal:

> The course of Mr. Vanderbilt, a citizen of the United States, is deserving of severe censure. His interference in this matter is in every way indefensible, and his assertion that he prevented for some time the recognition of Mr. de Irisarri, as the Minister of Nicaragua, is entirely unfounded, and certainly exhibits a mistaken estimate of his own influence. The delay in receiving Mr. de Irisarri originated, not in the representations or efforts of Mr. Vanderbilt, but in the political condition of Nicaragua and the apparent instability of the government. It is due to Mr. de Irisarri to say, that while he

---

[27] Cass to Lamar, January 2, 1858, ibid., 288.

[28] Ibid.

[29] H.G. Stebbins and Joseph L. White, former colleagues of Vanderbilt in the transit enterprise, were now his competitors for control of the route. Many believed that when Irisarri signed a franchise contract on his own initiative with Stebbins and White, the Nicaraguan was strictly on White's payroll.

has conducted himself as the faithful representative of his own government, he has secured the respect and confidence of this, by the whole course of his proceedings.[30]

Despite these myriad problems, Lamar was optimistic about his mission, and thought he could forward the ratified treaty by the first steamer after his arrival. Much to his chagrin, he found that Nicaragua was not enthusiastic about the accord, especially since the government feared it would open rather than close the door to filibusterism. Irisarri had even written his government that Nicaragua could not expect anything but aggression anyway, and they might as well sign the treaty as it was preferable to be filibustered by the U.S. government than by "private marauders"! Lamar was informed that the Assembly intended to adjourn before considering the treaty, but would reassemble just before the expiration date for approval, and at that time would ratify.[31]

Lamar did get an opportunity to discuss the ramifications of the treaty with Foreign Minister Rosalio Cortes, and Cortes in turn explained its provisions to President Tomas Martinez, first observing that the United States would abstain from all aggression against Central American territory, and would look with much disfavor on another country holding dominion over a part of the Isthmus. Cortes assumed that Great Britain would hold the same views, in light of the Clayton-Bulwer accord. The Minister then discussed the various provisions of the treaty. Articles 1-13 were general articles, the same as in all treaties of commerce and friendship. Article 14 defined the rights of the transit companies, i.e., for transit only, with Nicaragua retaining total sovereignty. Terminal ports were designated as free ports for transit goods, not to include troops and arms, in Article 15. By Article 16, the United States would guarantee all people and possessions passing through the transit route. It would be expected that Nicaraguan troops would enforce this, but in the event they could not, American troops would do so, after first advising the Nicaraguan government and then retiring when they were no longer needed. Article 19 prohibited the transit company from raising transit prices by more than fifteen percent for ten years after the establishment of the route. Writing to the Minister of Finance, Gregorio Juarez, about the provisions for a free port, Lamar referred to the treaty of 1795, negotiated by Thomas Pinckney, which provided that Americans could deposit their goods at the port of New Orleans, and export them with no other duty but the cost of renting a

---

[30] Ibid.

[31] Lamar to Cass, February 26, 1858, National Archives, M219, 11/6. Foreign Minister Cortes showed Lamar a copy of the letter from Irisarri.

warehouse. He assumed that similar arrangements would apply in San Juan del Norte.³²

In addition to the chronic frustrations that American diplomats suffered in Nicaragua, Lamar's burden was augmented by the continuing attempts of William Walker to reintroduce a band of filibusters into the country. Walker's arrival in San Juan del Norte in late November, 1857, had strengthened President Martinez' fears of a new general war, and had caused his government to take extraordinary measures against the foreign residents within the country. The order issued by the Commanding General of the Rivas Department that all alien males and females must report for an interrogation particularly offended Lamar's southern sense of chivalry:

> I wish to know whether this unmanly insult and outrage is not a proper ground for reclamation. It is due to the sex that such indignity and gross affront should not go unpunished. The idea that a rude uncultivated despot—and he a young man swaggering about with his arms—should drag our women to his cuartel for military examination! How uncivilized! And yet, how consistent with the character of this people.³³

After Walker was intercepted and returned to Mobile by the United States Navy, he immediately began fashioning a third attempt. In February, 1858, the Alabama legislature incorporated the Mobile and Nicaragua Steamship Company, and the next month, the Southern Emigration Society, with branches throughout the South, was formed for the purpose of "colonizing" Nicaragua.³⁴ With only minimal effort at camouflage, Walker's aims quickly came to the attention of Irisarri, who complained to the Department of State. Cass's reply reflected his weariness with the whole question of filibusterism, and with Irisarri's continual protestations:

> In respect to the apprehended invasion of Nicaragua through the agency of a company incorporated by the State of Alabama intended as is alleged in your note of the 16th instant "under the specious guise of

---

32 Ibid.

33 Lamar to Cass, March 27, 1858, ibid.

34 Scroggs, Filibusters, 369.

> emigrants to introduce large parties of filibusters" into that State, and to the measures by which it is proposed to defeat the suspected objects of the contemplated enterprise, the President instructs me to say that the officers of the United States have the most stringent orders to execute the neutrality law of April, 1818, and that, without the specific information which will warrant the interference of the law officers of the Government with suspected persons or movements, no other measures can, constitutionally, be adopted with the view of preventing the legitimate operations of the company referred.

Cass affirmed his belief that Alabama's legislature would not knowingly have incorporated an unlawful enterprise. Nicaragua, he said, had

> the unquestioned right to adopt such precaution as she may deem necessary for her own security or defence. But the President expects that in the exercise of this right, great care will be taken not to interfere with or infringe the equally sacred rights of American citizens who may not have committed any violation of the laws of that state.[35]

Lamar thought he had finally succeeded when, on March 26, 1858, the Assembly approved the treaty and forwarded it to the president for his signature. Martinez had hardly expected this, as his hostility to the agreement was well known, and his Legitimist party controlled not only the executive but the legislative branch of the government as well. Nonetheless, the Democrats managed to maneuver the treaty through by employing a parliamentary ruse, and the president was confronted with the results.[36] He therefore entrusted a sealed packet, purporting to be the presidentially-endorsed treaty, to Colonel Louis Schlessinger, a former filibuster and now an agent for the Stebbins-White company, for personal delivery to Washington. So anxious was Lamar to see the document on its way that he accompanied Schlessinger on the first leg of the trip from Managua to Granada, and he was astonished to learn, subsequently, that the treaty had not been signed and sent at all, but had in fact been returned to the Nicaraguan Assembly. Lamar was at a loss

---

[35] Cass to Irisarri, April 26, 1858, National Archives, M99, 10/138.

[36] Lamar to Cass, June 24, 1858, ibid., M219, 11/11.

to explain, but ventured the opinion that "the object of practicing this deception upon me was to prevent me from making known to my Government the fact that the President had written to Mr. Irisarri instructing him to propose some admendments [sic] to the treaty."[37] Cass directed Lamar to lodge a protest with President Martinez about the incident,[38] but Lamar had some even stronger advice for his own government:

> My own impression is that our Government will have to change entirely its policy toward this people. They are a low, ignorant and degraded race; false in word, treacherous in action, and vindictive in all their feelings. . .
> .. It is useless for our Government to establish any relations with them, founded, on their part, upon good faith and friendly feelings. One Man-of-War at San Juan del Sur would be worth more in bringing them to reason and justice, than any appeal which may be made to their hearts, or to their understanding.[39]

Perhaps the frustrations attendant upon his task were beginning to affect Lamar's judgment, or perhaps he was simply not the proper person for the job after all. He could not seem to grasp the feelings of insecurity of the Nicaraguans after nearly a decade of foreign intervention. He could not fathom <u>their</u> frustrations in recognizing the potential of the country and yet apparently being unable to control their own destiny. But for Lamar the worst was yet to come: a French adventurer, Felix Belly, had arrived on the scene in March, and Belly not only persuaded the presidents of Nicaragua and Costa Rica to grant an exclusive canal and transit franchise to a company which the Frenchman would form, but also to issue on May 1 a manifesto describing the American threat in such violent terms that it was scarcely credible. It said that a new invasion of filibusters was being prepared under the patronage of the American government as the means of definitively taking possession of Central America if she refused to surrender herself to the United States. The declaration further maintained that "all the official agents of the United States in Nicaragua have made themselves accomplices and auxiliaries of the invaders." But it reserved its major virulence for Lamar: "The Minister at present accredited in Nicaragua boasts in public of imperiously laying down this ultimatum, either the

---

37 Lamar to Cass, April 28, 1858, <u>ibid</u>., M219, 11/8.

38 Cass to Lamar, June 3, 1858, <u>ibid</u>., M77, 27/312.

39 Lamar to Cass, April 28, 1858, <u>ibid</u>., M219, 11/8.

taking legal possession of Nicaragua, by the ratification of the Cass-Irisarri Treaty, or by a new invasion of filibusterers organized at Mobile under the American banner." According to the manifesto, the Washington government had itself declared that it was absolutey powerless to prevent new filibusters and to protect the neutrality of Central America. Finally the document emphasized the inability of the Central Americans to defend themselves against a new onslaught:

> Three years of war and devastation have swept from the two republics any means of resisting a new attack of several thousand bandits; the cities of Nicaragua are destroyed in whole or in part, their commerce is annihilated, their population is decimated, and, after an obstinate resistance, which gives evidence of their patriotism, they may succumb to superior numbers if Europe will not deign at last to defend them against unprecedented attempts in the 19th century.

This last poignant observation was followed by the declaration that the supreme chiefs were placing "the independence and the nationality of the republics of Nicaragua and Costa Rica under the guaranty of the three powers which have caused to be respected the independence and the nationality of the Ottoman Empire—France, England, and Sardinia."[40]

On questioning by Lamar, the Nicaraguan government conceded that Martinez' signature was authentic, but deemed the document invalid because Martinez was in Rivas, and the constitution provided that when the president was out of the capital, he no longer exercised executive power. Under the circumstances, the acting president was Senator Augustin Avilez, who had not signed the manifesto.[41] Cass was understandably furious over the incident, and indicated as much in his instructions to Lamar:

> This absurd declaration that the United States were urging the annexation of this whole Isthmian region, is made with as much gravity as if the authors of it had the actual proof of the fact before them. The assertion is unworthy of refutation. . . .

---

[40] Lamar to Cass, July 26, 1858, ibid., M219, 11/18.

[41] Lamar to Cass, August 26, 1858, ibid., M219, 11/23.

Cass then proceeded to refute it, pointing out that Nicaragua "owes its political existence" to the implementation by the United States of its neutrality laws. Otherwise, there would descend on Nicaragua "bands of enterprizing men who would soon attain the control of its affairs and change the whole course of its policy—probably of its destiny."[42] The Secretary pointed out that normally when dealing with a major power in a situation such as this, the United States would simply suspend relations. Under the circumstances, she would show forbearance; nevertheless, Lamar was directed to

> give these governments distinctly to understand, that a suitable reparation will be insisted on, or the United States will no longer be restrained by the considerations I have adverted to, from seeking by more efficacious means, proper redress for these unworthy imputations.[43]

The treaty fiasco, the Belly contract, and the manifesto were beginning to take their toll on the Secretary of State as well as the American Minister. For a while their exchanges of ideas seemed to resurrect the ghost of the Palmerston-Chatfield cabal of earlier in the decade. Lamar wrote, "My advice would be for our government to take measures of its own for opening the route; and to plant the necessary force in the country to protect it without any reference to this government."[44] He referred to the "strategic position and virtual impregnability" of Castillo Viejo, the fort commanding the San Juan River at one of the cataracts, and recommended that American forces occupy it forthwith.[45] Cass responded by directing Lamar to make both Costa Rica and Nicaragua "distinctly understand that the American people, and government have yielded enough to the weakness of those republics, and without doing them injustice they will now take care and do justice to themselves." The Secretary said that naval contingents would be stationed at San Juan del Norte, San Juan del Sur, and Realejo

---

[42] Cass to Lamar, July 25, 1858, ibid., M77, 27/321.

[43] Cass to Lamar, ibid.

[44] Lamar to Cass, June 24, 1858, ibid., M219, 11/11.

[45] Lamar to Cass, July 4, 1858, ibid., M219, 11/16.

for the protection of American citizens and their property; and that commanders would consult with Lamar.[46]

By October the naval forces had arrived, and Lamar felt that things were taking a turn for the better. The Home Squadron flagship Roanoke, as well as the cruisers Savannah and Saratoga, were lying in San Juan del Norte. The Minister addressed a note to the Flag Officer assuring him "that your presence in the vicinity with the force under your command would materially facilitate . . . accomplishing an amicable and satisfactory solution of the present difficulties with these Republics."[47] The Merrimac was in the harbor of Realejo, and Lamar took advantage of its presence to converse on board with Costa Rican President Juan Rafael Mora, who was on his way to a Central American chief executives' meeting in Guatemala City. Mora assured Lamar that he would take the opportunity to promote good will toward the United States. Lamar responded by reading to the president a portion of the State Department position (previously supplied by Cass) with respect to the Monroe Doctrine:

> The feeling of the United States toward these countries had undergone no change. No spirit of annexation, of absorption or of aggression had been engrafted upon the Monroe Doctrine. It still pretends to nothing further than that the destinies of these countries shall be left in their own hands. It is simply a doctrine of non-intervention by the Monarchical Powers of Europe in the political affairs of this hemisphere—a doctrine which the peace and safety of the United States requires to be maintained at all hazard.[48]

Reiteration was not enforcement, however, and Lamar found himself trying to sort out the meaning of the mission of Sir William Gore Ouseley, who was active in Nicaragua and supported by the British fleet.[49] Ostensibly, Ouseley had come to negotiate a bilateral commercial treaty and to arrange for the resolution of the Mosquito question. Notwithstanding these instructions, he at first insisted on a general treaty which gave Great Britain the right to land troops

---

46   Cass to Lamar, July 25, 1858, ibid., M77, 27/321.

47   Lamar to Cass, October 28, 1858, ibid., M219, 11/29.

48   Lamar to Cass, December 2, 1858, ibid., M219, 11/33.

49   Lamar to Cass, December 26, 1858, ibid., M219, 11/34.

anywhere at the consent of the Nicaraguan government, or at San Juan del Norte to intercept filibusters without prior government consent. The British agent then gave Nicaragua an ultimatum regarding the Mosquito Territory which virtually amounted to acceptance of the Mosquito as an autonomous state, though not under British protection.[50] Fortunately for the Nicaraguans, the British government disavowed the treaty and returned it to Ouseley for renegotiation, instructing him to relinquish the Mosquito protectorate and annul the military and naval commitments he had made.[51]

While these diplomatic negotiations were going on, British capital was active. British financiers, notably Thomas Manning, a former consul and still a resident of Leon, were angling for a franchise contract to build a transit route. One proposal was to use the route up the San Juan River to the Serapiqui, up the Serapiqui to a point to be fixed, and then to build an $800,000 macadam road to San Jose, Costa Rica. From there, an existing road to Punta Arenas, Costa Rica's only port on the Pacific, would be utilized.

The new American Minister, Alexander Dimitry, who had arrived in September, 1859, watched these developments closely. He seemed reassured when the acting president, Senator Avilez, observed in a conversation that "they had had American contracts, French contracts, English proposals, but he was satisfied now that Americans, from every consideration of neighborhood, of community of interests, commercial and political, [will] ultimately [be] called to open and carry on the interoceanic service."[52] Therefore, Dimitry was startled when he learned that a Nicaraguan commission appointed to study the British proposal had in fact signed a contract. The American Minister reported to the State Department that Avilez had given a very lame explanation. The commission was supposed to draft a contract, not sign one. "Through a mistake," Dimitry said, the commission made a contract

> under a ninety years' lease of the route, with a supposed English company, supposed to be represented by a supposed agent in the Republic of Nicaragua! The absurdity of the thing would be inexpressibly ridiculous, did it

---

[50] Lamar to Cass, January 29, 1859, ibid., M219, 11/39, and April 28, 1859, M219, 11/43. British and Foreign State Papers, XLVIII, 667.

[51] Cass to Irisarri, May 4, 1859, National Archives, M99, 10/158. British and Foreign State Papers, XLVIII, 676.

[52] Dimitri to Cass, December 7, 1859, National Archives, M219, 12/28.

Perhaps the reason for Dimitry's equanimity was that he was becoming convinced that the transit was not going to be reopened under the auspices of anyone. One reason was physical: The bridges on the transit route were out, and the port at San Juan del Norte was rapidly silting up, with no one, apparently, disposed to maintain it.[60] The second reason, and probably the more significant one, was that the government did not want the route reopened. Dimitry received second-hand information that Avilez had declared:

> It is not to the interest of Nicaragua that [the transit] should go into operation—there is not a patriotic Nicaraguan who desires to see it re-opened; because all are convinced that its active operations must infallibly result in the sweeping of the country, by hordes of filibusters, on their way to the American possessions on the northwest coast of the Pacific.[61]

Dimitry's assessment was accurate. Belly was unable to deliver on his promises: the perfidy of business agents and financial angels alike, and the overthrow of President Mora of Costa Rica, his major mentor in Central America, in August, 1859, spelled doom for his enterprise.[62]

Aside from the transit issue, there remained the problem of the disposition of the Cass-Irisarri Treaty, negotiated on November 16, 1857. Although the Legitimist President Martinez seemed determined to avoid its ratification, the Democratic faction, led by Maximo Jerez, was more disposed to cooperate with the Department of State. Jerez was so annoyed with the recalcitrance of the chief executive that he remained in Leon, refusing to participate in the government even though it was ostensibly a bipartisan administration. Jerez even published a newspaper in the Democratic stronghold chiding the Assembly for its delay. The Democratic leader himself was under pressure by members of his party to take the treaty to Washington, equipped with plenipotentiary powers, and substitute his own ratification for that of the Assembly. An American correspondent noted that Jerez was not "systematically

---

[60] Dimitry to Cass, September 19, 1859, ibid.

[61] Dimitry to Cass, December 7, 1859, ibid.

[62] Cyril Allen, France in Central America, Felix Belly and the Nicaraguan Canal (New York: Pageant Press, Inc., 1966), 117-25.

opposed to the Americans," and was not "so brutally ignorant as the pretended Solomon of the Granadian aristocracy."[63]

Jerez did take the treaty to Washington, but it was encumbered with a number of Nicaraguan amendments. His substitution for Irisarri as Envoy Extraordinary and Minister Plenipotentiary was officially recognized on October 5, 1858.[64] Cass explained to Lamar that Jerez was received only after the Nicaraguan had given a clear explanation and disavowal of "the offensive language and imputations against the United States" contained in the notorious Manifesto. Jerez was empowered to conclude the treaty if the changes made by the Nicaraguan Assembly on June 28 were accepted. Cass indicated that the American government could no longer discuss the content of the treaty, but would accept one of the article modifications. With this limited concession Cass assumed that Jerez' mission was over, but gave the Nicaraguan time to submit the views expressed to his own government.[65] Jerez took the document back to Managua, but the Nicaraguan regime set it aside for consideration of the Ouseley treaty.[66]

Earlier, with the impending arrival of Dimitry, with the Ouseley treaty confronting him, and with time running out on his appointment, Lamar appeared to panic. On his own initiative, the American diplomat had negotiated a new treaty with Foreign Minister Zeledon which incorporated the Nicaraguan changes to the Cass-Irisarri treaty that Cass had already rejected. Lamar explained that these provisions were in the British treaty, and he thought they might now be accepted by the United States since there was no other basis on which a pact could be concluded.[67] The Lamar-Zeledon accord of March 16, 1859, was the last major official act of the frustrated American Minister. As his departure date neared, he began having second thoughts about some of his vituperative observations with respect to Nicaraguan officialdom. Trying to erase the record, he directed this last poignant request to Cass:

> I have also occasionally commented with some harshness upon the character and

---

[63] J. Debrin (Private Secretary to Lamar) to Cass, June 28, 1858, National Archives, M219, 11.

[64] Cass to Jerez, October 5, 1858, ibid., M99, 10/150.

[65] Cass to Lamar, November 2, 1858, ibid., M77, 28/14.

[66] Cass to Lamar, March 4, 1859, ibid., 28/32.

[67] Lamar to Cass, March 20, 1859, ibid., M219, 11/43.

conduct of individuals. It is my desire, in case it should become necessary to publish any of my Despatches, that the portions alluded to may be omitted—especially as subsequent official and social intercourse with some of the gentlemen spoken of has materially changed my opinion with regard to them.[68]

Jerez dutifully transported the Lamar-Zeledon Treaty to Washington, and there he found the Secretary of State surprisingly amenable. First, however, Cass pointed out that the President still considered the stipulations of the Cass-Irisarri treaty "just and mutually beneficial." He thought "that treaty should have been ratified by Nicaragua, without hesitation, and also, that the course of the government of that republic in the delays that took place, and in the other objectionable circumstances attending its actions, gave just cause of offence to the United States." The President's conviction "was still further strengthened by the rejection of that treaty and by the substitution of another without the knowledge" of the U.S. government. Nevertheless, in order to expedite normalization of relations between the two countries and to show the good faith of the United States, the President would submit the Lamar-Zeledon treaty to the Senate if one objectionable passage was removed. Article 16 stated: "The United States agree to use all legal means and reasonable vigilance to prevent the formation, within their territories, of hostile expeditions destined for those of the Republic of Nicaragua." Cass indignantly declared that

the government of the United States will consent to the insertion of no such provision in any treaty into which they may enter. They consider the proposition itself offensive. They choose to judge what laws they will pass and how these shall be administered without the intervention of any foreign Power. The retention of this clause in the treaty will ensure its rejection by the United States. Its omission . . . will be followed by the favorable action of the President.[69]

With this admonition, Jerez hastily sought permission of his government to drop the offending article. The Nicaraguan Assembly made the concession on July 25, 1859, and Luis Molina, who now assumed

---

68   Lamar to Cass, August 11, 1859, ibid.

69   Cass to Jerez, May 26, 1859, ibid., M99, 10/156.

the duties of charge' d'affaires for the Nicaraguan mission, so advised Secretary Cass.[70] Honoring his commitment, Cass then submitted the Lamar-Zeledon treaty to the Senate.[71] Unfortunately, the Senate was not as amenable as the Department of State. The Department found it necessary in June, 1860, to forward to the Nicaraguan government two Senate resolutions with respect to the treaty, plus amendments to certain other articles.[72] The treaty was returned from Nicaragua the following June with additional amendments.[73] However, by this time Confederate guns had fired on Fort Sumter, eleven states had seceded from the Union, and the nation no longer attached a high priority to a treaty with the Isthmian country. The era ended with no satisfactory diplomatic accord having been achieved. The decade had seen the settlement of the Nicaraguan-Costa Rican border dispute, however, with the State Department playing a major role in arbitration efforts, but none in the eventual—albeit temporary—resolution of the problem.

---

[70] Molina to Cass, August 30, 1859, ibid.

[71] Cass to Molina, September 27, 1859., ibid.

[72] William Henry Trescott to Molina, June 29, 1860, ibid.

[73] William H. Seward to Molina, June 4, 1861, ibid.

CHAPTER X

LEGACY OF AMERICAN INTERVENTION

The principle [sic] men of the Republic . . . including the Cabinet Ministers . . . have frankly stated to me that if they hereafter find that they cannot sustain themselves as an independent Republic, that they will ask formally to be annexed to the United States.[1]

<u>W.F. Boone, United States Consul at
San Juan del Sur, March, 1852</u>

There is in all this country a deep-seated terror that, when the Americans are admitted into it the natives will be thrust aside—their nationality lost—their religion destroyed—and the common classes be converted into hewers of wood and drawers of water.[2]

<u>Mirabeau B. Lamar, United States Minister
to Nicaragua, February, 1858</u>

These representatives of the American people may have overstated their cases, but a dramatic change occurred in Nicaragua during the 1850's not only in the life of the state but also in the attitude of the natives toward the United States. At the beginning of the era, due partially to erratic and inept American diplomacy, but more to American inattention, the Central Americans viewed the United States as a possible benevolent mentor who would reinforce Isthmian efforts to avoid the grasping paws of the British lion. By the end of the decade, the impression was that of an adolescent giant, stumbling about somewhat, unable to control its own citizens and without any definite foreign policy, and withal the major threat to Central American security.

One devotee of the muse Clio has observed that history is not what happened, but rather what people think happened. Whether or not a catastrophe befell Nicaragua during this period is unprovable, but it is certain that the Nicaraguans themselves felt that it had. The historian's

---

[1] Boone to Webster, March 16, 1852, National Archives, T-152, 1/61.

[2] Lamar to Cass, February 26, 1858, <u>ibid.</u>, M219, 11/4.

mission is to make past events intelligible, to find—or create—the patterns that can show us where we have been, and help us understand what we are. Unfortunately, he does not enjoy the luxury afforded the pure scientist who can operate with a controlled experiment. The historian can speculate and hypothesize ad infinitum, but he cannot recreate the event nor change the outcome. Without these tools, he is handicapped in determining the long-term effect of a historical phenomenon. So it is with Nicaragua in the decade of the 1850's. One can deal only with what happened, what those involved planned and ultimately realized, and what the subsequent life of the nation—in this case, Nicaragua—was like, with an occasional side trip into speculation.

Tomas Martinez remained in the presidency until 1867, and the Conservatives in control of the government at Managua until 1893. The period was characterized by relative peace, compared with the unsettled era from which Nicaragua had just emerged, but one of little democracy. The situation grew even worse, however, for a liberal revolt introduced to the chief executive chair one Jose Santos Zelaya. Zelaya was uniformly despicable and unpopular at home and abroad, and the American Secretary of State had publicly labeled him a "blot on the history of his country." Zelaya's rule, which ended in 1909, left the country in dire financial straits, with European creditors threatening diplomatic or military action. To forestall this eventuality, the United States intervened in 1912 with a contingent of marines and bankers. The approximately one hundred marines of the legation guard helped maintain peace for the next two decades, and the bankers managed Nicaraguan customs collections, the national bank, and the national railway. A brief respite in American intervention in 1925 resulted in internecine strife, and the marines stormed back, two thousand strong, in 1927. From then until 1933, the marines concentrated on establishing a dependable local security force, the National Guard, which would be apolitical and would maintain public order after the departure of the American military. With the advent of the Good Neighbor Policy, American military and financial representatives were withdrawn, and the leader of the National Guard, General Anastasio Somoza Garcia, used the leverage of the force at his disposal to catapult himself into executive power. The Somoza dynasty managed to maintain control of the fortunes of the Isthmian country until 1979.

United States diplomatic relations with Nicaragua, distracted during the decade of the Civil War, recovered with the ratification of a bilateral treaty in 1867. However, the accord did not construct a canal, and that issue remained to be revived sporadically during the next half century. In 1870, a U.S. Congressional appropriations bill provided money for canal surveys of Nicaragua and the Tehuantepec isthmus. This was not the last appropriation for this purpose, but until the end of the century, the amounts were so minimal that the resulting activity had little effect. The Clayton-Bulwer Treaty remained an impediment to official patronage of canal construction or to private financiers undertaking such a momentous task. By 1880, even U.S. officialdom began to chafe under the restrictive provisions of the British accord. President Rutherford B. Hayes publicly declared:

> The policy of this country is a canal under American control. . . . If existing treaties between the United States and other nations or if the rights of sovereignty or property of other nations stand in the way of this policy—a contingency which is not apprehended—suitable steps should be taken by just and liberal negotiations to promote and establish the American policy on this subject consistently with the rights of the nations to be affected by it.[3]

Nonetheless, the British refused to discuss modifications of the Clayton-Bulwer Treaty, and a bilateral accord with Nicaragua submitted to the Senate by President Chester A. Arthur in 1884 was not acted upon.

Toward the end of the century, the British attitude began to change. The Boer War and events in Europe and the world left Great Britain with few friends on the European continent and fostered a desire for Anglo-American accord. Also, the British generally approved the action of the United States in wresting the last of the Spanish-American colonies from their mother country, thereby creating new markets for British trade. At the same time, the Spanish-American War underscored the American desire for a shorter route by which to move its fleet from ocean to ocean than by Cape Horn. Finally, a bill in the U.S. Congress pointing toward a bilateral solution with the states of Nicaragua and Costa Rica promised to embarrass both the State Department and Whitehall. It was an admirable moment for the British to accommodate the United States on the canal issue. Accordingly, on February 5, 1900, British Ambassador Lord Julian Pauncefote signed an agreement with Secretary of State John Hay whereby the United States could construct, regulate, and manage an Isthmian canal. Although the treaty paid lip service to the principle of the neutrality of such a canal, the right to obtain an exclusive American franchise was unquestionably conceded.

Because of the French precedent in Panama, American attention by then was directed more toward that portion of the Isthmus as a possible route than across Nicaragua. Nevertheless, an act of Congress in 1901 authorized Theodore Roosevelt, in the event he should be unable to obtain satisfactory control of the necessary territory from Colombia, to deal with Nicaragua and Costa Rica. The administration's efforts to

---

[3] Ireland, Boundaries, 195.

secure Colombia's ratification of a canal treaty failed, but the Panamanian revolt of 1903 opened the door to negotiations with that new nation. Even after the completion of the Panama Canal in 1914, the United States had not lost interest in an alternate waterway across Nicaragua. Secretary of State William Jennings Bryan reached an agreement with Nicaraguan Minister (and next president) Emiliano Chamorro Vargas, providing that the United States would grant Nicaragua a payment of $3,000,000 in exchange for an exclusive canal franchise through that country, plus naval bases in the Gulf of Fonseca and on Corn Island. Though the outcry in Central America against the Bryan-Chamorro Treaty was long and loud, the U.S. Senate routinely approved it in 1916. That concession was never acted upon, but subsequently the Nicaraguan route was re-examined as one of the possible alternatives to the existing Panama Canal. The latter is too small to accomodate many modern ships, and the diplomacy leading up to the 1978 U.S.-Panamanian accord sparked a new interest in a site for a more modern and efficient transisthmian waterway.

Whether or not the canal would have been built or the transit road would have achieved more importance had it not been for American intervention is speculative. The battles on Nicaraguan soil among the American filibusters and financiers, Walker, Kinney, Vanderbilt, White, Morgan, Garrison, et. al., in which the Nicaraguans themselves seem to have been mere spectators, did leave the route and the issue in shambles. But the destruction to Nicaragua may have been more physical than ideological. A crucial issue at the beginning of the era was the question of Central American union. Mario Rodriguez has demonstrated in his comprehensive book on British agent Frederick Chatfield that it was Great Britain, to a large degree, which was responsible for the dissolution of the Central American Republic long before the Americans became actively interested in the Isthmus. And it was Chatfield who continued to play the advocate of disunion in what might be called the first American Period. With this type of British presence, it may have ultimately been in the best interests of Central America that individual American citizens forced the issue to the attention of the U.S. government, and caused the spasmodic attempts to enforce the Monroe Doctrine. If the American government had not been compelled to act to check British encroachment on the Isthmus in the fifties, it might have been too late after the Civil War. British dominance in the region, and British colonies in addition to British Honduras, might have been firmly established.

The cataloguing of Walker's trespasses against both the United States and Nicaragua is almost endless: injuring private capital in the United States, creating enormous destruction of life and property in Nicaragua, causing suspicion in Central America against the American people, adversely affecting relations between the United States and Great Britain, and destroying interoceanic communication via the San Juan River. In one sense, however, his activities may not have had a deleterious effect on Central American union. He certainly proved, by compelling the states to band together in order to expel him, that in cases of extreme and imminent danger the Isthmian republics could work together. Unfortunately, as events showed, cooperation ceased and internal strife resumed when the threat had passed. Martinez and Mora did make a post-intervention gesture toward union, but they received little encouragement in Guatemala City, and the effort was terminated when Mora was overthrown and killed in a counter-revolutionary attempt in 1861. Subsequent faltering steps were taken toward union in the Isthmus, notably the establishment of the Central American Court of Justice in 1908. Unfortunately, this high-minded endeavor met an early demise in 1918 when Nicaragua, at the instigation of the United States, defied the court's injunction against the Bryan-Chamorro Treaty. The irony was that not only had the United States been instrumental in the creation of the court, but also largely responsible for its dissolution.

Walker's own campaign was aimed at creating union in Central America, though hardly the democratic federation envisaged by its chief supporters. This is another irony and one that brings into sharp focus the nature of the era: the union was attempted by a foreigner, Walker, and largely destroyed by a foreigner, Cornelius Vanderbilt. Nevertheless, as the U.S. government was continually urging union among the Isthmian states that they might better resist British domination, in this rather perverse sense Walker was an ideological agent of his home government. If Walker did not achieve his goal of union for all five states, it is nonetheless probable that he contributed to union within Nicaragua itself. The pre-Walker split in Nicaragua between the Democrats (liberals) at Leon and the Legitimists (conservatives) at Granada was not only ideological but also commercial. Granada was oriented towards the Atlantic because of its trade via Lake Nicaragua and the San Juan River, while Leon's major port was Realejo on the Pacific. Perhaps the commercial question of free trade, which the liberals espoused, and high tariffs, which was a conservative tenet, was not resolved by the post-Walker transfer of the capital to the mid-point of Managua. But the move did tend to unify commercial views by making the economic concerns more national than regional. The transfer of the capital was ostensibly for ideological purposes, in order to avoid having to make a judgment between the competing claimants, but it was also partially caused by the fact that Walker had left the traditional capital, Granada, an empty shell.

There remains the recurring question of the filibusters' aims vis a vis the United States. Doubtless many of their supporters in the United States were so inclined because they looked upon the efforts as preliminaries to the annexation of Nicaragua and perhaps all of Central America to the United States of America. The example of Texas was still fresh in the minds of many, but there was little substance in these hopes of a renascence of what had been a unique situation. The fact that an identical event such as the annexation of Texas would never again occur was unknown to the filibusters of the 1850's. At least one of them, Colonel Kinney, seemed to have had in mind the recreation of the role he played in Texas, only this time he would be brought to center stage. In a letter written to a friend in Texas in April, 1855, before he encountered difficulties with the U.S. attorney and the port authorities in New York, the colonel intimated his intentions: "It requires but a few hundred Americans and particularly Texans, to take control of all that country. I have grants of land, and enough to make a start upon safely and legally. I intend to make a suitable government, and the rest will follow."[4] Unfortunately for the colonel, his high hopes were dashed almost before he left the United States through the surreptitious intervention of Joseph L. White of the Accessory Transit Company.

Conversely, Walker eventually made it clear that his plans included no such contingency as annexation. In fact, one of the major reasons for his repudiation of Nicaragua's anti-slavery statute, according to his own account, was to rule out—in the minds of Americans and Europeans alike—the possibility of annexation. Slavery was necessary, he reasoned, because the only way the regenerative Americans could hold Nicaragua after initial military conquest was to take control of the land; otherwise, the American contingent would be reduced to the status of "janizaries" or a "praetorian guard." However, "whites" (as Walker called the North Americans) could exploit successfully only with the use of African labor. It should have been obvious, the filibuster felt, that the reintroduction of slavery would preclude the chance of annexation, as the American Constitution forbade the importation of slaves from outside the Union. This would have meant having to drain the Southern states of slave labor, a commodity in which they were already in short supply. To the contrary, a dynamic, slaveholding, independent nation nearby would have provided employment for the South's "superabundance of intellect and capital." Balance would have been restored to Southern industry by having its unemployed "intellect" going to an area where no political obstacles would prevent it from getting the required labor. Walker even ventured that such an arrangement would have provided a safety valve for the United States and made it possible to avoid the coming "irrepressible conflict".[5] It is probable that the slavery decree caused Walker to lose more support than he gained, as afterwards the voices north of the Potomac espousing his cause were lonely and forlorn. But it was Walker's defeat by the Costa Ricans at the instigation of Vanderbilt which created the most despair among his adherents in the United States. If nothing succeeds like success, then nothing fails like failure, and the filibuster's expulsion from Central America appeared to write <u>finis</u> to his grandiose scheme. Cuba was also one of Walker's objectives, and those in the United States—including most of Washington officialdom during the decade of the 1850's—who felt that Cuba should naturally be incorporated into the federal union

---

4   Brownsville (Texas) <u>Flag</u>, May 5, 1855.

5   Walker, <u>War in Nicaragua</u>, 251-280 <u>passim</u>.

could never forgive Walker for a letter he wrote to Goicouria which was published in the New York Herald on November 24, 1856: "Cuba must and shall be free, but not for the Yankees. Oh, no! That fine country is not fit for those barbarous Yankees. What would such a psalm-singing set do in the island?"

The official attitude of the U.S. government with respect to annexation of Nicaragua probably never deviated very much from the position expressed by an American Secretary of State to the British Charge in Washington when the latter diplomat expressed some apprehension about U.S. interest in the Isthmian country. The Secretary said that it was U.S. policy to annex only empty spaces and unpopulated areas,[6] thereby making a distinction between North American Indians on the one hand and Central American Indians on the other. In truth, the major discrepancy between the anticipated course of the American government and that of the filibusters may have been in the direction that the extension of the Union would take. The filibusters were committed to beginning with Central America and subsequently incorporating Cuba and perhaps other Middle American territories. Although the premature publication of the Ostend Manifesto embarrassed American officialdom, the consensus in Washington was that Cuba would come first.[7] Then the question of Central America could be addressed. Most rational American diplomats recognized that annexation of Nicaragua, deep in the heart of an alien culture, would have been an untenable gesture. That nation did not possess the virtue of being contiguous to the United States, or at least merely separated by a narrow strait from mainland America. The same forces which objected to the incorporation of any or all of Mexico south of the Rio Grande on the assumption that the problems introduced by such an action would far outweigh the benefits, held steady with respect to Nicaragua. Nonetheless, if either Walker or Kinney had succeeded in his plan to first Americanize Nicaragua, some of the more obvious problems would have been removed. If this had occurred, the Nicaraguan's spectre of losing his nationality and religion, and becoming a "hewer of wood" and a "drawer of water" could have been eerily prophetic.

---

[6] Marcy to John F. Crampton, quoted in Marcy to Borland, June 17, 1853, M77, 27/177. Buchanan made a similar observation to Lord Napier, the British minister, in 1859: "We can only annex vacant territory." British Foreign and State Papers, XLVIII, 754.

[7] Franklin Pierce, in his inaugural address, implied that the goal of Cuban annexation was to be given first priority in foreign affairs. New York Evening Mirror, March 5, 1853. Letters from current and former officials and congressmen applauding this judgment crowded Secretary of State Marcy's desk. Marcy Papers, Library of Congress.

Perhaps the kindest thing that can be said abr
regard for Nicaragua itself in comparison with the
American individuals and institutions. Walker, who
citizen of that country, and Kinney thought of Nicaragua
live, to cultivate, and to develop, albeit that development hau
of exploitation. Vanderbilt and the financiers looked upon it as a h.
area of the Isthmus, therefore a site ideally suited for crossing an.
moving on. Wealth should be derived from an honest enterprise, and
even more wealth from a fraudulent one. The U.S. government
occasionally viewed the emerging nation as a possible commercial
partner, but more often as a persistent and nagging problem. Faced with
this mass of contradictions and the manifestations of the contradictions,
the Nicaraguans themselves were in turn baffled, xenophobic, desperate,
occasionally hopeful, but almost never sanguine or self-confident. The
real bruise inflicted by the "filibusters and financiers" may have been to
the spirit of the people of the country. They emerged from the era
perhaps more united, but surely less certain of their destiny and less
secure in themselves.[8] Their ambivalent attitude about Central
American union, and later about wardship of the United States, was
possibly a persistence of the shock of America's first intervention.
Withal, the focus of American interest in Nicaragua in mid-century
made that country a microcosm of United States-Central American
relations during the last half of the nineteenth century.

---

[8] An example of this was Nicaragua's reluctance to normalize
relations with the United States for a full decade after Walker's
intervention, and its deliberate procrastination about signing a
satisfactory transit contract with American capitalists during
the same period. Both cases of inaction seemed to stem from a
deep-seated fear of opening the door to any opportunity for
American intervention or exploitation.

BIBLIOGRAPHY

Collections of Private Papers

James Buchanan, Library of Congress, Washington, D. C.

Lewis Cass, Library of Congress.

John M. Clayton, Library of Congress.

John P. Heiss, Tennessee State Library and Archives, Nashville.

William L. Marcy, Library of Congress.

William Sidney Thayer, Library of Congress.

Daniel Webster, Library of Congress.

_____, Dartmouth College, Hanover, New Hampshire.

John H. Wheeler, Library of Congress.

State Department Archives (Record Group 59)

Dispatches from United States Ministers to Central America, 1824-1906, National Archives Microfilm Publication M219, Rolls 6, 9-12.

Dispatches from United States Consuls at San Juan del Sur, Nicaragua, 1847-1857, National Archives Microfilm Publication T-152, Roll 1.

Dispatches from United States Consuls at San Juan del Norte, Nicaragua, National Archives Microfilm Publication T-348, Rolls 1-6.

Dispatches from United States Consuls at Tegucigalpa, Honduras, National Archives Microfilm Publication T-352, Roll 1.

Diplomatic Instructions of the Department of State, 1801-1906, National Archives Microfilm Publication M77, Rolls 27-28.

State Department Archives (Continued)

Instructions to Special Agents to Central America, Vol. 2, Roll 154, Vol. 3, Roll 153.

Notes to Foreign Legations in the United States from the Department of State, 1834-1906, National Archives Microfilm Publication M99, Roll 10.

Public Documents and Compilations of Treaties and Documents

Comager, Henry Steele, ed., Documents of American History. New York: Appleton-Century-Crofts, 1968 (1934).

Gomez, Jose Dolores, Archivo Historico de Nicaragua. Managua: Imprenta Nacional, 1896.

Great Britain, British and Foreign State Papers, XLI-XLVIII. London: William Ridgeway, 1862.

_____, House of Commons, Sessional Papers, LXV-LXVIII. London: Eyre and Spottswoode, 1909.

Ireland, Gordon, Boundaries, Possessions, and Conflicts in Central and North America and the Caribbean. Cambridge: Harvard Press, 1941.

Miller, Hunter, ed., Treaties and Other International Acts of the United States of America, V-VIII. Washington: United States Government Printing Office, 1937.

United States Congress, Congressional Globe, 31st-36th Cong. Washington: United States Government Printing Office, 1849-1861.

Newspapers

Boston Daily Advertiser, 1856.

Central American (San Juan del Norte), 1855.

El Nicaraguense (Granada), 1855-1857.

Newspapers (Continued)

New Orleans Daily Crescent, 1850-1851, 1860-1861.

New Orleans Daily Picayune, 1848-1853, 1856-1861.

New York Daily Tribune, 1848-1861.

New York Evening Mirror, 1848-1861.

New York Evening Post, 1855.

New York Herald, 1848-1861.

New York Times, 1851-1861.

New York Weekly Post, 1855.

The Royal Standard and Gazette (Grand Turk Island, Turks and Caicos Islands), 1855.

Articles

Deaderick, David [Samuel Absalom], "The Experience of Samuel Absalom, Filibuster," The Atlantic Monthly, IV (December 1859), 653-665, and V (January 1860), 38-60.

"The Dispute with America," Blackwood's Edinburgh Magazine, LXXX (July 1856), 115-126.

Lockey, Joseph B., "Early American Diplomats in Central America," Hispanic American Historical Review, X (August 1930), 265-294.

"Nicaragua and the Filibusters," Blackwood's Edinburgh Magazine, LXXIX (March 1856), 314-327.

Peary, R. E., "Across Nicaragua with Transit and Machete," National Geographic Magazine, LX (October 1889), 467-494.

Rodriguez, Mario, "The Prometheus and the Clayton-Bulwer Treaty," Journal of Modern History, XXXVI (September 1964), 260-278.

Articles (Continued)

Scroggs, William O., ed., "The Walker-Heiss Papers. Some Diplomatic Correspondence of the Walker Regime in Nicaragua," Tennessee Historical Magazine, I (December 1915), 331-335.

_____, "William Walker and the Steamship Corporation in Nicaragua," American Historical Review, X (June 1905), 792-811.

_____, "William Walker's Designs on Cuba," Mississippi Valley Historical Review, I (September 1914), 198-211.

_____, ed., "With Walker in Nicaragua. The Reminiscences of Elleanore (Callaghan) Ratterman," Tennessee Historical Magazine, I (December 1915), 315-330.

Williams, Mary Wilhelmine, "The Ecclesiastical Policy of Francisco Morazan and the other Central American Liberals," Hispanic American Historical Review, III (May 1920), 201-213.

Books (Contemporary Accounts)

Doolittle, James Rood, Justification of Commodore Paulding's Arrest of Walker. Boston: Buell and Blanchard, 1858.

Doubleday, Charles W., Reminiscences of the "Filibuster" War in Nicaragua. New York: G. P. Putnam's sons, 1886.

Perez Zeledon, Pedro, Argument on the Question of the Validity of the Treaty of Limits between Costa Rica and Nicaragua. Washington: Gibson Bros., 1887.

Roche, James Jeffrey, By-Ways of War, The Story of the Filibusters. Boston: Small, Maynard & Company, 1901.

Squier, Ephraim George, Adventures on the Mosquito Shore. Gainesville: University of Florida Press, 1965 (1855).

Stout, Peter F., Nicaragua: Past, Present and Future. Philadelphia: J. E. Potter, 1859.

Walker, William, The War in Nicaragua. Detroit: Blaine Ethridge, 1971 (1860).

Books (Contemporary Accounts) Continued

Wells, William V., Walker's Expedition to Nicaragua. New York: Stringer and Townsend, 1856.

Books (Later Studies)

Aleman-Bolanos, Gustavo, Centenario de la Guerra Nacional de Nicaragua Contra Walker. Guatemala: Imprenta Litografia, 1956.

Allen, Cyril, France in Central America, Felix Belly and the Nicaraguan Canal. New York: Pageant Press, 1966.

Allen, Merritt Parmalee, William Walker, Filibuster. New York: Harper and Brothers, 1932.

Alvarez, Miguel Angel, Los Filibusteros en Nicaragua. Managua: Litografia La Prensa, 1944.

Bailey, Thomas A., The American Pageant. Boston: D. C. Heath & Co., 1966.

Caldwell, Robert G., The Lopez Expeditions to Cuba 1848-51. Princeton: Princeton University Press, 1915.

Carr, Albert H., The World and William Walker. New York: Harper & Rowe, 1963.

de la Rocha, Pedro Francisco, Revista Political sobre la Historia de la Revolucion. Granada: Imprenta Concepcion, 1947.

Duval, Miles P., Jr., Cadiz to Cathay. Stanford: Stanford University Press, 1940.

Ealy, Lawrence O., Yanqui Politics and the Isthmian Canal. University Park: Pennsylvania State University Press, 1971.

Estrada, Jose Maria, Juicio Particular sobre Cuestiones Politicas. Granada: Imprenta Concepcion, 1948.

Books (Later Studies) Continued

Floyd, Troy S., The Anglo-Spanish Struggle for Mosquitia. Albuquerque: University of New Mexico Press, 1967.

Folkman, David I., Jr., The Nicaragua Route. Salt Lake City: The University of Utah Press, 1972.

Greene, Laurence, The Filibuster. New York: Bobbs-Merrill, 1937.

Hamshere, Cyril, The British in the Caribbean. London: Weidenfeld and Nicolson, 1972.

Huck, Eugene R. and Edward H. Moseley, eds., Militarists, Merchants, and Missionaries: The United States Expansion in Middle America. University: The University of Alabama Press, 1970.

Karnes, Thomas L., The Failure of Union, Central America, 1824-1960. Chapel Hill: The University of North Carolina Press, 1961.

La Feber, Walter, The New Empire: An Interpretation of American Expansionism, 1860-1898. Ithaca: Cornell University Press, 1967.

Mack, Gerstle, The Land Divided: A History of the Panama Canal and other Isthmian Projects. New York: Praeger, 1944.

May, Robert E., The Southern Dream of a Caribbean Empire. Baton Rouge: Louisiana State University Press, 1973.

Meade, Rebecca Paulding, The Life of Hiram Paulding. New York: The Baker & Taylor Company, 1910.

Merk, Frederick, The Monroe Doctrine and American Expansionism, 1843-1849. New York: Vintage Books, 1966.

_____, Manifest Destiny and Mission in American History. New York: Knoph, 1963.

Munro, Dana G., The Five Republics of Central America. New York: Oxford University Press, 1918.

_____, The Latin American Republics. New York: D. Appleton-Century Company, 1942.

Books (Later Studies) (Continued)

_____, Relations between Central America and the United States. New York: Carnegie Endowment for International Peace, 1934.

Obregon, Loria, Rafael, La Campana del Transito, 1856-1857. San Jose: Libreria e Imprenta Atenea, 1956.

Rodriguez Beteta, Virgilio, Transcendencia Nacional e Internacional de la Guerra de Centro America contra Walker y sus Filisbusteros. Guatemala: Editorial del Ejercito, 1965.

Rodriguez, Mario, A Palmerstonian Diplomat in Central America. Tucson: The University of Arizona Press, 1964.

_____, Central America. Englewood Cliffs: Prentice-Hall 1965.

Books (Later Studies) Continued

Rosengarten, Frederick, Jr., Freebooters Must Die! Wayne, Pa.: Haverford House, 1975.

Salvatierra Sofonias, Guillermo, Maximo Jerez Inmortal. Managua: Progreso, 1950.

Sanchez, Rodrigo, Panorama Politico de Nicaragua, 1821-1940. Managua: Perez, 1940.

Scroggs, William O., Filibusters and Financiers. New York: Russell & Russell, 1916.

Sorsby, William and Victoria Sorsby, The Zambo-Mosquito Empire. Ms., Banco Central, Teguicigalpa, Honduras.

Soto Hall, Maximo, Nicaragua y el Imperialismo Norteamericano. Buenos Aires: Artes y Letras, 1928.

Tascher, Harold, American Foreign Policy Relative to the Selection of the Trans-Isthmian Canal Route. Urbana: University of Illinois Press, 1933.

Williams, Mary Wilhelmine, Cartographical and Geographical Data of Central America and the Caribbean. Baltimore: The Lord Baltimore press, 1919.

_____, Anglo-American Isthmian Diplomacy, 1815-1915. New York: Russell & Russell, 196 [1916].

Books (Later Studies) Continued

Van Severen, Ricardo Duenas, <u>La Invasion Filibustera</u>.
El Salvador: Director General de Publicaciones, 1962.

ABOUT THE AUTHOR

Dr. Wall is Professional Lecturer in Military History at Georgetown University and Professor of Latin American History at Northern Virginia Community College. His previous books include <u>The Landscape of American History</u> and <u>From the Law of Moses to the Magna Carta</u>.

… OF DAVIDSON COLLEGE